TWISTED BUSINESS

TWISTED BUSINESS

LESSONS FROM MY LIFE IN ROCK 'N' ROLL

JOHN "JAY JAY" FRENCH
AND STEVE FARBER

RosettaBooks®

New York, 2021

First edition published 2021 by RosettaBooks

Cover design by John Cappadona and Janet Evans-Scanlon

Book design by Janet Evans-Scanlon

ISBN-13 (print): 978-1-9481-2283-2
ISBN-13 (ebook): 978-0-7953-5309-3

Library of Congress Cataloging-in-Publication Data:

Names: French, Jay Jay, 1952- author. | Farber, Steve, author.
Title: Twisted business : lessons from my life in rock 'n roll / John "Jay
    Jay" French and Steve Farber.
Description: First edition. | New York : RosettaBooks, 2021. |
Identifiers: LCCN 2021027483 (print) | LCCN 2021027484 (ebook) | ISBN
    9781948122832 (hardcover) | ISBN 9780795353093 (ebook)
Subjects: LCSH: French, Jay Jay, 1952- | Guitarists—United
    States—Biography. | Rock musicians—United States—Biography. | Success
    in business. | Twisted Sister (Musical group) | LCGFT: Autobiographies.
Classification: LCC ML419.F745 A3 2021 (print) | LCC ML419.F745 (ebook) |
    DDC 782.42166092 [B]dc23

www.RosettaBooks.com
Printed in Canada

RosettaBooks®

OTHER BOOKS BY STEVE FARBER

The Radical Leap

The Radical Edge

Greater Than Yourself

Love Is Just Damn Good Business

THIS BOOK IS DEDICATED TO ALL OF
TWISTED SISTER'S DEVOTED FANS AND TO
EVERYONE WHO BELIEVES IN ENDLESS CHANCES.

AND TO MOM AND DAD—EVALINE FRENCH AND
LOUIS SEGALL. YOU BOTH SET THE PATH THAT
I WANDERED (AND SOMETIMES STUMBLED) DOWN,
AND SHINED A LIGHT BRIGHT ENOUGH FOR ME
TO SEE MY FUTURE . . .

CONTENTS

INTRODUCTION

"I HAVE BEEN TURNED DOWN MORE TIMES THAN A BEDSHEET IN A BROTHEL, AND COME BACK MORE TIMES THAN FREDDY KRUEGER, JASON VOORHEES, AND MICHAEL MYERS!"

—JAY JAY FRENCH

I was sitting in my older brother Jeff's apartment a couple of years ago. Jeff, who is a decade older than I, and I may have come from the same womb, but we grew up to live very different lives. He's been a teacher all his adult life, and I have been—as you're about to hear—in the rock and roll business. We never really talked about it much, but on this evening, for some reason, he turned to me and said, "How do you do what you do?"

"What do you mean, how do I do what I do?"

"Seriously," he said. "How do you do it? I don't understand your life."

"Well, I play guitar," I said.

"No, no. Your life, I don't understand your life."

"What do you mean, you don't understand my life?"

"Well, let's go back for a second," he said. "You're fifteen years old, and you start dealing drugs and then you drop out of high school, and you sue the board of education for violating your constitutional rights for handing out an underground newspaper, and your drug use spirals out of control, and you're just dealing, dealing, dealing and making a lot of money. And you're dealing heroin, and you take a ton of LSD and you smoke so much pot it looks like Chernobyl in your bedroom. And just when it looks like it's all falling apart, you decide to just give up drugs and start a rock band, but it's not just a regular rock band, it's a transvestite rock band.

"So you go from being a hippie to a female impersonator, and you join a band in New Jersey, and you call yourselves Twisted Sister, and for the next ten years, you kill yourself to become a famous band. And ten years goes by, you're slugging along, and finally you get a record deal. Now you're thirty years old and your band just takes off with 'We're Not Gonna Take It' and 'I Wanna Rock' on MTV, and now you become one of the biggest bands in the world. And then just at the peak of everything, when everything looks great, it all falls apart. You get divorced, the band's sued for millions of dollars, you guys break up, you wind up filing for bankruptcy, and you have nothing.

"And then, unbelievably, you decide to get married again, but this time you need to start all over because you're out of the music business, so you get a job as a stereo salesman, and you're selling stereo equipment. Everything's moving fine. You have a kid who seems to be doing okay, but you're selling stereos. Then out of nowhere, Sevendust, an unknown band from Atlanta, calls you, and they want you to produce their record, and you've never produced a record before, but you agree to produce this record, and you decide to manage them, and the record sells almost a million copies.

"Now you're making more money than you've ever made in Twisted Sister, and you buy a weekend house in Long Island, and now your career is going on the upswing, and everything is looking absolutely amazing. And then Sevendust fires you. You get Afib and you need a heart operation, and your wife leaves you for another guy. And then everything falls completely apart again. And just when things are completely trashed, your band decides to reunite for a benefit for September 11 to raise money for the Widows and Orphans Fund for the New York City Police and Fire Departments and Emergency Services. And the band gets back together, the reaction worldwide is astonishing, and all of a sudden everybody in the world who you thought could care less about you guys because you hadn't been together in eleven years wants you back. And for the last fourteen years you've become one of the biggest bands in the world on the festival circuit, and your career has just gone on and on like this.

"This, to this, to this, to this, to this, to this," he said, moving his hand up and down like an elevator.

"True," I said. "I was turned down more times than a bedsheet in a brothel and came back more times than Freddy Krueger, Jason Voorhees, and Michael Myers."

"I, on the other hand, was a schoolteacher," said Jeff. "I wanted a trajectory that was nice and even. I figured if I could get a job as a teacher, I would have maybe a twenty- or thirty-year career." (Which he did.) "And I'd get a great pension, and then maybe I could get a private school gig." (Which he did, along with another great pension.)

"My life has been smooth and even, but your life is like a roller coaster, Jay Jay. I have one question for you."

"What's that?"

"How the hell do you do it?"

And I looked at him and said, "Jesus Christ. I don't know. That sounds freakin' awful."

But then I thought about it.

"Well, you know what, Jeff? I'm an entrepreneur, and entrepreneurs are born with asbestos underwear. We can take the heat. And the world needs people like you, and the world needs people like me."

How about you? Were you born with asbestos underwear, or do you need to hop online and order yourself a pair? Or are you more of the steady Jeff type? These are good questions to ask yourself as you read my story and, I hope, reflect on your own. Each of us has our own unique story to tell, to be sure. Mine is just a little more, um, out of the ordinary than most people's. And there are lessons to be learned at every twist and turn.

Every successful businessperson has some kind of theory that underlies how and why they achieved success. That theory comes from how life affected them. Their habits, skills, and knowledge at some point coalesced into a life and business pattern that brought them to a goal.

You may know me as the guitar player for and the founder of the iconic metal band Twisted Sister. But I'm also an entrepreneur, and being an entrepreneur is the foundation of everything that I have been in my life. I've managed the band for over forty years. I own the brand (trademark) and do all the licensing deals. I'm a business guy. Rock 'n' roll just happens to be my business.

In Part One of this book, I'll share my early story. In short, I was born in New York City in 1952. I lived through and was part of the epic events of the 1960s. I started Twisted Sister in the 1970s, which became one of the most popular bands worldwide in the 1980s. I became a successful manager and producer of other artists in the 1990s. I brought Twisted Sister back, bigger than ever, in 2003, and the band continues to be one of the biggest bands of all time.

On top of this, I have had a long career of managing the band. I've been doing business since before I understood what business was—from selling cookies for the Boy Scouts to selling tons of drugs. Now, in addition to managing Twisted Sister, I'm a professional speaker and business consultant.

Over the years, in addition to developing a successful speaking career, I've written for Inc.com, an online business magazine. My articles are about the challenges young entrepreneurs confront, with solutions I learned through the prism of the life of a rock star. One of the most significant of these is reinvention. I have been reinventing myself for decades, even before I picked up a guitar. So have you, I bet. Think about it.

We reinvent our lives from the moment we start to realize any sense of self.

The first time you stood up and stumbled a few steps into your mama's arms, you reinvented yourself. This goes on throughout your life as a human being. You reinvented yourself on the first day of every school year when you laid out your clothes the night before.

You reinvented yourself in high school, in college, for each job interview, on every date, at every new job, when you got married, when you had children, and, if you run your own company, you still have to reinvent your business to stay ahead of your competition and take better care of your customers.

Reinvention in business is what keeps you in business.

I come from the entertainment world, where reinvention is built into every hit record, every successful TV show, movie, book. You can bask in your success for a couple of weeks, and then there's the fans' attitude: "What have you done for me lately?" Being in the entertainment business is a high-pressure environment where success seems to last for a minute and failure lasts for hours, days, or even years.

The tools of reinvention became clear to me after reading Angela Duckworth's book *Grit*. According to Duckworth, grit is the part of one's personality that differentiates those who succeed from those who don't. The secret to outstanding achievement is not talent, she says, but a special blend of passion and persistence.

Grit may be an aspect of a long-distance runner or an Olympic skater's success, but whether you're an athlete or an entrepreneur, it's only a small part of the overall picture. Companies, too, need way more than grit alone to thrive.

Reflecting on my own business journey, I started to write down the elements that have led to my success. And here's what emerged:

- **T**enacity
- **W**isdom
- **I**nspiration
- **S**tability
- **T**rust
- **E**xcellence
- **D**iscipline

Notice a pattern there?

Yes—it's TWISTED. More important though is the fact that these words, and the principles and practices behind them, accurately describe how and why Twisted Sister succeeded. And, conveniently, they afford me a simple yet effective structure to be able to teach business reinvention to others.

Yes, that's right. I teach business reinvention. Doesn't every rock musician?

Well, as you'll soon see, I'm more than a musician—I'm a manager, a licensing expert, a marketing guy, and a people leader. An entrepreneur, in other words. But these were the things I did, the roles I played—not the lessons I taught to others.

That all changed when I met my collaborator and cowriter, Steve Farber, at a business conference in Chicago in the spring of 2009.

My wife, Sharon, who worked at Forbes.com at the time, was speaking on a panel at that meeting. By that point, I considered myself an accomplished businessperson, and I was always interested in what other successful entrepreneurs, executives, and operators had to say about their own experience. If nothing else, I'm a perpetual student. So I tagged along to support her and see what I could learn in the process.

As one of the speakers, Farber presented his Extreme Leadership framework, called the Radical LEAP, which stands for Love, Energy, Audacity, and Proof. His perspective on love being, as he says, "just damn good business" resonated with me.

One of my pet peeves in business has always been those dysfunctional people whose lives are dedicated to making other people miserable. I hate them. They destroy people. They do not cultivate love. So when Steve opened the discussion for questions, I jumped up and grabbed a microphone. I said to Steve, "I get your *love* concept, but what do you do when you're dealing with someone who's just a son of a bitch?"

That led to a conversation between the two of us—with the audience looking on—that left me even clearer on what I already knew:

don't replicate these people; don't perpetuate their actions by emulating them in yours. If you get beat up, screwed, stabbed in the back, walked on, and run over, and you find yourself feeling like *now it's someone else's turn* to take it from you—don't do it. Just don't. If you pay the abuse forward, so to speak, you're personally participating in a very dangerous myth and helping to propagate a nefarious lie.

The more we talked, the more Steve started to convince me I had a lot of knowledge I could offer, and that because I had so much experience as a performer, I could easily become a speaker and a teacher.

"I think you could do this," Farber told me. "And you have a remarkable story to tell." Then he invited me to make my keynote speaking debut at his Extreme Leadership conference that was going to take place the following May in San Diego. When I told him that the band was going to be on tour on those dates, he moved the conference to August. That's how much he believed in me.

And he was right; I do have a remarkable story to tell.

Since then, I've embarked on a new tour of sorts: I share my ideas by speaking and teaching at live and virtual meetings, events, and conferences around the world. And now by sharing them with you in this book.

Twisted Business is a story unlike any other about the music business in particular or the business world in general. When I started the band that would become known as Twisted Sister, I didn't really understand what it was going to take to be successful. Now I do. And, as you will see, this is hard-earned knowledge gained from trying to make it in a notoriously savage business. And the lessons you're about to learn apply to any type of business, large or small.

I don't care if you want to start a craft beer company, a car company, or a venetian blind company; it doesn't matter if you work for a Fortune 500 behemoth or a scrappy technology start-up; it doesn't matter if you're an investment banker or if you're driving an Uber to earn a few extra bucks as a side hustle—the dynamics of what it takes to be successful in business are essentially the same.

Yes, I'll say it again: I do have a pretty fascinating story to tell. I think you'll find it's entertaining, illuminating, broadening, surprising, and educational. Yes, I'll tell you about the music, but we're also going to dive into politics, art, relationships, and, of course, business. That's a combination most people don't expect to come from a rock musician—let alone a metal guy. But the lessons I've learned in my storied adventure apply to businesspeople of all stripes: corporate careerists, entrepreneurial warriors, executives, and solo venturers. They will apply to you.

And not to worry. You don't have to be twisted to learn from the T.W.I.S.T.E.D. business model.

But it wouldn't hurt.

PART ONE

TWISTED LIVING

IN THIS SECTION, I'M GOING TO SHARE SOME OF THE TWISTED EVENTS OF THE EARLY PART OF MY LIFE, BEFORE I BECAME A ROCK STAR. I HAD NO IDEA AT THE TIME THAT THESE EXPERIENCES, INCLUDING BEING A PRETTY SUCCESSFUL DRUG DEALER TO MAKE THE MONEY I NEEDED TO BUY GUITARS AND SEE SHOWS, WERE GOING TO BECOME THE BASIS OF A SUCCESSFUL BUSINESS CAREER.

BEFORE I TAKE YOU BACK TO THE BEGINNING, I WANT YOU TO KNOW THE RATHER UNORTHODOX AND HARD-EARNED CONCLUSION I CAME TO AS A RESULT OF MY ADVENTUROUS YOUTH:

 THERE IS NO PLACE FOR DRUGS AND ALCOHOL IN THE BUSINESS OF ROCK AND ROLL.

YES, YOU READ THAT RIGHT. THE TWISTED SISTER THAT YOU KNOW, THE BAND THAT FINALLY MADE IT TO THE BIG TIME, WAS BUILT ON A PHILOSOPHY THAT THE USE OF DRUGS AND ALCOHOL WERE NOT ALLOWED.

BUT IT WAS NOT ALWAYS THUS.

1

HOW IT BEGAN

IF YOU WERE TO HOP IN A TIME MACHINE and talk to my teachers in fifth and sixth grade, the ones who routinely suspended me for talking too much in class, they would tell you, "John Segall has no focus. He has no organizational skills. He will never amount to anything."

Now tell them that little Johnny will grow up to be Jay Jay French, a successful rock star in a band with a huge international following. You know what they'll say? They'll tell you you're crazy because: 1) time travel is not possible and 2) little Johnny just doesn't have it in him. He exhibits none of the qualities it takes to make any of that happen. I probably would have told you the same thing. It's not that my talents didn't exist in a nascent form—it's just that no one, including my young self, recognized them at the time.

All I wanted was to be a rock star.

I was a music fan from about eleven. I used to get really sick. I'd get slammed with head colds and chest colds, and I spent a lot of my childhood feeling like I got hit by a New York City Transit bus. I was stranded at home for weeks at a time.

To keep me occupied, my mother gave me a transistor radio. One afternoon in 1963, I was listening to WABC, which was the number one AM radio station in the United States at the time. I didn't really know what a "greatest hits countdown" was, but they started playing down the latest songs: number five, "The Night Has a Thousand Eyes," by Bobby Vee with the Johnny Mann Singers; number four, "Up on the Roof," by the Drifters; number three, "Go Away Little Girl," by Steve Lawrence; number two, "Walk Right In," by the Rooftop

Singers. And the number one song that week was "Hey Paula," by Paul and Paula. I'd love to tell you that it was a song by Chuck Berry or Little Richard or James Brown that struck me like a lightning bolt and lit the fire of music in my being. But it wasn't. It was a cheap, stupid pop tune called "Hey Paula."

But there was something undeniably special about it on that particular day: It was number one. I was so impressed. And I thought, *Why is it number one?*

The next week, I started listening from number twenty. When they got down to number one, "Hey Paula" was it again. Same for the following week.

I started listening to that radio station every waking minute. They played the same twenty songs all day long. "Walk Like a Man," "Wild Weekend," "Up on the Roof"—they'd play them all over and over. Yet number one, week after week, was "Hey Paula."

I was fixated on this number one phenomenon, but I had no idea how it worked. I asked my mom, and she also didn't have a clue. So, I came to the obvious conclusion: it was a worldwide vote. It had to be. People around the globe just called a phone number and cast their ballot for the best song.

After four weeks of "Hey Paula" holding the top spot, a timeless, universal truth dawned on me: it is the top song in the world and it will remain that way now and forever. And then, on the fifth week, tragedy struck. The weekly countdown obliterated my adolescent rock music paradigm when "He's So Fine" by the Chiffons took the top spot away from "Hey Paula."

"Who is responsible for this?" I cried to my mother. I mean, I literally cried. I don't know if she was bemused, amused, or just thought it was a stupid question. She obviously didn't know the inner workings of the music industry, but she clearly recognized my deep interest and the pain I felt in the moment.

I didn't care about school, but this craziness was something I was passionate about. I was on a mission to figure out how to get my beloved "Hey Paula" back to its rightful place in the top spot. I surmised that it had to involve the number of records people were buying (which may have been the first indication that I was a budding entrepreneur) and that maybe there was something I could do about that.

I begged my mother to take me to a record store. She took me up to 107th Street, where there was a tiny little record shop in her best friend's apartment building. I stepped in with amazement. It was a dusty, smoky, cramped place with 45s arranged on wooden shelves. A little old lady with thick horn-rimmed glasses sat behind a shabby wooden desk. The countdown surveys from WABC, WINS, and WMCA were spread out in front of her. I picked them up and read them with wonder.

"Do you have 'Hey Paula'?" I asked her.

She nodded.

"How much is it?"

"Forty-nine cents," she said.

"If I buy it," I asked, "will it go back up to number one?"

Now that crusty little old New York lady could have easily scoffed at me and said, "Are you an idiot, kid? It's all run by the mob. It's all about payola, you shmuck. Pay for play."

But she didn't. "Maybe, son. Maybe," she said.

She gave me hope, so I bought the single. And guess what happened? Nothing, of course. I mean, nothing in terms of helping "Hey Paula" shoot back to number one. But in that moment, my obsession with the charts, and the industry behind them, exploded.

With each week's new countdown survey, I'd write the song list on cardboard from my father's laundered shirts, take it to school, make copies, and put them on every desk in the class. No one else gave a shit, but I was an eleven-year-old on fire with an obsessive passion for the songs.

Around that time, my father, like all good Jewish parents, started talking with me about my professional future. To say the least, a career as a rock star was not what he had in mind for me. "You should start thinking about joining me in my jewelry business, John."

"Okay," I said. "You make a lot of money?"

"Well," he said, "you can if you sell diamonds. That's how you make your money. But I don't do that."

"Why not?" I asked.

"It's dangerous," said Dad. "If you notice, I carry my jewelry case with me, but I don't keep it in the house. I don't want our apartment to be a target for robbers and thieves. And if I had diamonds, we'd be even more vulnerable."

Two months later, I was standing in the building lobby with the superintendent's son, Stanley, and another tenant named Herb Hamburger. (We had a Frankfurter in the building, too, believe it or not.) We were on our way to the basement to work on a school science project. Suddenly, we heard someone screaming, and three guys ran in from the mail room on the other side of the building and—right in front of us—attacked and tried to rob an old man, beating him on the head with their gun butts. I stood there, shocked, clutching my science project in my hands. I couldn't believe what I was seeing.

One of the robbers stopped and saw me, Stanley, and Herb Hamburger witnessing the crime. He ran up to me and held a gun to my head. "If you scream, I will shoot you," he hissed.

So, you know what I did? I screamed. I screamed so the whole building could hear me.

At that moment the super and the doorman, who had been in the basement turning on the boiler, walked into the middle of the chaos. Like a freakin' Wild West showdown, the doorman drew his revolver, and the three thugs stopped what they were doing (including, may I remind you, holding a gun to my head), and fled the scene. As it turned out, the mark was a rabbi who lived in the building. He was also a diamond dealer, and they almost killed him.

After I got over the trauma of the whole event, I told my dad, "I don't think the jewelry business is for me."

My mother was a reform Democrat political consultant who worked for many politicians, including John Kennedy and a litany of famous New York City Democrats, like Paul O'Dwyer, Ted Weiss, Bill Ryan, and Jerry Nadler. Mom was connected in New York and Washington. She had serious clout.

Working with my mom at the JFK for President
Upper West Side headquarters. Eight years old.

One day she said to me, "You know what, John? When you turn sixteen, I'm going to get you a job in Washington as a page for Congressman Ryan. Then you'll go to law school, and you'll get into politics, and that'll be your direction in life."

That sounded okay to me. I mean, the jewelry business obviously wasn't safe, so I figured I'd start thinking about pursuing a political career. I was already tagging along with my mother to civil rights marches and lefty meetings, and I was absorbing the liberal life. Being a professional politician seemed like a natural extension of the person I was becoming.

Then, on November 22, 1963, Lee Harvey Oswald killed President John F. Kennedy.

"Mom," I said. "I don't think politics is too safe, either."

So, I couldn't be in the jewelry business because I'd end up like the Diamond Rabbi, and I didn't want to be in politics because . . . you know . . . Kennedy. Then, one Sunday evening, in the living room of our apartment on the Upper West Side, it all became clear.

There's a cliché often heard from guys my age. It has to do with the early sixties' confluence of the hit radio phenomenon and the growing ubiquity of television in households across America: I saw the Beatles on *The Ed Sullivan Show* and I knew I wanted to become a rock star.

That's exactly the way it was for me, and I remember it very clearly. I saw the Beatles on *Ed Sullivan* and I wanted to do that, too. I didn't know what "that" was, exactly, except it looked fun. You had girls screaming. You were a millionaire. You were on TV. You were playing rock and roll. And—contrary to jewelry and politics—it looked relatively safe. This was the perfect axis of all great things.

If at that very moment someone had tapped me on the shoulder with a magic wand and said to my eleven-year-old self, "Okay, John. You shall become a rock star. And you will have a gold record. But there's just one thing: it shall not come to pass for nigh on twenty years and six months," I honestly think I would have said, "Screw that; I ain't waiting around." And I would have turned my attention to something more attainable. But there was no prescient genie watching *Ed Sullivan* with me that evening. So I turned off the TV and set my naive little sights on rock-and-roll stardom.

Every summer, from the time I was six years old, we would go to Briel's Farm in Wallkill, New York. In 1961, the farm was sold to a couple named Carl and Ann Rodman, who decided to turn it into a summer camp called Camp Thoreau.

It wasn't until 1968 that my mom let me know a secret about their past. By that time, I was doing drugs and all this crazy shit. She looked at me one day and said, "You know, there's gotta be a dossier on you in Washington, because your father and I were members of the Communist Party in the fifties."

"Whoa! What are you talking about?" I asked.

"Well, you know Briel's Farm."

"Yeah, of course."

She went on to explain to me that this was essentially a family summer resort for Communists and political left wingers who lived in the New York City area, and that my guitar teacher in 1962, a camp counselor named Mike Meeropol, was the son of Julius and Ethel Rosenberg. As a little boy in short pants, I knew nothing about who they were at the time. It didn't come up. There was no proselytizing at the camp. There were no politics involved. It was just a summer camp. A camp, as it turns out, where the guitar teacher was the son of a couple who'd been executed for a federal crime involving Communism.

Then my mother said, "And remember last year, when you went to camp at Shaker Village?"

"Yeah?"

"Well, who was in your bunk?"

"Ben Cheney."

"Ben Cheney is the brother of James Cheney, the civil rights worker who was killed in Mississippi. You do know that, right?"

"Yeah," I said.

"So who do you think goes to camp at Shaker Village?" she pressed.

Kids whose parents were left-wing radicals, apparently. We were called "red diaper babies," and we essentially went to one of three camps in upstate New York over the summer: Buck's Rock, Lincoln Farm, and Shaker Village.

This was a lot to take in. After a couple of minutes, I asked my mother, "Are you still a Communist?"

"Oh, no. We left the party years ago."

"So why did you leave?"

"Well, in 1956 Stalin invaded Ukraine and turned out to be the thug everybody thought he was. That was the end for most of us."

I replied, "I thought you could never leave the party, or that's what I've heard. Because once you're in, you can never get out."

"Well, yes, after we left, they did send a couple of guys to the apartment. This was when we lived on Twenty-Fourth Street. Sometime in 1957. We signed out in 1956, and they came the following year."

Apparently, the way the story goes is that my father, who had this unique ability to be insane on demand, turned all that explosive charm on the interlopers.

"You motherfuckers better get out of here or I'll kill you both!" my father screamed. And he did so in such a manner that the comrades never came back.

This was part of the foundation that started to create who I was going to turn out to be.

So, thanks to the son of notorious traitors, at Briel's Farm I had my first taste of playing guitar—and I wanted more. My older brother played a little, and he taught me a few things, but I didn't have a guitar of my own. I asked my father to buy me one.

"It's only twenty-five bucks," I implored.

"No."

But I did get that guitar. Thanks, as strange as it may sound, to the Boy Scouts.

Yes. I was a Boy Scout. Not a typical pastime for a Jew in New York City. For a kid in Wis-

Age twelve.

consin or Minnesota or Iowa, sure, but not for guys with my background in my neighborhood. But I liked it. I liked earning merit badges and progressing through the ranks. I liked accomplishing things and excelling in whatever I put my efforts into. Like selling cookies, for example. We associate cookies with the Girl Scouts, but the Boy Scouts sold them, too. It was an important part of the troop's revenue, and I was determined to do it better than anyone.

During the cookie drive of 1963, I stormed through our building and knocked on every door. I relentlessly pushed and cajoled my parents' friends. I hustled, shucked, and jived and sold like crazy until I reached 110 boxes, which set a record for the most cookies ever sold and established a new Boy Scout benchmark.

But for all my success in the business of cookie sales, I could not get my dad to budge on buying me a guitar. In 1965, even though I still didn't have the most important tool of the rock trade, I started looking the part by growing my hair long.

My scout master was appalled. "You can't have long hair," he told me. "It's against the rules." Somehow, that just didn't strike me as a valid reason.

By this time, I was working toward my Eagle rank, the pinnacle of success in the scouting world. While I was reviewing all the requirements to make sure I had everything I needed to advance, I learned that I had to have a letter from my religious leader. Now, my parents were not religious. They didn't call themselves atheists; they were Jews. But they were non-practicing, and, therefore, we didn't have a religious leader. My dad said he knew lots of rabbis associated with the jewelry business, and he was sure one of them would be more than happy to write a letter on my behalf.

"I don't think that's right," I said. "They don't know me. And, besides, why should I need that kind of thing to get my Eagle Scout?"

My father, who had to have been impressed with my sense of righteous indignation at age twelve, agreed to back me up. I told my scout master, "If I'm not good enough without that letter, I'm quitting."

He couldn't believe it, but quit I did—and only three months before the next cookie drive. The Boy Scouts lost their star salesman on a matter of principle.

I soon got a call from the scout master. "John," he said. "You sold one hundred and ten boxes of cookies last year. I know you're no longer a scout, but would you mind selling for us anyway this year?"

"Are you serious?" I said, incredulous. "I'm not good enough to be in the Boy Scouts because I don't have a letter from a religious leader, but you want me to sell your cookies?"

My father, who was standing nearby, overheard this insanity and gestured to me to cover the receiver. "How much is that guitar you want?" he whispered.

"Twenty-five bucks."

"Tell him you want ten cents' commission for every box you sell, and we'll sell hundreds of boxes and you'll get a guitar."

So I struck the deal. Days later, my father and I hopped in the car, and he drove me down to the jewelry district. We sold 242 boxes of cookies. I broke the record. Smashed it. I made $24.20. Dad, big spender that he was, threw in the remaining eighty cents, and I bought my first bass guitar.

Now all I needed was a band.

The first attempt at making a band occurred on the night of November 9, 1965.

Why would I remember that date? Because after our first (and only) rehearsal after school that cold fall day, the five other guys and I walked around my neighborhood talking excitedly about how the rehearsal went. All of a sudden, as we stood on the corner of Ninety-Third Street and Columbus Avenue, we looked up and all the lights in the city flickered and then went out. It was the night of the great East Coast blackout. Here we were, six thirteen-year-old guys, standing around a totally dark city. After wandering around in the dark for a couple of hours, we decided to call ourselves The Lost 6.

The Lost 6 never did rehearse again.

There were a couple of kids in the neighborhood who had similar aspirations as me. Paul Herman was a budding drummer. A Chinese kid named Bing Gong was a singer. And I, of course, had my guitar. We started rehearsing together and called ourselves John, Paul, and Bingo. Which, I would still argue, was a stroke of band-name genius.

We learned two great songs and entered our band to play at the Joan of Arc Junior High School Eighth Grade Talent Contest. The first was Bob Dylan's "Like a Rolling Stone," because it had been a big hit, and, frankly, anyone could sing Dylan, even someone with

LEFT TO RIGHT: My brother, Jeff; my sister-in-law, Ricky; my niece, Eliza; my dad, Lou; my mom, Evaline. **SITTING:** Me and my dog, Bagel.

my terrible voice. I believe that God created Dylan so I could sing cover material. If you can sing Dylan in tune, it sounds wrong. So, I was the perfect singer for that one. We opened with that, and it went pretty well.

We also chose to do a song by a counterculture Village band called the Fugs. They were called the Fugs because they couldn't call themselves the Fucks. So John, Paul, and Bingo followed "Like a Rolling Stone" with a song called "I Couldn't Get High":

> *I went to a party the other night*
> *I wanted to fill my brains with light*
> *But I couldn't get high*

When an eighth grader starts singing "I couldn't get high" at a school function, it's not too hard to predict what happens next. They pulled the plug and threw us out. We lost to a tough-guy group from the neighborhood called the Bats.

John, Paul, and Bingo broke up, and I started hanging around and playing music with our vanquishers.

The Bats had Orlando Viera, Carlos Avalaras, and Chris Wallace from Ninety-Ninth Street, where they rehearsed in the basement apartment of the drummer, Carlos. Other neighborhood musicians at the time—Manny Hernandez, Hector Melendez, Freddy Rivera, and Louie and Rudy Echeverri—all became members of multiple bands that broke up and reconstituted every twenty minutes or so. We all loved the same music, and we'd be in a lot of different bands as the years went on. That bass that I bought with my Boy Scout money finally came in handy, as I was recruited as the bass player for the Bats.

At the time, I still thought I was somehow going to graduate, go to college, and pursue a traditional education. It never even occurred to me that I'd follow another path.

OFF THE PATH TO GET ON THE PATH

WHEN I WAS A JUNIOR IN HIGH school, I heard black activist H. Rap Brown give a speech at Columbia University. It got me so energized, I started a riot at my school, Brandeis High School, the next day.

It all started innocently enough. I brought in some folks from Students for a Democratic Society (SDS)—infamously known at the time for staging anti-draft occupations of campuses around the US—to put on a dissent-charged play in the common area. I don't know exactly how it started, but suddenly students and teachers alike were screaming and pushing and running around. It was chaos.

I sprinted around the school kicking in doors and yelling something along the lines of "Get out now! Rise up! Emancipate yourself!" I don't exactly remember what I yelled, as I was pretty stoned at the time, but I emptied the school out.

The next day, I got expelled. I wasn't going to class, anyway, so I didn't really care. But my mother cared. A lot. She challenged the administration. "How could you expel my brilliant child? He only has a year and a half until graduation. You must let him return to school."

The school acquiesced and made me sign an agreement that I would not be disruptive any longer. But then, about a month later, some friends broke into the print shop and stole the print block, which included the official heading of the school newspaper and the signature of the principal. True to my agreement with the administration, I had not been involved, but I knew it was happening, and I knew why.

The teachers had recently been on strike, forcing schools to shut down for nine weeks. As a result, classes hadn't started until November. As part of their settlement, the teachers had agreed to make up for the lost time by extending all classes by five minutes for the rest of the year. Nobody had consulted the students about that decision; we were not pleased. We felt we were being punished for something we did not do.

I had no part in the break-in, but I did join in exercising my right to free speech. We wrote a fiery anti-teacher diatribe and printed it with the stolen print block. In between the official school header and the signature of the principal, we published and distributed an op-ed saying that all the teachers should be banished to Long Island, and that Long Island should be sawed off from the rest of New York so it would float out to sea and the teachers would all drown in the middle of the Atlantic.

It was political satire. We didn't actually mean that the teachers should all drown in the Atlantic. The Hudson River would have worked just as well. But the administration (who obviously had no sense of humor) said that what I'd written constituted a breaking of my no-disruption vow, so they threw me out of school again.

So I sued the board of education for violating my constitutional rights. My parents supported me. They went to the Emergency Civil Liberties Committee for help. We found out from them that there were two other kid-originating lawsuits going on at the time. A thirteen-year-old girl named Alice De Rivera was suing the city because Stuyvesant High School was boys only and she wanted to go to school there, and a fourteen-year-old kid named Joshua Mamis (whose brother, Toby, is now Alice Cooper's manager and a good friend of mine), who sent around a petition to have the principal replaced following the student lockout during the NYC teachers' strike. He was threatened with suspension or expulsion and sued the school on the grounds that any of these actions violated his constitutional rights to petition.

Josh won, and Alice won, which is why Stuyvesant went coed.

By the time they got around to me, the judge was really angry and the board of education had had enough. They knew they'd have a major fight on their hands, and they knew my mother was politically powerful. They asked her what it would take for this thing to just go away, and she passed the question along to me.

I hated Brandeis—all my friends were at George Washington High School up in the Heights (or "G-Dubs," as we called it). I'd always wanted to go there, but I didn't want to take French, which was one of their requirements. "If they let me go to G-Dubs," I said, "I'll drop the suit."

By this time, I had gotten heavily into dealing drugs. One thing about that activity was, in an odd way, kind of positive. I was sort of a wallflower when I was a teenager, but when I was dealing, I was Mr. Magnetic Drug Dealer. Everyone wanted me to go on all the revolutionary activities, and everyone wanted me at their parties.

Understandably, most people don't want to talk about the positive elements of dealing and doing drugs, but the truth is I became really self-confident, really street smart, and really good at math. I mean, if it weren't for dealing, I wouldn't be half the man I am today, which is a horrible thing to say—and, kids, I don't recommend it as a career choice—but because of the dealing, I became an emboldened, popular guy. I started thinking that I liked this kind of thing. I knew my future job wasn't to become a big drug dealer, but I just liked the ride. And I somehow felt that it would eventually lead me to a rock star future. What I didn't anticipate, of course, was the terrible price I and others would pay as a result.

Despite all this, I managed to get through the first year at G-Dubs without incident. It was, actually, an uncharacteristically quiet period. Then in the summer of 1969, a teen magazine called *Ingenue* contacted me for a piece that would ultimately be titled "High School Revolutionaries: Heroes and Troublemakers," and they did a feature on me. And I have to admit I was liking the notoriety.

After I did the interview, they told me they wanted to do a photo shoot. I agreed, and sometime in the summer of 1969, we shot the pics. I didn't give it another thought.

Age seventeen.

The night before the shoot, I was hanging out with Vicki Sue Robinson (who, by the way, later recorded the hit "Turn the Beat Around"). At that time Vicki was just another hippie friend of mine. We both fell asleep in Central Park and woke up the next morning at 8:00 a.m. I called my mother to let her know I wasn't dead, and she reminded me that I had a photo shoot at ten o'clock.

So I showed up at my photo shoot wearing the clothes I'd slept in the night before, and that was the picture they used in the magazine.

When I got back to school that fall, I had one year left until graduation. All I had to do was lie low. Be invisible. But then that article came out. Thanks to *Ingenue*, I was all over the fucking place as the High School Revolutionary poster child. I may as well have set up shop and hung out a shingle saying, "Revolutionary for Hire."

One day, a group of students came to me and said, "Hey, man. You know our administration is racist, right?"

"What's racist about it?" I asked.

"We think the school advisory board funnels all the Black and Puerto Rican kids into vocational colleges. We want to set up a table in the lobby where parents can review the suggestions by the guidance counselors, to prove that this is happening."

"That's a good cause," I said. "But don't involve me. I'm just trying to sell dope and play my guitar and graduate." I had no intention of going to classes that year. I was just dealing every day, doing great business at the bleachers and having a good time, and I didn't want anything to get in the way of graduating.

"No, you don't understand, man. You brought it to Brandeis. Now we need you to do it here."

I really didn't want to get involved, but they inflamed my inner liberal and convinced me to help. Now, we could have printed flyers and given a few soapbox speeches in the cafeteria, but since I had just been profiled in a major magazine as a revolutionary hero and/ or troublemaker, that wasn't going to cut it. Instead, I led a student takeover of the principal's office.

The police raided the school and arrested everyone. Well, almost everyone. I was in the bathroom at the time. The parents were informed that their kids were arrested and went down to the Tombs at 2:00 a.m. to get them out. They were eventually given a court date and released to the care of their horrified parents.

You'd think a terrifying experience like that would have put an end to our adolescent social uprising, but you'd be wrong. This was just the beginning. Our one act of rebellion led to a series of daily events that went on for the rest of the year. Riots in the school. Marches in the hallways. Every. Single. Day. It got so intense that the police actually set up a precinct office in the school gym at the bottom of the bleachers, where all the druggies and junkies and dealers hung out. I'd deal drugs daily right over where the police had stationed themselves.

As for me, well, my revolutionary responsibilities took precedence over my studies. I didn't go to class all year. Even though my last year of high school had started quietly enough, it was clear that I was not going to graduate.

Politics and social justice aside, I still wanted to be a rock star. The music industry is a notoriously savage business. I sold drugs to make money for music. Guitars and concerts cost more money than I could earn selling model planes and pens at Berman Twins on Broadway for eighty dollars a week.

I was dealing pot and acid in 1968, but I'd never taken LSD. One day, I had the thought that it might be a good idea to sample what I was selling.

My first acid trip was on April 9, 1968. I'll never forget the date, because it was the day of Martin Luther King Jr.'s funeral. It was the afternoon. I was in Central Park, and I took a whole tab of acid. I started getting this weird sensation and thought it would be best for me to go home.

When I closed my bedroom door, the entire room visually exploded. All my posters came off my wall and started swimming around. Everything was melting and pulsating, and I looked down at my chest, where I saw my heart throb like a cartoon version of a love beat.

I somehow got it into my head that I had to tell my parents and walked into the living room, where they were watching King's funeral on TV. While they sat there, I saw them turn into giant hogs. I said to myself, "If I tell these two hogs I'm OD'ing on acid, they're going to put me in Bellevue Hospital."

I raced out of the living room and into the bathroom. I took my clothes off and took a shower, thinking maybe I could somehow force myself straight. I don't know what the temperature of the water was, because I couldn't really feel it. I looked up at the nozzle, and paint was pouring from where the water should have been. I was soon covered in liquid sheets of yellow and red and green. Then my head comes off my body, floats over to the windowsill, and turns itself around to watch my headless torso take a remarkably colorful shower.

At some point, my head went back over to my body and reattached itself. And when all the colors turned to black and white, I said, "You must be coming down, so just hold on."

My father knocked repeatedly on the door. "You okay, John?" I apparently had been in there for four hours.

"It's hot today," I kept saying. "I'm taking a cold shower." Seeing it was April, it wasn't the most credible response.

When I finally felt normal again, I walked back into the living room, and my parents were there. There were no more hogs. Just them. "Hey, what's wrong with you?" my dad asked. What was I supposed to say? *No problem, Dad. Just a bad acid trip. Everything's cool?* Instead, I ignored the question and went back to business as usual.

Around this time, my good friend David Schiff suggested that we blow out of New York for a while and go to Bermuda. He'd been there before, loved the place, and had a friend we could crash with.

He may as well have invited me to Planet Zepton. I'd never been out of the United States; hell, I'd never been south of Brooklyn. As far as I knew, Bermuda was somewhere in the Bahamas, wherever that was. How would we even get there? It cost real money to fly to the other side of the planet. And, besides, I didn't have a passport.

"Do you have a library card?" he asked.

"Yeah," I said.

"That's all you need to get into the country," he said. "And it's off the coast of Virginia, about a ninety-minute plane ride. And tickets are $42.50 each way."

"Mom," I said soon after. "I'm going to Bermuda."

David and I wound up living in Bermuda for three weeks, and I had the most amazing time of my life. I was only seventeen years old at the time, but the friendships I developed in Bermuda have stayed with me all my life. Some of my closest buddies are Bermudan, and we've maintained a close relationship for fifty years. And I met my first serious girlfriend there, too.

Gail Horneffer was stunningly gorgeous, older than me, and, I thought, way out of my league. She also happened to be the great-granddaughter of Robert E. Lee. Nonetheless, back in the States she started dating me, a Jew revolutionary from New York. I think she partly did this just to piss off her mother. It was around that time that I decided I would be dropping out of school.

The following May, Gail asked me to visit her in Richmond, Virginia, where she was living.

Two days later, on May 4, four students were killed at Kent State during an anti-war demonstration. This caused almost immediate rioting at college campuses around the country. Gail's apartment was around the corner of the University of Richmond, and police and fire trucks were everywhere. This was no longer a nice quiet time to get to know my girlfriend, so I got on a returning Greyhound bus back to Manhattan. My mother didn't want me to go to Richmond in the first place, as I had never been out of NYC (except to Bermuda).

When I got back to my parents' apartment, we talked about the continuing student unrest and the rampant racism around the country. At this point I proclaimed to my mom that I didn't need a high school education and I wasn't going to return to school.

My mother wasn't thrilled. "You only have two more months until graduation," she said, incredulous.

"Thing is, Mom," I confessed, "I haven't been in school this entire year; I haven't been to class once."

"So, what are you going to do?" she asked, resigning herself to my decision.

"Don't worry about me. I'm going to be a rock star."

I don't think I really believed that at the time. I just needed to shut the conversation down. It sounded good, and I was feeling invincible. As half of the hippie golden couple with the great-granddaughter of a Confederate commander, I moved out of my mom's and in with Gail and her brother, Steve, who rented an apartment on the East Side. And we were all crazy into drugs. Like I said: invincible. I was dealing and getting fucked up all day and going to rock concerts almost every night. Over the next two years this was my life: drugs, concerts, jamming with bands, and buying new guitars and amps with my hard-earned dope dealer's cash.

Drug use among hippies who hung out at the Fountain in Central Park started innocently enough with pot. But over the next four years it spiraled into every imaginable confluence of drugs: hash,

Long, curly hair and LSD. 1971.

acid (multiple brands like brown dot, window pane, peace tabs, purple and orange Owsley, mighty Quinn), STP, MDA, MDA 2, psilocybin, mescaline, and DMT, to name a few. And I did 'em all. In great amounts. All the time. So did most of my friends.

And then came my fateful date with heroin, which had hit the scene in early 1971. And it brought this whole invincibility theory of mine to a screeching halt.

My mother had known about my drug dealing, and that started to weigh heavily on my conscience. So, in the spring of 1971, I got a legitimate job working at Berman Twins, the hardware-and-stationery-and-everything-else store in my neighborhood. But I was hardly separated from the drug scene, because the owner's nephew also dealt drugs. And we had quite a time together. We got stoned in the basement. We got high on the roof.

One day another employee came in with some heroin he wanted to exchange for weed. I made the trade for a bag of H, which I promptly snorted in the bathroom. When I walked back into the store, the guy asked, "Where's the bag?"

"I snorted it," I said.

"That's not good," he said.

"What do you mean?"

"That bag had four doses of heroin in it."

Now, I prided myself on my ability to consume drugs. I was tough. I could control my hallucinations. But even I could not control four doses of heroin at once. The enormous euphoria I felt now turned to fear. My heart alternated between pounding hard and slowing down. I started sweating.

The store was only two blocks from my parents' place, so I ran there, even though I didn't live there anymore. I was having a hard time breathing. I was panicking. What was I supposed to do? Tell my mom I've just OD'ed on heroin?

Something told me there were some problems you just don't take to your mother—at least not yet. Instead, I went into the bathroom (do you see a pattern here?), shoved my hand down my throat, and commenced throwing up with the 100 percent commitment I give to everything I do. I threw up, then threw up some more. Think firehose. I kept retching and heaving until I was upchucking blood.

I was naked in the tub, covered in blood and vomit, when my mother, who does not miss a trick, asked through the locked door, "What's going on in there, John?"

I said, in my best not-overdosing voice, "I'm okay. I just ate something bad."

Then I threw up some more. And some more. To myself I was saying, "Man, I really, *really* screwed up this time. I'm probably going to die." Mercifully, I had finally thrown up enough that the world stopped moving and everything calmed down. I looked around and thought, "Maybe it's time to stop this drug thing."

I realized I needed to take a break from the New York drug

scene. I was tired of the people. Drug dealers, users, hippies, musicians, and revolutionaries can be lovely people, and I was one of them, but I needed a break from the crazies. Call me perceptive, but after the heroin episode, I sensed I was approaching the end of the line with my drug-dealing ride. So I decided to go to Amsterdam for a while. I mean, what better place could I choose than the recreational drug capital of the Western world?

Earlier, when I was getting my passport with my best friend, Victor, who was going to be traveling with me, a guy who told us he was a journalist from *TIME* magazine asked us about our travel plans. As a spoof, I told him we were heading to Amsterdam to pursue "the elusive Great White Hash." It sounded good at the time. It sounded downright Melvillian. We were embarking on the quest for our generation's equivalent of Moby Dick. To us, it was just a gag. A funny story that we'd made up on the spot.

It was a little less funny when he wrote the story and it appeared in the July 19, 1971, edition of *TIME* and, instead of calling me Ishmael, the shmuck used my real name.

I called my mom from Kennedy Airport just before we got on the plane. She asked, "Did you do an interview for *TIME* magazine?"

"Why?"

"Because I think they quoted you."

I hung up and bought a copy. I opened to a story called "Rites of Passage: The Knapsack Nomads," and there I was. "'Thousands of my friends are going,' observed ponytailed John Segall, 18, as he queued up to get his passport in New York. 'No one will be left in the city this summer except the junkies who couldn't rip off enough people to get the bread to go.'"

I called my mother back, but instead of busting my chops for saying something stupid, she reminded me to keep a low profile when breaking the rules. "Did you have to give them your name? Did you have to spell it correctly?"

"Mom, I thought that was a joke. I didn't believe it when he said he was from *TIME* magazine."

"You're an idiot. You know that, don't you?"

Rites of Passage: The Knapsack Nomads

SUMMER in Europe has become a rite of passage for American youth, the Woodstock of the '70s. Young vagabonds have always tripped out to Europe for the warm months, but there is something different about Exodus 1971. Most of the new wanderers are not highly motivated students seeking culture or well-heeled dollar scions out to raise hell. They are generally the same bunch of kids who would normally have had summer jobs lifeguarding at the pool or dispensing hamburgers at MacDonald's. Only this year few summer jobs are available for students. The unemployment rates top 15% for the 16-to-19 age group, and 9.9% for those aged 20 to 24, the highest in seven and ten years, respectively. The youth fares have given students and recent graduates a fresh chance to get away from it all.

The new nomads travel light: a few old pullovers wadded into a knapsack and a few hundred dollars stuffed into their jeans. Many of the girls are unsupported by anything but their male companions. While some of these not-so-innocents abroad may have well-planned itineraries, most are rather aimlessly following crowds of their countrymen in a quest for good vibrations. They are joining millions of footloose European youths, who are wandering far and wide from Hammerfest to Gibraltar—and points even farther out. Whatever their mother tongue, the youngsters manage to communicate. They speak a sort of *Jeunesperanto*, and they share much the same style of dress, penchant for folk music and smoking habits.

"Thousands of my friends are going," observed ponytailed John Segall, 18, as he queued up to get his passport in New York. "No one will be left in the city this summer except the junkies who couldn't rip off enough people to get the bread to go." Said Conrad Young, 23, as his plane circled London's Heathrow Airport for a landing:

"Maybe I'll go to Switzerland. Or maybe Spain. Anyplace with lots of young people. Just follow the crowds."

Old-fashioned hedonism remains an attraction. "I'll roam until my book of traveler's checks gets down to the last leaf," said Viet Nam Veteran Steve Verich of Akron, Ohio, traveling in West Germany. "When I was in the jungle, I vowed that if I ever got out alive, I'd

SHARING QUARTERS IN COPENHAGEN

spend a long time in Europe—drinking the local brand and making it with all the chicks until I got my fill. Then I'd return home to do something constructive. But now my traveler's checks are nearly gone, and I still haven't any notion of what I should do back home, or even who I really am."

Most young Americans abroad share one obsession: getting by on the least amount of money. Unlike the conspicuously consuming adult U.S. tourists

of an earlier day, they spend little for gifts, souvenirs, meals or lodging. The challenge of "living free," seeing Europe on a shoestring and with a sleeping bag, has elements of reverse snobism that appeal to the professed antimaterialistic instincts of youth. Ken Stephens, 29, of St. Petersburg, Fla., figured in Amsterdam that he can last two months on only $180. Bill Hyman, 23, said in London that he was getting by on $3 a day or less. The pinchpenny ethic usually requires sleeping in youth hostels (from 65¢ to little more than $1 a night), hitchhiking and mooching meals from friendly Europeans. One compromise with comfort, however, is a money saver: a new category of Eurailpass for students 14 to 25 costs only $125 for two months' unlimited second-class travel and sleeping on trains. All together, 104,000 Eurailpasses were sold in 1970, and travel agents expect sales to rise by 45% this year.

A whole underground lore of overseas moneysaving is being built up by waves of knapsackers. New tips are communicated almost instantaneously through a transnational grapevine. Among recent intelligence reports: sleeping in London's St. James's and Green parks, though normally forbidden by police, is being tolerated this year. University cafeterias in Germany and Switzerland sell rib-sticking meals for less than a half dollar. Specially cheap flights within Europe are offered by the British Student Travel Center and other official youth organizations to full-time high school and college students who have convincing identification. Sample one-way prices: London to Paris $13.20, London to Leningrad $48. Belgian railroads give 50% reductions to students. The municipal steam baths of Copenhagen, Stockholm and Oslo charge only $1 or less for steam bath and swim. Troubled trav-

TIME Magazine—July 19, 1971.

So in addition to ambition, a love of rock and roll, an entrepreneurial spirit, and physical stamina, let's add my mother's confidence in me to the list of traits that have made me successful.

When I arrived in Amsterdam, I asked the woman in whose house we were staying what I should do to see the sights.

"There's a big park called Vondelpark," she told us. "You should go there. A lot of hippies there."

Nothing provides relief from New York hippies like European hippies. Except Vondelpark, which was packed with New York hippies. Right away I ran into ten guys I knew from Central Park. In this new-but-familiar setting, the entrepreneurial juices kicked in, and I decided, what the hell? I have a skill. I have experience. So, why not deal drugs in Amsterdam?

I researched the market and found out hash was legal—and a dollar a gram. That was all the business plan I needed. In New York at the time, hash was ten dollars a gram. It may not have been the elusive Great White Hash of legend, but I decided to buy some and start selling it.

Now, I can hear all you business types saying, "Hold on. Just because hash retails for one-tenth what it does in New York, you can't arbitrage it in Amsterdam, because people won't pay your markup."

Not true. I realized that maybe the idiots coming over from the States won't know how cheap it is right away, so I'd sell it for five dollars a gram—which to the uninitiated was half the price of US hash, so it sounded like an amazing deal.

Listen, when you're dealing in Europe in multiple currencies, and everyone's on acid, you take advantage of this kind of thing.

I parked myself at the Milky Way, the English name for one of the two big hash clubs, the Melkweg, and started barking, "Hash! I'm selling hash!"

Every day, newly arrived Americans would come to the Melkweg, hear me hawking, hear the low, low price, be blown away by what a "steal" they were getting, and load up on the merchandise. Of course, they'd come back two days later with a customer service complaint.

"Hey, man, it's only a dollar around town, and you charged me five."

Hippies by the waterfront.

"Did I force you to buy it?"

"No."

"Well, that's how much I charge. You could have gone to Sven or Horst or somebody else, but you didn't. You came to me, and now you know." (That kind of street moxie would come in handy a few years later when I was dealing with music executives.)

As you can see, instead of taking a break from drugs, I found a new lease on the business. Then four days into this renewed life, I was smoking hash at Vondelpark when a cop came up to me.

"What do you have?" he insisted.

Sweat sprouting on my forehead in anticipation of the worst, I showed him my stash.

He broke my plate of Afghan hash in two and handed me half.

"You're only allowed this much," he said.

"Oh my God," I said. "I love this town."

By this time, Victor and I had gone our separate ways. But just before we'd left for Europe, he had fallen in love with a New York woman whose name I can't remember. (When you consider how much dope I was smoking, it's amazing I remember anything at all. So, for the purpose of this narrative, let's just call her Victor's girlfriend.) Unbeknownst to me, he'd persuaded her to come to Europe. One day, she and I happened to run into each other at Vondelpark and, naturally, she wanted to see Victor.

"I don't know how to find him," I said. "Last I saw him, he was headed to Yugoslavia."

"Okay," she said, rapidly adjusting to the news. "I only have a week. I want to hitch through Europe. Want to come with me?"

The truth is, I had come to Amsterdam to get away from all the Central Park idiots, and now they were all here. I was struck with a blinding flash of the obvious: it was time to leave the Netherlands and head off with Victor's girlfriend.

"Sure," I said.

So Victor's girlfriend and I hitched to Paris. Along the way we shared hotel beds, but there was no sex. You read that right: the Future Rock God led a chaste relationship with his buddy's girl.

In Paris, someone stole our passports. At the American Embassy, I proved my identity with a library card—a *library card*—and vouched for the identity of Victor's girlfriend. (I did know her name at the time. I really did.) And that's all it took to get our passports replaced.

In any case, Victor's girlfriend was anxious to absorb as much of Europe as she could in one week, so off we went to London. Talk about ending up in the right place at the right time!

This, you have to understand, was London in the summer of '71. Here's what that meant to an aspiring rocker like myself: "Who's Next" by the Who, Rod Stewart's "Every Picture Tells a Story," and the Rolling Stones' "Sticky Fingers" were all on the radio. As we walked down the London streets, phenomenal, earth-shattering music was blasting from every shop. "Move on Up" by Curtis Mayfield was the single of the summer, and that is exactly what I felt like I was doing.

The first day in London, there was a free concert at Hyde Park by Chris Spedding. Rock hard cores will recognize Spedding as a session guitarist and producer who's worked with everyone from the Sex Pistols to Paul McCartney. I mean, rock was *happening* in London.

By this point, Victor's girlfriend had to go back to the States. We never got naked together, but I *did* get her to take half my clothes back to New York, because, as a good Jewish boy, I had overpacked.

Back in Amsterdam, my first errand was to find a pay phone. I needed to call home to assure my parents I wasn't dead. Thousands of hippies were lined up to do the same, including Victor. He told me, "I'm living in a hotel for hash dealers. You've got to live with me."

I took him up on that. Right as we walked into this hotel, a half pound of Afghan hash was serving as a paperweight on the check-in sheet. This was better than the cop in the park who advised me on proper inventory practices. I thought, *Oh my God, this is the greatest hotel on planet Earth.*

Our days followed a routine. We got up in the morning and got something to eat. Then we went back to the hotel room and got fucked up, then headed to the park to deal drugs. Because there's nothing like a routine to encourage regular work habits.

By this time, Victor was shooting opium every night from a silver-plated set of works engraved with his name. You could buy your own set of hypodermic needles and have your name engraved on the silver plating of the hypodermic needle. It would have been romantic if it wasn't so messed up.

I said, "Victor, come on, man. I didn't come here to watch you do this on a nightly basis. Let's go out."

Nodding, he replied, "No, man. You go. I'll be fine."

We spent the summer that way—Victor stoned in our room and me being something of the house dealer at the Paradiso and the Milky Way. There were free concerts in the park. It was the ultimate place to be as a kid neck-deep in hippie youth culture. But changes were coming when we got back to New York.

My girlfriend Gail's drug use was bumming me out. Victor's drug use was bumming me out. Selling drugs for a living was bumming me out. I started to wonder, where's my rock-and-roll life? Where's the dream I had? All the years of dealing, what was it all about?

Dealing was never about making money. It was about buying guitars, traveling, being able to see all the rock concerts, and laying groundwork for my success. And I had done that. It was time to move on.

I said to myself, "I'd better get serious and get a band together, because the time is fading for this whole drug thing."

At nineteen, you feel you're immortal, but I had had enough life-threatening experiences to question my immortality:

I was almost murdered at gunpoint at the age of ten by the robbers in the building.

I was almost murdered at gunpoint at the age of twelve by a punk in Central Park who pulled a gun on me.

Someone pulled a knife on me during a drug deal in an elevator in Harlem.

I almost died on the roof of my building smoking dope in the elevator tower when I leaned on a gearshift and someone turned the elevator on. If my friend hadn't grabbed me by the shirt, I would have been crushed to death.

Then there was the acid overdose. Then the heroin overdoses. (Yeah, there was more than one.)

But before I let drugs kill me, I wanted to find out how it felt to die.

As I've said, whatever I do, I do 100 percent, even if it's crazy. *Especially* if it's crazy.

The crazy psychedelic in question was DMT, or dimethyltryptamine. This is the chemical your brain releases when you die. When people who've had a near-death experience report seeing a white light, it's because their bodies release DMT at death.

DMT makes LSD feel like a nicotine buzz. It's like shooting LSD into your jugular vein. But it only lasts about ten minutes, so if you can withstand this unbelievable amount of psychedelic activity in your brain, you will see shit that you would never believe you'd see. I was warned that if I did DMT, I would need people to hold me down while I was on it.

I smoked the DMT at the dealer's house. I lay back and felt like a supersonic transport at takeoff. All of a sudden I was walking in the Aztec pyramids. I was seeing hieroglyphics on the wall. I was seeing pharaohs. I was walking *through* pharaohs. I was walking through the pyramids. It was an explosion of light, color, and time that I can't possibly explain to you except that when it ended I had a guy sitting on each arm and a guy sitting on my chest.

Later I read Timothy Leary's essay on DMT, which described almost to a tee what I saw. Because, believe it or not, I did it one more time. It was after I did DMT the second time that I said to myself, "If I don't do psychedelics for the rest of my life, it really doesn't matter, because I've seen it all."

You know how when you make up your mind to do something different, the universe conspires to help you along? In my case, as I came to realize the drug scene was going sour, the universe helped in a big way. Now it was time to *really* end the drugs. Unlike rockers who do drugs to do their shows, I had to *get rid* of drugs to do rock, before they got rid of me.

One day, two former high school friends came into my room, pulled out a knife, and put it up to my throat. Then they helped themselves to whatever I had—half a pound, maybe a pound of weed and four or five hundred dollars.

My mother, in her infinite, intuitive wisdom, picked that very moment to walk into the room.

Of course, these former pals of mine knew my mom, so they said, "Hi, Mrs. Segall," like it was an episode of *Leave It to Beaver*, only one of them was holding a knife to my back.

"Everything okay here?" my mother asked.

"Yeah, everything's okay, Mom," I said, forcing a smile.

She walked out and they said to each other, "I think we should go now," so, the gentleman that I am, I walked them to the front door.

I opened the door and told them, "Nice to see you guys. I guess you're off my Christmas list." I shut the door behind them.

My mother asked, "Did you just get ripped off?"

"How did you know?"

"You were white as a ghost," she told me.

"Mom, I'm done. The dealing is over," I told her. And it was.

As for the drug taking, that needed to go with more ceremony. After all, I still had a handful of drugs in my black box, and I couldn't just let them go to waste, could I?

One of my (now former) customers, who was a timpani player for the Radio City Music Hall band and living with two Rockettes, invited me to the Easter show at Radio City. I had never been there, so I jumped at the chance. To return the favor, I gave him and his Rockette roommates a bunch of acid in exchange for my front-row ticket to the show.

As my druggie swan song, I decided to take every drug I had left all at once. And I'm not talking about a few Advil here. I had mescaline, psilocybin, angel dust, THC, STP, LSD, and an assortment of other little goodies.

OFF THE PATH TO GET ON THE PATH

I'd had enough experience to know that I could handle just about anything coursing through my system, so this was just the last exercise in the "I can take more than you" contests I'd had with friends over the years. But if I was going to leave the drug life behind, I was going to go out in a blaze of glory. This was to be my last hurrah.

Goodbye, hippie John Segall. Tomorrow, I will be a former drug-user.

So, I swallowed everything in the box and off I went to Radio City Music Hall for the 1972 Easter show.

Radio City is so stunningly gorgeous, it looks like a hallucination anyway. But there I was, sitting in the front row, tripping balls on the kitchen sink–full of recreational drugs tap-dancing through my nervous system.

The featured movie was *What's Up, Doc?* starring Barbra Streisand and Ryan O'Neal, then after an intermission, the Easter show began. And everything in that theater was exploding.

Onstage, my friend was playing timpani. The two women he was screwing walked out with crosses, and I started laughing my ass off. The girls saw me, and they started laughing so hard they almost dropped their crosses. They may have been tripping, too, I don't know. But what a show.

When it was over, I stumbled out into a one-dimensional collage of color on Sixth Avenue. I was wasted, but somehow I made it home and, given that you're reading this story all these years later, you know what happened the next morning. I did, indeed, wake up.

"That's it," I said. "That's the end of that."

I was reborn. And I could feel change coming.

I WANNA ROCK

SURE ENOUGH, ONCE I CLEARED the decks of drugs, my new life of music-making started to seek me out. In a chance encounter that June, I found myself in the elevator of my apartment building having a conversation with a well-known music attorney, Peter Thall, who not only lived in the building but had asked me on a couple of occasions if I would babysit his daughter, Emily. Peter knew me as a musician primarily because I used to crank up my amp and play guitar with my window open. I'm sure I had a lot of fans in the building because of that.

"Are you in a band?" he asked me.

"Not currently," I told him.

"Do you want to audition for Wicked Lester? They already have a record deal." Peter was representing their record producer, Ron Johnson, so he knew they were looking for a guitar player. I jumped at the chance. He gave me the phone number of a guy named Gene Klein, who was the band's main man.

When I called, Gene told me that the band had made a record for Epic, but he and his partner, Stan Eisen, didn't like the direction. He said they currently sounded like Looking Glass (who had recently had a hit record with the song "Brandy") and that they wanted a heavier sound, more like the English band Slade. Then he asked me how I liked Led Zeppelin and Jimmy Page's guitar playing.

"I've seen Zeppelin five times in the last three years," I said.

Satisfied with my answer, Gene said, "Are you playing anywhere that we can come and see you?"

It just so happened that I would be jamming with a local band called Scout at a church dance that coming Sunday afternoon. And, true to his word, Gene came to the gig.

When I walked off the stage at the end of the set, Gene came up to me and told me to take my glasses off.

"Why?" I asked.

"Because you look too Jewish," he said.

I'd never heard that before.

"If you join the band," said Gene, "you'll have to change your last name." My name was still Segall back then. "It sounds as Jewish as you look."

When I asked him why it was a problem to seem Jewish, Gene explained that the new band was going to portray itself the way English bands look and sound; therefore, their band member names had to sound English, too. That's why Gene Klein was going to call himself Gene Simmons, and Stan Eisen was changing his name to Paul Stanley.

I had never thought that my real name was an issue until that moment. Looking back now, Gene was echoing what most of the Hollywood power brokers in the '40s and '50s told their latest stars. Basically, "You gotta change your name, kid!"

I think that there were two forces at play. One was that many famous (and not-so-famous) entertainers removed ethnic references to their last names to make themselves more palatable to the masses, and the other (in the case of KISS) was a real homage to the English rock bands of that era and the desire for American bands to sound British.

Gene was right. The moment I joined Silver Star (the band that became Twisted Sister), I was told that all the members had stage names. Mel Anderson was now Mell Star, Billy Steiger was now Billy Diamond, Michael O'Neil was now Michael Valentine, and Kenny Neill was now Kenneth Harrison Neill. I called myself Johnny Heartbreaker for about six months—I thought about Jonathan Livingston-Segall for a minute—then settled on Jay Jay French during the spring of 1973. That name and my ubiquitous sunglasses became my new image after looking in a mirror one night while putting on makeup prior to a show at a club called the Capricorn, on Route 17.

The actual inspiration, heretofore never divulged, of the name came from one of my blues guitar heroes, BB King. JJ French, BB King, get it? Short, to the point. I added the long spelling (Jay Jay) so as not to make it that obvious.

Gene then went on about how all the great English bands play through Marshall amp stacks—something very few American artists (except, notably, Jimi Hendrix) did at the time.

They were taking the band through a heavy metal makeover. The members of Wicked Lester looked like the Grateful Dead. Gene and Paul told me that beards were out (I didn't have one) and that the other members of Wicked Lester didn't know they were all going to be fired.

Apparently, I'd passed the first phase of the audition, because they invited me to come to their rehearsal space and jam with the band. When I met the other guys, I was introduced as a friend, not a potential band member. The jam sessions went on for about two weeks and seemed to be going pretty well, as far as I could tell. Then, suddenly, they stopped calling me.

I figured I wasn't good enough, and even though I was a little disappointed, I got over it and moved on pretty quickly.

I soon found myself playing in an Allman Brothers cover band called Maxwell Benjamin and the Downtown Boogaloos. We all moved into a big commune on the top of a mountain in Wilkes-Barre, Pennsylvania. We baled hay as a favor to the farm owners during the day and rehearsed at night. We played a lot of Allman Brothers and some Zep as well. All the guys in the band were veterans of the New Jersey bar scene, so we got an agent right away.

At the end of the summer, we played one show in Greenwood Lake, New York, which was just over the border from New Jersey. In those days the drinking age was eighteen in New York, but it was twenty-one in Jersey, so kids would drive over the border, see bands, get hammered, then get arrested when they came down the hill to come home.

The gig that night was a disaster. The guitar player got punched in the mouth by a jealous boyfriend, and I got my amplifiers stolen. After that, the band rapidly fell apart. It was now the end of the summer of '72, and—once again—I had no band. I thought to myself, *Jesus, what am I going to do next?*

Around that time, I started subscribing to a music magazine called *Fusion*, and with my subscription, I got three free albums. The cover story of the September issue was about David Bowie, and the albums were *The Rise and Fall of Ziggy Stardust and the Spiders from Mars*, Lou Reed's *Transformer*, and Mott the Hoople's *All the Young Dudes*.

In a flash, my music world changed.

I loved the music and image of David Bowie, and especially the rock-god image of his guitar player, Mick Ronson. I didn't want to look like a member of the Allman Brothers anymore. I wanted to look like David Bowie. This was what Gene and Paul had been trying to tell me. This English glam look was the new thing, and I wanted to be a part of it.

Soon after, a close friend of mine told me about a new band called the New York Dolls, and he dragged me to a show to see them play. And man, they looked great. The audience was not the old hippie crowd. They were glam fans and Andy Warhol–looking characters.

The Dolls were very English-looking and Warhol-style androgynous. But their playing?

God-awful.

Around that time, I heard that David Bowie was coming to New York to play Carnegie Hall, so I ran out and got tickets. The show was amazing. They played almost all of the *Ziggy* album, and I was mesmerized by Bowie. Watching him onstage, I knew I wanted to become a glam god. The following week I went to see the Dolls, who were playing weekly at the Mercer Arts Center, and—lo and behold—Bowie was sitting right behind me. I knew then and there that this was a scene that I wanted to be a part of ASAP!

Soon I got a shag haircut, which felt like a betrayal of my hippie roots, but I was on a new, exciting path of discovery.

Shaggy and blonde.

I had promised my friend Charlie I would go see the Dead with him that October, but that would be my last Dead show. Charlie and I used to jam every Wednesday night after he finished working at a film editing house. The guy who worked in the booth next to him was named Wes Craven. Yes, that Wes Craven. Charlie, Wes, and I jammed every week. We also were all Deadheads. Charlie even worked on the Dead crew during their 1972 summer tour of Europe.

So, living up to my commitment to Charlie and Wes, I went to see the Grateful Dead one last time. I had seen the Dead twenty-six times before, and I loved every performance. But that night, for the first time, I wasn't high on acid or anything else. It was my very first sober experience of the Dead. And I realized something that night: the Grateful Dead was the worst band I ever heard in my life. I walked out of Roosevelt Stadium and never saw them again. I never even played an album of theirs after that.

I was now in full glitter/glam mode, and that was the way it was going to go for me for the next couple of decades. No more hippie bands with scraggly hair and beards. It was going to be makeup and costumes and glam for ever and ever, amen.

I started looking in the *Village Voice* classifieds for glam bands needing guitar players. I answered an ad from a band who said they had a record deal. The phone number looked familiar. It was Gene Klein. He told me that they'd filled the guitar position, but he invited me to their rehearsal loft on East Twenty-Third.

A couple of weeks later, I went down there with a close friend, Tommy Jahelka. The loft was big, and on one side of the room was all the gear. The amps were Marshall stacks. I was introduced to the new guitar player, Paul Frehley, also known as Ace. Peter Criss was now also in the band. They began to play the old Wicked Lester songs, but they were now super loud and heavy. Ace's playing was really good. Much better than mine. He also had the look. Sitting in a chair in front of the band was the producer Ron Johnson.

I could tell that there was a powerful, professional vision for the brand they were creating. They had just changed their name from Wicked Lester to KISS, and although they hadn't yet adopted what would come to be their iconic makeup, they looked great. Even the amps were set up to make a statement. In every sense I could see the future in this band. Yes, the Dolls were better known at that point and had already been on magazine covers, but KISS seemed built to conquer. And as an added bonus, they not only had a vision, but unlike the New York Dolls, they were great players and singers.

Given what you know about what a phenom KISS turned out to be, you might think I'd have been envious that Ace got the guitar gig. And you'd probably be right, except for one thing. That afternoon, I overheard a conversation that showed me I'd actually dodged a bullet.

At one point in the rehearsal, when the band had stopped between songs, Ron Johnson declared that he thought they were ready to go out and perform. Ace agreed.

Incensed at his guitar player's temerity, Gene pulled Ace to a corner of the room and pointed his finger in Ace's face.

"Don't you *ever* give your opinion as to when we are ready," Gene sneered. "Only I say when we're ready, do you understand me?"

What an asshole, I thought. That kind of shit would never have gone down with me. I wouldn't have lasted ten minutes.

So, as I continued my search for a band, I kept on learning songs and practicing my playing until the right opportunity came along—which I knew it would.

Throughout my life, I have believed that the more your life intersects with others, the greater the chance that valuable connections will present themselves. Nothing could be a greater example of this than a phone call I received on Friday, December 15, 1972, from Tony Petri, the drummer I had played with in Maxwell Benjamin and the Downtown Boogaloos that previous summer.

"Hey, John," Tony said. "You're still into David Bowie and Mott the Hoople, right?"

"Yes," I replied.

"My new booking agent is looking for a guitar player for a glitter band," he told me. "Interested?"

"You're fucking damn right I am!" I screamed.

Tony gave me the number for Lou Mang of Mang Bros. Productions, and I called right away. Lou passed me along to Armell Anderson, the drummer of a new band called Silver Star.

Armell picked up the phone and was quick to tell me that his stage name was Mel Star.

"Okay," I said.

"Are youse into glitter?" asked Mel Star in a thick Jersey accent.

I told him that I loved Bowie, Lou Reed, and Mott the Hoople and that I knew how to play all the songs.

"When can you audition?" he asked.

"Right now," I said.

The audition would be held in one of the band members' houses in Ho-Ho-Kus, New Jersey (a thirty-minute drive from my apartment on the West Side). I told Mel that I didn't drive, and he offered to come into Manhattan to pick me up.

On Tuesday, December 19, at 7:00 p.m.—just four days after that fateful call from Tony—Mel Star knocked on my door. Expecting to see some white, Italian, mobster kind of guy, because that's how Mel sounded on the phone, I pulled open the door and saw nothing of the sort.

Mel was Black.

Okay, cool, a multiracial band, I thought.

I was entering a whole new world of people I had no history with. Just, apparently, a love of the same music, the same look, and the desire to become a famous band. I was excited about the prospects, but I did have one problem from the outset.

"What's with the name Silver Star?" I asked Mel. "Is this someone's idea of a glitter band name? It's terrible," I said.

"I named the band," said Mel, coldly. "And I like it."

That was not the best way to start a pre-audition conversation, so I quickly pivoted to our mutual love of the music, and I asked Mel to tell me his plan for putting the band on the club scene.

Mel said that we could get gigs right away playing six nights a week, and we would get paid $150 per night. That's $900 a week, $3,600 per month. The band paid the house renters $300 per month to rehearse. Gas was twenty-three cents a gallon, electricity was twenty dollars per month, and a truck rental to move all our gear was twenty-five dollars a week. After all the bills were paid, we could each make $100 per week take-home pay. Not bad money for 1973.

But there were added benefits. Mel also told me that there were girls all over the house, and if I got in the band, I could fuck any of them except the lead singer's girlfriend. I couldn't believe what I was hearing. Did he actually say that?

"It's true," Mel assured me. "For some reason, chicks dig guys dressed like chicks."

I had come off five years of heavy drug use and drug dealing, but I was always a serial monogamist—I only had one girlfriend at a time. Was this how life in a real rock band was? A hundred bucks a week and all the girls you could want?

I auditioned and was made a member that very night, so the answer came quickly. Not only was I an immediate Silver Star member, but one of the other house renters was moving out, so, if I wanted, I could move in right away. And in that moment, my answer was clear and obvious: I wanted.

Michael, the singer, had an incredible Jim Morrison–like effect on women, so there were girls all over the place. He wasn't smart, but he had the strongest animal magnetism I had ever seen. Aside from the fact that I had no car anyway, living in the band house clearly had its advantages. Also, my relationship with my mom wasn't great right then, and I needed the space. In a matter of hours, I had become the new guitar player and roommate in one fell swoop.

After the audition, I was sitting in the kitchen when a kid named Sal Randazzo, a loud, obnoxious young drug dealer who was a friend of Michael's, sat next to me and introduced himself. He also had a thick Jersey accent and started telling me that on his way to the house that evening, a "n——" cut him off on the Garden State Parkway.

My jaw dropped. I couldn't believe what I'd just heard. Didn't he realize that Mel, the drummer and namesake of the band, was Black? Did he care? Did Mel care? Was Mel used to this kind of suburban ignorance? I sure wasn't. I was only fifteen miles from Manhattan, but the way this kid was talking, I may as well have been sitting at a kitchen table with a fat guy named Bubba somewhere in the wilds of Mississippi. As much as I had been dealing drugs and traveling around the world, I had never experienced this kind of ignorance.

As extreme as my life had been up till then—what with all the drugs and craziness and fringe elements—my friends were actually quite intellectual and liberal. We all shared the same feelings about the important issues of the day. We were against the Vietnam War, and we did not harbor any racism. In my circle of family and friends, I never heard racial slurs. First of all, the occasion would never come up to use it. Second, if my father ever DID hear you say it, he would kick your ass. That kind of language was not tolerated, let alone encouraged. Racial epithets were never part of my friends' or my vernacular.

I was a voracious *New York Times* reader; these people would have found *Highlights* to be a challenge. I came out of a political family and a socially conscious scene. None of that mattered in this New Jersey bar band world. It was all about the music and getting laid.

I went back to my parents' apartment that night feeling really torn. The guys were all great musicians and seemingly committed to becoming a famous rock band. If I committed to this band, then I was doing a 180 and leaving not just the dealing and drug use behind, but everything good I ever cared about, too.

I wanted it so bad, though. I jumped in headfirst, and my glitter-rocker ride had officially begun.

Leaving the peacenik, hippie, revolutionary, anti-war world behind and moving to the sticks, I soon learned that our audience, the guys coming to see Silver Star, were white, blue-collar kids with— let's just say—a different view of the world and the people in it.

Over time, I started to understand that a functional, undeniable racism existed among our following. And, in fact, it was endemic to the American culture. While I wasn't going to let it stop me from becoming a rock star, it sure shocked the hell out of me. Oddly, Mel didn't seem to be bothered by it, so, for the time being, anyhow, I chose to ignore it as best I could.

We hit the bar scene and took off. Despite our early success, I couldn't let go of my disdain for the name Silver Star. The name just sucked, and I took every opportunity to remind everyone, which, needless to say, pissed Mel off to no end.

At rehearsal one night in early 1973, we had a big fight about the name, and Michael, who had a legendary drinking problem, bolted from the scene.

Later that night, Michael, drunk out of his mind as usual, called me from a pay phone in a bar.

"I have the perfect name for the band, man," he slurred.

"What is it?" I asked, humoring him.

"Twisted Sister."

Holy shit! What a great name. I hung up the phone and raced down to the basement to tell the rest of the band. Everyone loved it—except Mel, of course. But the name stuck.

When I saw Michael the next day, I slapped him on the back and told him how much we loved the name.

"We're going to use it," I said, excited.

"What name?" he said.

He had no idea what I was talking about; he had absolutely no recollection of the previous night's phone call. As far as he could remember, he'd never heard the words *Twisted Sister* before.

So, with one of the greatest band names ever, we launched ourselves into the local bar scene.

Sunshine In. Our first concert appearance—August 12, 1973.

Back in the day, in New Jersey and Long Island, where we mostly played, a lot of the club owners were old-time Italian guys. I couldn't tell you if they were mob or not, but they told classic stories like, "Yeah, back in the day, Sinatra used to play here" and "Mel Tormé used to play here" and "We had the Dorseys play in this room back in the forties." Capisce?

Some of these clubs added a kind of "variety show" element to the night's entertainment lineup. I can't tell you what their entertainment strategy was, but the club owners loved to book bizarre acts to accompany their bands. We found ourselves on bills with some weird guys. And I say that as the founder of a transvestite metal band.

Let's take Charles Lamont, X-rated hypnotist, for example. He would hypnotize an eighteen-year-old couple and command the girl to get on her knees. Then he'd put a guy on a chair ten feet away and say to the girl, "Okay, sweetheart, he's got a ten-foot dick. Now blow him." She'd hold her hands out like she's holding a gargantuan cock and start bobbing her head. And the guy sitting in the chair would be moaning in ecstasy.

The first time I saw this, I thought, *This can't be happening.* But we played with Charles Lamont a lot, so I saw this routine many times. One night, Lamont gave me some sound financial advice. He said, "Hey, kid. What are you doing to save money?"

"What do you mean?"

"Mail yourself five dollars a week for every week that you work professionally. Find a post office box and just mail yourself five dollars. When you retire, you're gonna have a lot of money." Then he went onstage to hypnotize some kid into thinking he was taking a shit on the stage.

Another of our illustrious show mates was John Valby, aka Dr. Dirty, who wrote obscene, politically incorrect versions of famous songs.

Like this unforgettable hit . . .

(To the tune of "Yesterday")

Leprosy
All my skin is fallen off of me
Now it hurts me when I have to pee
Oh I believe in leprosy
Syphilis
It just started with a simple kiss
Now it hurts me when I take a piss.

We played with these guys all the time.

Let us pause for a moment and take stock:

I'm in a band called Twisted Sister. We're transvestite rockers, and we're doing these floor shows with a perverted hypnotist and a psychotic songwriter.

Which, of course, raises the obvious question: "Could it possibly get any weirder?"

Yes. Yes, it could.

But it never got any weirder or worse than the time we opened for Mr. Jiggs, who was, in fact, a chimp.

What the fuck, you may wonder, does a performing chimp do? Well, I'll tell you, but first let me say that about ten years ago I met John Scher, a very famous rock promoter. We were talking about all the legendary shows that played at his Capitol Theater, and I was sharing with him the history of Twisted Sister.

"What's the weirdest gig you ever did?" he asked me.

"Well, John," I said. "We performed with a chimp called Mr. Jiggs."

"What? Mr. Jiggs?" he said. "I used to book him in the Capitol Theater! In fact, I had Fleetwood Mac and Mr. Jiggs on the same day."

"Who headlined?" I asked.

"Fleetwood Mac, of course," he said.

I said, "Well, *we* opened for the *chimp*, okay?"

Anyway, the chimp had an act tailored for clubs. For example, there was a huge club called Dodd's in Orange, which had a giant, square bar in the middle of the floor. We'd get on the stage to play our set, and they'd put Mr. Jiggs up on the bar with a rolling cart stocked with alcohol, cigarettes, and a lighter. Mr. Jiggs would walk around the bar, mixing drinks for people and lighting cigarettes.

That's it. And we opened for this. So, when people say to me, "Give me an idea of the most humiliating gig you could ever imagine," that's the answer they get.

In the fall of '73, the gas crisis kicked in. And as a working band in Jersey, we were constantly driving from gig to gig. In the space of a few months, because supplies were short, gas rose from twenty-five cents a gallon to around sixty cents a gallon. Some government genius came up with a sophisticated fuel-rationing program that said if you had an even-numbered license plate, you could buy gas on an even-numbered day, and if you had an odd-numbered license plate, you could buy gas on an odd-numbered day. But if you needed to gas up on a Sunday, you were shit out of luck, because all the gas stations in the Northeast were closed.

Gas thievery was so rampant that most of the gas stations rented giant trucks to block the driveways on Sundays, so that the petrol robbers couldn't get in. It was horrible.

I'd always been a good talker, and ever since my days in the Boy Scouts and later, selling drugs, I knew how to make a good deal. One day, I walked into the gas station near our house in Ho-Ho-Kus. I said to the young owner, "Hey, man, you like rock and roll?"

"Yeah," he said.

"Well, we're in a band, Twisted Sister. Do you go to Dodd's in Orange?"

"Yeah," he said. "I love Mr. Jiggs."

Pretending not to hear that, I named a list of other clubs, and he responded affirmatively to each one.

"Well," I said. "We play in all those clubs, and we'll get you into any show we play for free if you guarantee that you will always fill us up—including Sundays."

He agreed, so on any given night, we would show up at his station with our band cars and trucks at 4:00 a.m., when nobody would see, and fill our tanks. In exchange, he got all the free drinks and admissions he wanted.

This is how we survived. It was street sense. We had to. You could not be without gas when you're driving to clubs around New Jersey. And we managed to pull it off nearly disaster-free. Nearly.

Our agent usually kept us fairly local, but one time he booked us up in northwest Massachusetts, a good 150 miles from our house. It took a long time to drive there, and you can imagine how bad it would be if you couldn't get the gas you needed to go there and come back. It would take more than one fill-up to do the round trip, so you would need access to gas no matter what.

As you already know, Michael, our singer, had a bad drinking problem. On the day that Michael and I, along with our roadie, Don, were to drive the show truck up to the gig, drunk Michael caused us to leave late, which meant we'd arrive late—something that music venues don't particularly appreciate.

I called the club owner and lied my ass off and told him the transmission of our rented truck blew out, and that we were stuck waiting for another truck. He couldn't fault us for that, right?

Now already four hours late, we were tooling up the New York State Thruway when we suddenly heard a loud bang. And, you guessed it, the transmission blew. Of course, there were no cell phones in those days, so we just sat and waited for the state police, who eventually came and filed their report.

The cops called the local U-Haul guy, who towed our truck to another U-Haul place, where we moved all the gear from our ten-foot rig into a twenty-four-footer, which was way too big for our gear but was the only available size. So while we drove, we could hear our equipment flying around in the back.

We arrived to set up at 10:00 p.m., which wouldn't have been such a big deal except that we were supposed to have started playing at nine. What could I do? I told the stage manager the truth—that our transmission really did blow out. And that's the last time I ever lied. About a transmission, anyway. Even though we got off to a bad start, we played through the weekend and everything went fine.

TWISTED SISTER

Twisted Sister original lineup.

On Sunday, Michael, Donald, and I were preparing to head back down to Jersey and, of course, all the gas stations were closed, and we didn't know anybody who could hook us up with gas. Fortunately, the owner of the club, who was also the mayor of the town, got his brother to fill up our truck, and we started the drive back down to New Jersey.

But somewhere around Exit 26 on the Thruway, we were just about to run out of gas. By then we determined we were seven miles from the Hunter Village Inn, which was one of the ski resorts we played. So, we figured we had just enough gas to get there, and we could park the truck, stay overnight, fill up on Monday morning, and go home.

The route up Hunter Mountain is a winding, two-lane road of hairpin turns that's tough enough to navigate in perfect weather. But this was winter. There was snow. And to top it off, we were in a twenty-four-foot U-Haul being driven by a drunken rock singer.

So, as we worked our way up through the nail-biting turns, the snow started falling in great white sheets. We had five gallons of gas to make it to the top of Hunter Mountain. This was no-man's land. If anything went wrong, we were going to freeze to death.

Then the windshield wipers broke. So while Michael's driving, Donald's hanging off the side of the truck, trying to wipe the snow off the windshield to keep it from blocking Michael's vision. Then Michael made a wrong turn and plowed us into a snowbank.

People have asked me, "In those early days of Twisted Sister, what made you think you were going to succeed?" Thinking back on events like this, I honestly don't have a rational answer.

Somehow, calling on some superhuman strength, Donald and I pushed that twenty-four-foot truck out of the snowbank and got it back on the road. Somehow, we found our way back onto the main road, navigated up through the hairpin turns, and just as we pulled into the driveway of the Hunter Village Inn, the truck ran out of gas.

The next morning, we filled the truck up and drove home to New Jersey.

That's what life was like the first year of Twisted Sister.

One day in the spring of '74, some producers approached us in a club and told us they wanted to make a record with us. Naturally, I thought that this could be our break.

They booked some time in a studio in Manhattan, and Michael, true to form, didn't show up because he was still drunk from the night before.

Even though that wasn't totally surprising behavior from Michael, his lack of professionalism deeply disappointed me. More and more this kind of mentality permeated the band, and I was wondering when the bottom was going to fall out. But the band kept getting more popular, the money kept coming, and that summer we were asked to play the Mad Hatter, where we had been the house band the year before. This time we wanted a lot more money, so they hired us for one month instead of three.

Next we were hired by a rival club in the Hamptons called the OBI East. It held three thousand people! Bars with bands in the tri-state area during the seventies and the eighties generally held one hundred people, two hundred people, maybe three hundred people. The drinking age was low and the number of kids going out to listen to cover bands was high, but three thousand was more than we'd ever played to.

By the end of the summer of '74, we'd blown away every other local band. We were making $500 or $600 a night. Multiply that times five or six nights and that's $3,600 a week. That's pretty good money, even by today's standards. We enlarged our road crew and bought more equipment. Things were really sailing along, with the band and with my girlfriend, Maureen, who had become the love of my life.

That fall, Maureen and I went to Aruba, but we came back to bad news. My brother called to say, "Mom just collapsed and she's in a coma."

I raced into the city to meet everyone at the hospital where my mother, the genius, Evaline Segall, was in a coma. The doctor told us, "We don't know what happened, but she may not come out of it."

I was shocked. But I knew I had the band and I had Maureen,

and that somehow that would help me deal with this crisis with my mom.

Over the next six weeks, my mom got better. She came out of the coma and voted in the off-year elections that November using an absentee ballot. Everything seemed to be fine with me and Maureen, but by then the band was starting to have meetings to deal with the growing drinking problem among our members. I don't know if he was just defensively lashing out, but in the middle of one of these intervention-like meetings, Michael told me that Maureen was screwing a bartender from one of the clubs.

It was an unexpected non sequitur, and it threw me.

"How do you know that?" I asked.

"I know, and you're an idiot," he said.

Well, Maureen and I did have an open relationship. As far as I recall, it had even been my idea. It was my way of being Mr. Liberal. We weren't married. You do what you do, I do what I do. Don't ask, don't tell. It sounded great in theory, but hearing this news crushed me on the spot.

I confronted Maureen, and she admitted to the affair. And then she laid down the shocker: not only had she been cheating on me, but she wanted to break up. I was crushed. It added insult to a number of injuries. My mom was still in the hospital and might be dying. I was super pissed at Michael. And the band was on the verge of disintegrating.

In the first week of December, the band played a gig at the Sahara Club in Adams, Massachusetts. They put us up in their rooming house, which was a barracks-type layout with eight beds. A whole family lived across the hall. And since it's hunting country up around Adams, Michael had brought his gun so he could get in some hunting during the day before the show.

After the gig that night, our bass player, Kenny, was walking down the stairs as one of our roadies, Greg, was going up. As they passed each other, somehow Kenny's cigarette ash fell on Greg's chest. Greg was shit-faced on quaaludes and, feeling drunkenly aggrieved, he went right to Michael, who, of course, was also plastered.

"Kenny put a cigarette out on my chest," slurred Greg to Michael.

Michael, incensed at this violation, immediately went on the hunt for Kenny. He ran into the room where Mel and I were hanging out, blissfully unaware of the burgeoning conflict.

"Where the hell is Kenny?" he shouted at us. "The bastard put a cigarette out on Greg's chest!"

Mel and Michael were buddies; they went to school together and knew each other better than anyone else in the band.

"Shut the fuck up, will ya?" Mel said. "You're just fucking drunk."

"Fuck you, Mel! Fuck you!" Michael shouted. "Don't you fucking tell me that shit!"

"Go fuck yourself, Michael."

Michael grabbed his loaded gun from the corner of the room and pointed it at Mel's chest.

"What the fuck you gonna do?" Mel said. "Fuck you, you drunk mick."

"Fuck you," Michael spit back.

There I was, twenty-two years old, and I vividly remember watching this scene take place and thinking, *I'm about to witness a murder.*

The two faced off against each other for what seemed like days until Michael lowered his weapon and said, "I don't need this gun to kick your ass, you dumb motherfucker."

He threw the piece to the floor, and they started wrestling and punching each other. Hearing the racket, a bunch of people ran up to our room and pulled the two of them apart.

Hearing what had just gone down, Greg the roadie, knowing he had precipitated this whole thing, panicked and, in a moment of clearheaded wisdom so characteristic of the drug-addled brain, decided to get the hell out of Dodge and run the ninety miles back to New Jersey. Barefoot. And stoned. In December.

We got in our cars and raced down the road after Greg. We finally caught up to him and loaded him into the car. Out of his mind on angel dust or something, he cried, over and over, "I broke up Twisted Sister. I broke up Twisted Sister. I broke up Twisted Sister."

By the way, Greg and I are friends to this day. He's thanked me for changing his life and helping to get him off the drugs. He recently sent me an incredible email that said, "Without you, I don't know if I would be clean today." It made my day.

The truth is, Greg didn't break up Twisted, because it was going to happen without him. That weekend was the end of the band.

When I got back to New Jersey, Maureen left me.

Two days later, my mom died.

PART TWO

TWISTED
BUSINESS

FROM SELLING COOKIES AND DEALING DRUGS, I KNEW WAY MORE ABOUT BUSINESS AND MAKING DEALS THAN MEL AND THE OTHER GUYS IN THE BAND UNDERSTOOD. IN THE BEGINNING, I WASN'T A BUSINESSPERSON. I WASN'T RUNNING THE BAND. I WASN'T THE MANAGER. I WAS JUST A MUSICIAN. IT WASN'T UNTIL THAT FIRST ITERATION OF THE BAND BROKE UP THAT THE WHOLE ENTERPRISE FELL INTO MY LAP.

THAT'S PART OF HOW I AS AN EVENTUAL ROCK STAR WOULD ALSO BECOME A BUSINESS CONSULTANT, BUT IT WOULD TAKE DECADES OF BUILDING MORE BUSINESS KNOWLEDGE AND RUNNING THE BAND—THROUGH THE HIGHS AND LOWS— BEFORE I WOULD BE QUALIFIED TO ADVISE OTHERS. ALONG MY UNFOLDING TWISTED PATH, WHETHER I KNEW IT OR NOT, I WAS LEARNING LESSONS THAT WOULD BECOME THE FOUNDATION OF MY CONSULTING. THOSE LESSONS ARE THE BASIS OF THIS SECTION.

WHEN I STARTED THE BAND THAT WOULD BECOME KNOWN AS TWISTED SISTER, I DIDN'T REALLY UNDERSTAND WHAT IT WAS GOING TO TAKE TO BE SUCCESSFUL. NOW I DO: IT'S THE T.W.I.S.T.E.D. METHOD, AND I'M GOING TO TAKE YOU THROUGH IT, STEP BY TWISTED STEP.

TENACITY

TENACITY IS THE ABILITY TO OVERCOME obstacles and keep pushing for a goal. It's the drive to confront issues and challenges, solve them, and move on to the next ones. Without tenacity, you've got nothing. If you can't keep going when all hell is breaking loose, then you have no chance.

I was either the smartest guy because I kept pushing for my goal or the dumbest because I didn't know when to stop. It takes an enormous amount of tenacity to succeed in any worthwhile endeavor. And I have an enormous capacity for it. So did the band. Fortunately.

Tenacity is in our DNA; it's part of the very fabric of Twisted Sister's journey. Persistence, we learned over and over again, overcomes resistance. Now to you that may sound like a motivational speaker's platitude, but it was our direct, personal, day-to-day experience.

Until I was twenty-two years old, I never had trauma in my life. To be clear, yes there were the crazy drug-fueled episodes, the near-death experiences, the fear of getting busted, going to jail, and having a police record. Those, however, were short-term problems that for the most part lasted no more than one day. In fact, the more I got away with stuff, the more invincible I felt.

This time it was different. This was long-term, perpetual, and very deep pain.

Tall with bellbottoms—1975, during depression—149 lbs.

Maureen, whom I was madly in love with, broke up with me. The first version of Twisted Sister, which had been together about two years at the time, broke up. And my mom died. All in the same week.

This particular confluence of tragedies put me in a spiraling, black hole of depression. I thought I wanted to commit suicide, and I didn't want to tell anybody how I felt, not even my brother. It was just killing me. I couldn't sleep. I couldn't eat. I wrote a song called "Can't Stand Still for a Minute" with the line, "I can't stand still for a minute, there's too many memories in it."

Everywhere I looked, I saw my mother walking down the street or Maureen walking around the corner. Nobody knew how depressed I was. I never told anyone. I was in real pain and nobody saw it, because a thin rock star was kind of normal. A thin body and bushy hair kind of made me look the rocker part. So nobody recognized that I was in real and severe pain.

My mother's funeral service was on December 10, 1974. We had people over afterward. When everybody left, it was just me and my dad sitting there in the living room, looking at each other.

In my whole life, my dad never told me he loved me. He never said he loved my mom, either, and I don't really know what their relationship was like. He was a traveling salesman, so he was gone a lot.

"Wow, man. It's just the two of us left," I told him. "We haven't had the best relationship. So I'm gonna make a suggestion."

"What?" said Dad.

"I have a feeling that going to therapy is not exactly something that you want to do, so I'll make a deal with you."

"Okay?"

"Well, you know you beat me pretty bad as a kid. I did stupid shit, you used to whip me with a belt periodically. That was really pretty traumatic to me, but I don't hate you, and I forgive you for that. I will forgive you for what you did to me if you forgive me for what you think I did to you, which was drop out of school, embarrass you, deal drugs, almost get arrested, all the dumb shit that I did that you probably figured was going to kill me. If you can forgive me for all the stupid stuff I did as a teenager, I will forgive you. We'll shake on it, we'll never talk about it again, and we'll move forward. Deal?"

He shook my hand and said, "You got a deal."

"I only have one request."

"What?"

I said, "I don't know how much longer you have. You've been smoking cigarettes for, what? Like fifty years now? Maybe if you can stop smoking, you'll be around a little bit longer. Maybe if I ever get married and have a kid, you'll get to meet your grandkid. Do you think you can stop smoking cigarettes?"

He looked at me and he said, "Do you remember what you told me when I asked you to stop smoking weed? Do the words *go fuck yourself* sound familiar?"

I said, "Yeah."

"Go fuck yourself."

"Okay, fair enough."

We shook hands and, until he died, we had a great relationship. We'd call each other every week. My dad remarried and he'd come visit with his wife. We'd talk about baseball games, but we never again touched upon our past.

On the day of my mother's funeral, I started writing a diary, which became my lifeline. Over the next nine months, my written reflections about how I processed my depression became a template for my eventual abilities to overcome everything and to finally understand the different kinds of chaos that come at all of us in life.

It took nine months, but one day I woke up and the weight of the world was finally off my shoulders. I thought to myself, *Wow, depression's kind of like a cut on the hand. If you give it enough time to heal, it can heal.* That's how it was for me, anyway. Others may have underlying physiological or chemical issues that complicate the recovery process, but when I came out of the depression, I realized I could come out of anything. I could persist. I could be tenacious. Nothing would ever set me back as badly again.

I kept diaries for fifteen years. Keeping a diary, especially in business, is important because it helps you to build perspective, allows you to learn from your specific experiences, and gives you a greater ability to confront, solve, and move on. To be tenacious, in other words. It's allowed me to retain the details of the life and times of Twisted Sister and to see that tenacity is really our unsung theme song.

The guys in the band that made it—the band that everyone knows: Dee Snider, Eddie Ojeda, Mark Mendoza, AJ Pero, and me—were not the original members. Far from it. After going through four singers, three guitar players, two bass players, and seven drummers, the band that you know is actually the eleventh iteration.

We fired Michael after he pulled the gun on Mel. The guitar player, Billy, left with Michael, and starting in January of 1975 we rebuilt the band over and over again.

Through it all, I was sinking deeper and deeper into emotional despair. The pain of losing my mom and the pain of losing Maureen was too much to bear. Looking back on that black hole I was in, I see that I should've gone to a therapist. I should've taken medication of some sort, some psychotropic drug, but I didn't. I just toughed it out. But I didn't know how long I could last. The pain just got worse.

We muddled through another version of Twisted Sister with a guitar player named Keith Angelino, whom we named Keith Angel, and a singer named Frank Karuba, who was known as Rick Prince. That version of the band stumbled around for all of nine weeks.

Rick Prince was more of a Rod Stewart than a glam guy. So for a time, believe it or not, we went from being a David Bowie cover band to a Rod Stewart cover band. Rick sang like Percy Sledge. We did "When a Man Loves a Woman" and other stuff you wouldn't expect Twisted Sister to do.

We were doing okay—we were getting gigs, we had an agent—but we weren't the same Twisted Sister. We didn't seem to have the same value, but we were working. Then one day, after nine weeks, Rick just never showed up again. He never came to rehearsal, and we never heard from him again.

I said to the guys, "You know, I can't rely on singers anymore. I'll take over singing."

The problem with my taking over singing, as I have mentioned, is that I would actually have to sing. Still, that version of the band trudged through the spring of '75. Summer came, and we got a job again in the Hamptons as the house band at the OBI—the Oak Beach Inn—the biggest club in the Hamptons.

Well, that June it rained every major weekend, so the numbers in this club were terrible. It held three thousand people and we averaged maybe nine hundred a night. The club owner, who was paying us a lot of money, fired us, which was easy because we only had a one-month contract.

By that point, my relationships with Mel and the guitar player, Keith, who had taken Michael's place, were becoming strained. The original bass player, Kenny, and I were still there, but as we turned into August of '75, we were starting to fray at the edges and our popularity was dropping. My agent said to me, "You need a lead singer that sings Led Zeppelin, man. I know just the guy for you—his name is Danny. He sings in a band called Peacock. You should meet him."

So Danny Snider came down in August of '75. He watched me singing my Lou Reed and said, "Wow, I thought you guys did all these other songs."

I said, "We do, but I can't sing them."

He said, "Well, I'd like to join your band."

And I said, "Okay, sounds great."

I went into the dressing room to tell Mel and Keith. "There's a guy out there, Danny Snider. Our agent sent him down. He could be our lead singer."

Mel said, "We don't need a lead singer, John. You're great." Which didn't make any sense at all. But unbeknownst to me at the time, they were planning to quit the band and steal the equipment.

I went back out to where Danny was and told him, "Hey, man, thanks, but no thanks. I'll keep your number around."

Two weeks later, we were playing at the Rock Palace in Lake Caramel. The next morning, the Monday following Labor Day weekend, I get a phone call from Mel. "Keith and I quit. We have the gear. You ever wanna see the gear again, we want $2,500."

"You're holding it for . . . what . . . ransom?"

He replied, "We want $2,500 if you want it back."

I don't remember how or what happened, but I'm reasonably sure no SWAT teams were involved. We settled the ransom amount for $1,000. I gave him the money and they gave back the gear, which would have been a satisfactory end to that chapter, but when we got the equipment back, it was smashed to smithereens. Assholes.

I wanted to give up, and, in fact, I did for a while. I got a job as a waiter at Terrace on the Park Caterers in Flushing Meadow Park. Kenny took a job at a Korvette's department store. Around the end of October, Kenny called me and said, "God, this job sucks."

"Man, being a waiter sucks, too," I told him. "I do seven shifts a week. I have to wear a short-haired wig. We gotta do something."

That next Saturday night, I went out with some of the waiters. They were bombed and got into an accident on Park Avenue while I was in the car, and they ran. When they ran, I ran, too. I found out later this was because they were undocumented and the car they were driving was stolen. Long story short, the driver of the other car was beyond intoxicated and somehow the whole thing went away.

That accident could have turned into an unmitigated disaster, and since it didn't, I took it as a sign and decided I was now officially out of the restaurant business. I quit my job and called Kenny.

The band begins to take shape—1976.

"It's time to put Twisted Sister back together," I told him. And then I called Eddie Ojeda and asked him to join us, too.

"Yeah, man. That would be great," he said.

So now we had Kenny on bass and Eddie and me on guitars, but we still needed a drummer. I saw an ad in *Rolling Stone* magazine for a guy named Kevin John Grace, who was looking to play in a glitter, glam-ish kind of band. We called him, and that was the beginning of version three of Twisted Sister. Next, we filled in our singer slot by hiring Danny.

Since I was now known as Jay Jay, I wanted to name him Dee Dee, but the Ramones already had one of those. So we settled for plain old Dee.

By this time, I had come to what, to me, was an obvious conclusion: there's just no place for drugs and alcohol in the business of rock and roll. They hampered our success and just caused too damn much misery. So, as we brought new guys into the band, one non-negotiable was that they couldn't drink or do drugs of any kind during work hours. A little light indulgence on their own time was their business—but showing up at rehearsals or gigs drunk or high would be cause for firing.

But Kenny, I discovered several years later, was secretly an alcoholic. I loved him; he was a great guy. I just had absolutely no idea that he drank a case of beer a day since he was ten years old. One day in 1978 he told me he'd joined AA and, unbeknownst to me, he'd brought members of his church down to see our show.

Now, here's the thing: our show is not for the pew and chapel crowd. We're incendiary. We curse a lot, to say the least. It's part of our brand image. Our fan club, for example, is called the Sick Mother-fucking Friends of Twisted Sister. And Kenny brought his church group into this viper's den called Zaffe's in Piscataway, New Jersey.

Afterward, he told me, "Hey, man. My church people saw that show, and they say the devil speaks to you and Dee. I have to quit the band."

Now, I wanted what was best for Kenny, but I was a bit confused. "Kenny," I said. "Let's review this for a second. You drink, we don't. We don't do drugs. We just work hard six days a week and rest on the seventh, but the devil speaks through us? How does that work, exactly?"

"You've got a point there," said Kenny.

For the next eight months, we did everything to keep Kenny in the band. We even hired a minder to stay near him in the bars. But after the summer of 1978, it became apparent that this wasn't going to work.

"So, here's the thing, Kenny," I said. "I don't want you to quit because of your church friends' opinions. But here's how we all have to look at it: we're playing in bars every night, and the last place an alcoholic needs to be is in a bar. I don't want you to be exposed to the very thing that could kill you. I love you, and I want to save your life, so I think you should resign."

He did, and Kenny and I are friends to this day. You know what Kenny does for a living? He fixes church bells. That's fucking poetry.

Like other bands, we got our start playing in bars. The Beatles, the Rolling Stones, and others got their record deals within a couple of years, then spent the next eight years trying to make it. Then went on to hate each other's guts.

Unlike other bands, we spent a full decade trying to make it in the bars. We couldn't get a record deal because nobody liked us. We had to be our own record label. We couldn't get anyone to make merch for us, so we made our own. We were our own press and promotion agency. We did everything ourselves and became really, really good at all of it.

But the goal never changed: become rock stars. Which meant we needed a record deal. We came close over and over and over again, with each attempt ending with a crushing blow of rejection or a tragic, unforeseen circumstance.

As the band kept getting rejected, we started to develop this approach to overcoming the relentless setback: we mourned it, we reflected on it, we retooled, and we reapplied.

It's tough to deal with rejection, but you have to learn how to do it.

We learned to mourn the rejections and reflect on the failure. Why did it happen? Was the song or the production bad? Did we have a bad show on an important night?

Then you retool. You come up with another way to do it. You change the song, you change the arrangement, you change the stage show. Then you reapply it. That's what successful businesses do: they mourn, reflect, retool, and reapply.

We reapplied. We sent countless demo tapes to the record labels but with no success. Despite not getting a label, the band had become very popular, and we drew crowds. We were making a lot of money, so we could sustain ourselves.

When Kenny left in December 1978, we replaced him with Mark "The Animal" Mendoza. Mark brought a heaviness in sound to the band; things started to really take off creatively and the band's popularity exploded.

UPPER LEFT: Leaping in air. Onstage at Mad Hatter, Stonybrook—1977
UPPER RIGHT: On stage at Speaks on Long Island—1978. Nothing but water in that can. **LOWER LEFT:** Telling off the audience. Calderone Concert Hall, October 31, 1978. **LOWER RIGHT:** Me and Dee wrapped

Six months later, in the summer of 1979, we met Eddie Kramer.

Eddie was one of the most famous record producers in the world. He worked with Led Zeppelin, Jimi Hendrix, the Rolling Stones, and other small-potato artists like that.

One night, a girl comes into a bar (I know that sounds like the beginning of a bad joke, but stay with me).

"You know who's coming down to see the band tonight?" she said to me.

"Who?" I said.

"Eddie Kramer."

"How would you know Eddie Kramer, and why would you know he's coming here to see us?"

"My mother is a teller at a bank up in Airmont, New York," she said. "Eddie Kramer is a customer of hers. They were making small talk and my mom asked him what he was up to tonight. He said he's going to a club called Detroit to see a band called Twisted Sister.

"I'm telling you," she insisted. "Eddie Kramer is coming to your show tonight."

I went back to the dressing room and told the guys what I'd just heard. And, true or not, we were nothing less than prepared. It was one of those nights during the summer of the 1979 gas crisis, so there were only thirty or forty people in the audience. But that didn't matter to us. We played a hell of a show.

Then who comes backstage to see us afterward but Eddie Kramer, in the flesh. "You guys are great, and I'm signing you to a production deal."

And, oh my God, right then and there we signed a deal with Eddie.

I didn't even know what a production deal was, but I didn't care. It was Eddie Kramer. What it meant was that he would produce our demos, arrange for our recordings, and then he had one year to get us a major record deal.

We did the demos. We did the tapes. A year went by and guess what happened?

Nothing. He couldn't sell us anywhere.

So we released the records on our own.

Live at Detroit—Portchester, NY, 1979.

If nothing else, we'd have something to give away to our fans. A few of the records even ended up in Sam Goody's retail store, which sounds kind of cool except for one small thing: unbeknownst to us, Eddie Kramer, in order to get us affordable studio time, had made a deal with the studio that if Twisted Sister got a record deal with the tapes, the band would pay the studio owner four times the $6,000 they'd given him to record the demos. Hold that thought. I'll come back to it in a bit.

What followed was a succession of monumental near misses.

In the winter of '81, our co-manager, Mark Puma, suggested that he and I take the demos to the Midem festival in Cannes, France. It's the music equivalent of the film festival in the same locale, and I was told that more deals get signed at that event than all the deals done around the world in the rest of the year. So, armed with the Eddie Kramer demos, we went to Midem to shop for a record deal.

What a scene it was.

The main hotel had hundreds of rooms, each one occupied by either a music publisher or record label. Thousands of managers, artists, and song pluggers wandered the halls over the four-day conference. You either came to Midem with a prescheduled fifteen-minute appointment to make your pitch, or you met someone from a label or publisher at one of the bars or restaurants during the event and, if you were lucky, got invited to their room to take your shot at a deal.

Every room had the same setup: a desk, a couple of chairs, a cassette player, and sometimes a turntable. On each desk was an ever-growing pile of demo cassettes and records, each one holding the hopes and dreams of an aspiring band or artist.

You either were frozen in fear of the ferocious deal making or you relished it. I relished it, of course. Mark and I marched into these meetings with the Eddie Kramer demos in hand. We also had 45 RPM singles, which we had made with professional record sleeves to make it even more official-looking. We even made up the record company: Twisted Sister Records!

Working with legendary producer Eddie Kramer (front),
engineer Rob Freeman, and Eric Block.

Recording at Electric Lady Studios—September 1979.

Our very first meeting was with Freddy Cannon, a former car salesman from Detroit, who was working for the French record label Carrere Records. Freddy was one of these guys who ended everything he said with "babe."

"Babe, babe, babe, love you, babe. I love you, babe. Babe, babe, babe. Man . . . love you, babe. Babe, you got a deal, man."

He pulled out a three-by-five index card and filled it out. "Babe, here is the deal, babe: $50,000, three albums. You're going to come over to France, babe. You're going to record with a band called Saxon, babe. This summer is going to be your summer, babe. Babe. Babe, babe, babe, babe."

Well, that was fast. It looked like we had already accomplished what we'd come here to do, but just in case we decided to meet with as many labels and publishers as possible.

So with Cannon's three-by-five "contract" in our back pocket, we took more meetings and collected more business cards. For example, we had a nice meeting with Trudy and Peter Meisel, who were running Hansa Records from Berlin. And the last business card we took was Peter Hauke's. Peter was from a production company called Rockoko Productions that had offices in LA and Frankfurt.

As you'll soon see, these were great people to know; we'd be glad we'd taken those meetings. But we already had a deal with Freddy Cannon, so—mission accomplished!

I went back to New York and announced to the band, "We got a deal! Freddy Cannon and Carrere Records are signing us!"

Carrere was a great label back then. This was the big-time. Now all we had to do was wait for the contract.

There were no fax machines in those days; this was the telegram era. A long-distance call was like eighty cents a minute. God forbid you'd make one.

We waited with anticipation, but we never heard from Freddy Cannon. Not a word, not a peep, not a whisper. The band had sent me over to Europe to get a record deal. I thought I brought one back, but Freddy Cannon just evaporated into the ether, babe. As did our record contract. Babe.

So . . . that deal was over, but we weren't.

Shortly thereafter, we found out that Hansa, run by our new friends the Meisels, was making a big move to the US under the name Handshake Records, and they were interested in signing us. They hired the legendary former head of Epic Records, Ron Alexenburg, to be their US president. We were told that Handshake had signed three projects that were all slated to come out shortly and that we would be the next release after these first three had been smash successes.

Their first album was of Pope John Paul II's appearance at Yankee Stadium; the second was a compilation of greatest hits from Johnny Carson and *The Tonight Show*; and the third was a band called the Pet Clams.

And then, riding in the draft of those blockbuster albums, would be none other than Twisted Sister's big debut record.

Take a guess at what happened next.

Pope album? A bomb. Carson? Tanked. Pet Clams? Well . . . when was the last time you listened to the Clams' greatest hits? Right. There was no such thing.

And after the abject failure of those three albums, Handshake, for all intents and purposes, folded its tent.

So, yet again, in the spring of 1981, we were facing the very real possibility that we were never, ever going to get a record deal.

But we weren't dead yet. As a last-ditch effort to save our career, we reached out to the holder of the last business card we'd collected at Midem: Peter Hauke of Rockoko Productions.

Peter came to meet us in New York, loved us, and gave us a letter of intent to sign the band. He headed off to LA for some meetings, and on his way back to Germany, we met him at JFK Airport and handed him the demo tapes, which he would take back to Germany to finalize the deal. Once again, we were psyched.

Then a couple of days later, my lawyer called. "Are you sitting down?" he asked. This was either a really good or really bad sign.

"Peter Hauke had a heart attack on the flight back to Germany."

"What do you mean, he had a heart attack?" I asked. "Is he dead?"

"I don't know," said my lawyer. "But the deal sure is."

I felt like I was at the end of my rope. So, on my twenty-ninth birthday, July 20, 1981, I gave our comanager, Mark Puma, an ultimatum:

"If we don't have a record deal by the time I'm thirty—one year from today—then I'm out."

And, honestly, I thought that it was a likely scenario; I just couldn't see a pathway at that moment.

Little did I know that within a month of that proclamation, we would be thrown a spectacular lifesaver.

A Twisted fan told us that on his recent trip to England, he'd picked up a copy of *Sounds Magazine*, the country's most influential heavy rock newspaper. And there, in the number one position on the magazine's "Personal Heavy Metal" chart, was Twisted Sister.

Sounds sent Gary Bushell, a senior writer for the mag, to check us out. He became an instant fan and wrote a glowing profile of us called "Sister Sledgehammer." He also called Secret Records, a UK-based rock label, and sang our praises to the company's president.

Secret checked us out and liked what they saw and heard. They were interested in signing us, they said, and they were sending a representative to the States to make it official.

Given our track record with potential record deals, we were so cynical at this point that we took bets that the guy's plane would blow up on the way over. And that if that didn't happen, he'd die in a car crash when he got to New York. And if that didn't happen, he'd be mugged and murdered between his car and our office.

Miraculously, though, he survived and was still interested in signing the band. We shook hands, and when he left, the guys in the band said nothing. At first. Then the bets started.

Ten bucks says he dies on the way back to the airport.

Fifty bucks that the IRA blows up the plane on the way back to England.

A hundred bucks he gets taken out by an errant bullet in a drive-by shooting.

No one, however, bet that when he got back to London, the worst blizzard in 150 years would completely wipe out his offices, but it did. And, once again, we thought, the deal was dead.

But it wasn't. Not this time. The company eventually recovered from the snowstorm, and our deal proceeded.

We were finally on a nice, smooth track to our first album with a major label.

And then, one day, we got a phone call from Hal Selby, the owner of Electric Lady studios—the very studio where we had recorded the Eddie Kramer demos. Hal was—let me say this nicely—a connected family guy, if you know what I mean. Remember, this was the same studio where Eddie had made a deal that if Twisted Sister got signed with those tapes, the band would pay the studio owner four times the $6,000 they'd given him to record the demos.

Well, we'd never gotten a record deal with those tapes, so we obviously didn't owe him $24,000. Right?

Hal summoned me to the studio and told me he wanted his twenty-four grand.

"But we didn't get a record deal," I said.

"Yeah, you did." He reached into a drawer and threw our single on the table.

"That's a free record," I said. "We give it away to our fans."

"Yeah? Well, I bought it at Sam Goody's for a dollar. So, you owe me $24,000 or I'm breaking your legs."

Oh my God. I just got threatened by a mobster.

Now, you already know that Twisted Sister played in bars. What you don't know is that most of them were mob bars. As in *owned by mobsters* kind of mob bars. And we played in them for ten years. We worked for the extended families of every possible version of *Goodfellas*. In fact, Henry Hill worked in one of our bars. Tiny Tony, Sal, Vinnie, Fat Scottie—all these guys, they all worked at these bars.

Nobody ever threatened me, ever, and, occasionally, I even borrowed money from a couple of club owners. At this point, Mark and

I picked up the phone and got to work. I had to call up a guy who knew a guy who knew a guy who knew a guy. Tony the Fork, Tommy the Shoe, Billy the Chair—guys with names like that. I tried to get the hit called off, but as far as I knew, I still had a target on my back.

We ultimately reached out to our friend Larry Tortorici, the owner of a large nightclub called Detroit in Portchester, NY. My efforts paid off.

Larry had a sit-down with Hal Selby and, with a little bit of coaxing from some of Hal's associates, an agreement was reached to have the physical threat against me called off for a payment of $10,000.

And, believe it or not, $10K just happened to be the same amount of money that Secret Records had given us as an advance. We gave Hal the dough, and he called off the hit.

Elated about our English record deal, we bought ads on the radio that said, "Twisted Sister thanks its fans for ten solid years of support" and "Thank you, Twisted fans! We're off to London to make our record. Goodbye! It's been great!"

The day the contracts were delivered from England, I brought them to my band for signing. And on that day, the British went to war in the Falkland Islands. I said to myself, "There won't be any resources left to print our records. There will be no nickels for the cutting head. They're going to use it all for missiles and bombs. We're never going to make this record."

But this time, the story had a happy ending. We headed to England and, after ten years of tenacious striving, we finally made our first album. As we returned home to New York, the label told us the record would be released Labor Day week in 1982, and that they would bring us back to England to do our first promotional tour.

We were ecstatic. Our tenacity had finally paid off. A deal, a record, and a European tour. This. Was. It.

So, of course we bought more radio ads: "Thank you, Twisted fans, for all the years of your support!" And we blasted our own original music behind the ads so listeners would think our record was released on the radio, which it wasn't. Smart marketing on our part.

Then, the day before we were to return to England for our much-hyped and anticipated tour, the phone rang. Now, given the story you've heard so far—given that every time we'd come close to success, something blew it apart at the last possible minute—you may be thinking that the ringing of that phone couldn't possibly have been a bad sign. There's just no way that things could fall apart again.

But you'd be wrong.

The record label had just gone bankrupt.

We'd had crushing disappointment before, but this was truly the lowest point. I felt like my guts had been destroyed. Eaten out. Caved in. Still, I had to convince myself that this was not the way it was going to end.

Since we had already told the entire planet that we were going to Europe, we knew we only had one possible option: we would go to Europe. Hell, if the defunct label had wanted us, there had to be another. And we would go and find them.

All we needed was the dough, which, as you may have guessed, we didn't have. But we knew people. We knew . . . you know . . . *guys.* And those guys had money. So, driven by our urgent need, we made a prudent financial decision and took out a loan from some very dubious people.

Like Larry Tortorici, for example. Even though Larry was a good friend of ours, I didn't know anything about his business. I didn't know that among his many ventures was his financing of the Lufthansa heist the movie *Goodfellas* would one day be based on. He was just Larry to us. Dubious Larry, sure. But he offered us the cash we needed, so I went over to his nightclub to pick it up.

When I showed up in jeans and a T-shirt, his brother, Tony, said to me, "Whatever you do, I don't want you walking through the main ballroom, because it's a big night tonight and you're not dressed appropriately. So just go into the back room and pick up the money."

Which I did. And it was stuffed into a brown paper bag, just like Wells fucking Fargo.

Having bagged Larry's cash, we took off for England for what would become our tipping point experience, when we agreed to appear on a live British TV show called *The Tube.*

The TV studio was in Newcastle, which is way up north. It just so happened that the day we were doing the show, Mick Jones from Foreigner was getting an award at the same location. Attending with Mick was Phil Carson, a London-based executive for Atlantic Records.

Mick Jones lived in New York City, and he'd heard our radio advertising. Phil knew our manager Mark Puma, and when Phil saw Mark at the TV studio, he asked, "What are you doing here?"

Mark told him, "I'm here with Twisted Sister."

Mick replied, "Oh, Twisted Sister. I hear them in New York on the radio all the time."

Not wanting to let go of such an influential potential fan, Mark suggested that Mick and Phil hang around to see our performance on *The Tube.*

Phil declined, because he had to get back to London, but he explained that he'd just bought a new thing called a VCR. "I'm taping the show, so when I get home, I'll watch," Phil promised.

Phil Carson. Holy shit. Now the pressure was really on. Backstage that night, we were thinking—rightfully so—that this was going to be our last shot. If we didn't get signed after this, it was really going to be over, once and for all.

Eight million people tuned in for that live show. That's sixteen million ears and eyeballs. We hit the stage, the lights went up, and in true Twisted style, we blew the roof off the place. The next morning, every record label in the world called to sign us, including the legend Phil Carson. Phil had worked with the likes of Led Zeppelin, Yes, and AC/DC, and now he wanted to sign Twisted Sister. We were ecstatic.

There was a problem, however. Phil was with Atlantic, which sounds great except for one small problem. For some reason, the president of Atlantic in the US, Doug Morris, simply hated our guts.

A month earlier, Doug had told the entire team at Atlantic US, "The next person who uses the words *Twisted Sister* in my presence will be fired. They are, without a doubt, the worst band in the world.

I don't want them on my label, and if you mention their name, you're done."

Phil called us and said, "Gentlemen, I am signing you here in the UK, but I have to tell you that I had a very interesting conversation with our record company president in New York."

I said, "Really, and what would that be?"

"Well, I called him up," Phil recounted. "And I said, 'Dougie, my boy, I really like this band. I want to sign them, but they're American, so I wanted to tell you about it.' Doug then asked me, 'What's the name of the band?' and I told him, 'Twisted Sister.'"

He went on to tell us that Doug started cursing and screaming. "You got to be kidding, they're the worst band in the world."

"Well, how do you know they're the worst band in the world?" Phil had asked. "Did you ever see them?"

"No!" shouted Doug. "I don't need to see them. They suck. They suck by proxy. They suck, they suck, they suck!"

"They may suck, but they're going to make me a lot of money," said Phil.

With a sigh, Morris relented, saying, "Fine, you keep them over there."

So Phil signed us and we made a record, *You Can't Stop Rock and Roll*. "I Am, I'm Me" was the first single released, and it hit the top twenty.

We were a hit in England, but when we got back to the States, we found out that because Doug hated us so much, our label wasn't going to release the record in the US market. They said it was because we'd gone over budget by $4,500.

Def Leppard had gone $2 million over budget. Metallica, $3 million. The Beatles, $8 million. Twisted Sister went $4,500 over budget, and that was, according to them, good enough reason to keep the record on the shelf. They told us if we wanted them to release the record, we had to pay them $4,500 or give up more recording rights to the label. I don't remember which option we took but they both sucked. They ultimately released the record but gave us no tour support. We rented two cars and drove around the country

Signing our Atlantic Records recording contract in Jimmy Page's kitchen—March 1986. **LEFT TO RIGHT:** AJ, Eddie, Dee, me, record company president Phil Carson, Mark Mendoza, Mark Puma.

for a year. We also returned to Europe for the summer festival season, where we played regularly with Whitesnake, Ozzy, Meat Loaf, Blue Öyster Cult, Motorhead, and Thin Lizzy. Back in North America, we played endlessly in the States and Canada and finished the fall and winter season by touring with Queensrÿche and Dio and playing every dump and dive imaginable.

Exactly one year after Doug Morris, our nefarious nemesis, tried to prevent us from signing with Atlantic, I was doing a press event at Atlantic Records' headquarters. Doug walked by, saw me in the hallway, and asked me to come into his office. *This is going to be interesting*, I thought.

"Jay Jay," said Doug. "Do you have any idea how many records you sold?"

"I don't have a clue," I said, because it was true. We'd been out there touring our asses off on our own dime, but I had no way of knowing the record stats.

"Well," he said, "you sold one hundred thousand albums in the last year, and, as you know, I haven't put one cent into your band."

Then he pulled out a stack of telexes from promoters around the country and read them to me.

"'Doug, Twisted Sister played in California. Blew the place apart. How come we got no promotion?'

"'Doug, Twisted Sister played in Florida. They were great. How come we got no promotion?'

"'Doug, Twisted Sister played in Canada. How come we got no promotion?'

"You know what, Jay Jay?"

"What?" I said, feeling a sense of I-fucking-told-you-so gratification washing over me.

"I was wrong," said Doug. "Next year is going to be Twisted Sister's year. If you guys give me the right video for this new MTV thing, I will make you the biggest band in the world."

Now, understand, I'm a cynical New York Jew. I didn't buy this for one second. When I left the room, Patti Conte, the effervescent head of Atlantic's publicity department, bounded up to me with anticipation. She was a good friend of ours and a fan of the band.

"How did your meeting with Doug go?" she said, bouncing on the balls of her feet.

"He says he's going to make us the biggest band in the world," I told her.

"That's great!" she said.

"No, it's not," I told her. "He's full of crap. This guy isn't going to do anything for us. He hates my guts and he hates the band." I then told her about that MTV thing.

Her face lit up. "Jay Jay!" she said. "Don't you know what MTV is?"

"No. Not really."

She explained it to me. I was starting to get the picture.

"And do you know who owns MTV?" she asked.

"Uh, no. Who?"

"We do," she said. "American Express and Warner Elektra Atlantic do!"

Doug kept his word. He spent the money and brought in the right producer, video director, and crew.

And we gave him the video for "We're Not Gonna Take It."

In my experience, family, love, and job are the three pillars to life. If you have all three and then lose any one of them for a time, you have the others to hold you up. When I was twenty-two, I lost all three. It was my tragic troika. But I came back nonetheless. Again and again.

And against all odds and apparent logic, Twisted Sister did, indeed, prevail.

By 1985, we were the third-biggest band in the world.

That is tenacity.

In business, tenacity is about keeping going, staying current, and reinventing—no matter what it takes.

But it's not about tenacity for tenacity's sake.

We need wisdom to keep us coming back to the right path.

Zeppelin Field, Monsters of Rock Festival with Ozzy Osbourne, Blue Öyster Cult, Meatloaf, Whitesnake, Thin Lizzy, and Motörhead. View from stage. Nuremburg, Germany— September 4, 1983.

WISDOM

TWISTED

WISDOM COMES FROM YOUR ABILITY TO study everything you need to know about the business you're in. But it's not just what you know, it's what you don't know, too. Never stop asking questions. Always remain curious.

I'm never embarrassed to say, "I don't know that" or "I need to know that." Just when you think you know everything, you may find out you know nothing. Wisdom is about looking at the whole picture of a puzzle, even before all the pieces are in place, and understanding what's missing.

I believe in partners and partnerships. I'm not a solo artist. I've always believed in collaboration. I don't believe I have the tools to catch everything or the infinite wisdom to know it all. I need to bring other people into whatever I'm doing.

One night I was having dinner with Ahmet Ertegun, the late former chairman of Atlantic Records. Atlantic's incredible history goes back to the early years of blues and jazz and the launch of Led Zeppelin; Emerson, Lake & Palmer; AC/DC; and Twisted Sister. Much of that was under Ahmet's leadership, so I asked him how he accounted for his incredible track record.

"Success is easier if you don't mind who gets the credit," he said.

I thought that was an extraordinary statement. He went on to tell me that he needs somebody else to let him know if a band is going to work or not.

"Without that," he said, "I don't have an ongoing business. So I hire kids to figure it out. I may love Ray Charles, I may love Nina Simone, I may love Miles Davis. I know where my passion is, but if I don't have someone else's perspective to help me see the value in music outside of my personal preference, I'm not going to survive in this business."

Most people don't want to admit that anybody else deserves the credit but them. But I've always been a team player, and I've always believed in partnerships. I don't go it alone. I never have. Even before I became a rock star, I had the wisdom to understand the importance of collaboration.

When I realized I wanted to be a rock star, I knew right away that I had limitations. I don't write songs and I can't sing, so I needed a singer and a songwriter. I needed other guitar players. I got a band together because I knew I needed people to work with. I didn't know this was wisdom until I started taking a look back at my life and understanding why I made the choices that I made. I didn't care about singing or songwriting—that was Dee's job, and he was great at it. I realized I needed to understand the strength of each band member.

At some point on my journey, I understood that I wasn't going to be one of the world's great guitar players. I was really good, but not world-class. And I was okay with that. Instead, I was going to channel my talent toward being a rock star—which is a very different intention and outcome. It's less a function of musical talent and more about business savvy, management, marketing, image, and packaging. I had inherent talent in all those things and the wisdom to recognize what I could and couldn't do.

Regardless of the hours you put in, sometimes the path you originally thought you wanted to be on may not be the one that ultimately leads you to your success. As my self-awareness, and the wisdom I gained from it, grew over time, I readjusted my path.

When I saw the Beatles on *The Ed Sullivan Show*, I just wanted to be famous. But as I learned to play guitar, I became much more serious about my craft. I changed course. I even took jazz lessons in order to get studio work.

When Bowie and Ziggy Stardust entered my life and changed my twenty-year-old perspective, I changed course again and focused on achieving that certain look and feel. And I developed a burning desire to perform live. I had learned enough about how to play the guitar, and that enabled me to hit the stage with the right band.

So, as a boy watching the Beatles, I started out just wanting to be famous. Then I had the goal of being a great musician. And later I pivoted and landed on a different path, which brought me to the realization that I really wanted rock stardom, which, in retrospect, is what I wanted in the first place. It just took me a long time to recognize it. I still marvel at some of the world's best guitar players and recognize that I'm not one of them. I can't play ten thousand notes to three people, but I can play three notes to one hundred thousand people. When I started my journey, I never understood that difference or how my dream of being a great guitar player could or would change. I chose a path to be a great performer because that was where my natural talents took me.

At the time, I was not aware that a *musician* and *rock star* embodied very different skill sets. I have come to learn over time that no rock stars I know are musicians and no musicians I know are rock stars. They have very different job qualifications.

I came to the realization that I wasn't really a musician around 1977, when I learned the guitar parts to the Lou Reed song "Sweet Jane." His guitar players were rock legends Steve Hunter and Dick Wagner. The parts were really hard to learn, but I mastered them, at which point I said to myself, "Well, I'm good enough to play by ear and to figure out whatever song I want to play, so now I'll turn my attention solely to my image." I proclaimed myself knowledgeable enough to get by as a guitar player and decided that I could become famous without having to put more time into learning my instrument.

And the truth is, my playing has not evolved since then. I still can't read music, and I know no music theory.

But there is a cliché in my business: "It's close enough for rock 'n' roll."

Now it was time to be a rock star, so how I looked onstage became way more important. Making sure I was always ready to play anywhere, no matter what the conditions, and being professional enough to deliver a consistent performance were now more important than anything else.

Hanging out with Brian Johnson and Angus Young of AC/DC.

The one aspect, however, of my playing that I really still care about is the sound of the guitar. My playing style evolved from a love of the sound of Mike Bloomfield's playing, not just the technique. The sound is what drew me to love Clapton's playing. I tried to get the sound created by Eric Clapton and Peter Green, his replacement in John Mayall's Bluesbreakers bands. John Mayall's 1966 album *Blues Breakers with Eric Clapton* set a standard for guitar tone that forms the foundation of thousands of blues players of my generation. The tone of a Gibson Les Paul model guitar plugged into a low-power Marshall combo amp fused with a vibrato created by one's fingers is my sound.

As the band morphed from style to style, my blues roots became overshadowed by the need to sound like a heavy metal band. To that end, especially after Mark Mendoza joined the band with his huge amplifiers and his take-no-prisoners style of bass playing, both Eddie Ojeda and I increased our amplifier firepower: bigger, louder, heavier.

Tenth lineup.

We were greatly influenced by Judas Priest, and after we played a show with them in 1979, I wanted that same kind of sound: very loud volume and distortion that, when controlled and played in unison by two or more guitar players, provides a thick heavy layer to an industrial sonic palette that supports the very foundation of the definition of heavy metal.

So, in a way, although my technique didn't evolve, it didn't really need to. The sonics of the band as a whole did, and that became our calling card.

It's hard to describe exactly what it's like to harness volumes that exceed 117 decibels (the sound of a supersonic plane at takeoff). When you perform in arenas or stadiums in front of one hundred thousand people, there is a sense of control and an almost spiritual electro-motive force that probably comes closer to being on a battle-field. It's really that kind of intense.

Me and Eddie with Steven Pearcy and Robyn Crosby of Ratt, plus Fiona Flanagan (Atlantic recording artist).

I'm often asked if I feel lucky to have made it. I personally, and we as a band, worked our asses off to be the best live band in the world. The goal changed along the way, and we adapted. That was my strength. That was what I was built for. I became a rock star, but I'm also a real musician who changed my focus in order to succeed. I had the wisdom to know it was crucial to reinvent and change direction.

On top of changing my focus from being a great guitar player to becoming a rock star, I was also starting a new path—as a businessperson. Even early on, it made sense to me to try and understand the business aspects of the business we were in. I saw the full picture of what success would mean, and I knew, even without knowing what those other pieces would be, that there were other things I was going to need to know in order to succeed.

When Mel and Keith stole the gear and quit the band and Kenny and I had to start all over again, I realized that I had to take the reins of managing the new band. I wanted to handle it, but I was terrified of talking to club owners and representing myself as a manager. *These guys are gonna step all over me,* I thought.

Since it was common knowledge that the Jersey and Long Island bar scenes were run by the mob, I wasn't super confident that I'd have the acumen, confidence, and cojones to sit in a room with these guys and ask for our gig money without getting my head shot off. I needed a godfather to guide me through and watch my back. I had the wisdom to know I needed a mentor, and Kevin Brenner taught me everything I needed to know.

Kevin was the most powerful and influential booking agent in the tristate area. He had the biggest and most popular bands, and he really knew how to wheel and deal with the club owners, many of whom were "connected."

Besides being a brilliant agent, Kevin also owned some clubs and/ or was a secret financial backer of many of them. Because he could control who played where, he could make or break a band; therefore, he was both hated and loved by club owners and artists alike.

Remember, even though the bar scene was huge in those days, it was all geographically located within a hundred-mile radius from Manhattan, and there were hundreds of bars and clubs in that area. Kevin's company, CTA, wasn't the only booking agency, but they controlled the biggest rooms and worked the biggest bands like Zebra, Rat Race Choir, Baby, Swift Kick, Twisted Sister, and dozens more. Each band had certain strengths, which made them effective for different audience sizes; some were only suited for smaller clubs that held up to three hundred people, but the bigger bands, like us, could regularly fill the rooms that held over two thousand people, and we could play them five nights a week, fifty-two weeks a year, and never leave the confines of the hundred-mile tristate area. Those halcyon club days disappeared when the drinking age was raised to twenty-one years old, and, consequently, many of the clubs lost a huge chunk of their clientele and dried up overnight.

But back then, Kevin Brenner controlled it all. And we were his number one band.

Kevin was the best negotiator I'd ever met. I studied everything he did, and he taught me many management skills that I use to this day. When we finally made it to the big leagues, I really wanted to bring Kevin with us. But for reasons that I never understood, he either couldn't or wouldn't make the jump.

Kevin Brenner was one of the unsung heroes of Twisted Sister, and he was the best mentor I've ever had. He died suddenly many years ago but not without him knowing that we had become bigger than any of us thought possible.

Now, I am a social creature by nature. And I'm a street guy with plenty of bravado. But even back then, Kevin helped give me the wisdom to know that I shouldn't be in charge of everything.

I could size people up pretty quickly, and if I concluded someone could handle something better than I could, I let them handle it.

Hiring Dee, for example, was wise. He may have been a hyper, egotistical, narcissistic, self-absorbed motherfucker, but he was committed. And he was truthful. He was professional and he did what he said he was going to do. That was so important, because it freed me up to learn the business side of the equation.

Soon, learning the business became more important to me than the music. Learning how to become a great live bar band, and the biggest live bar band, became my primary focus.

Keith Richards says the difference between him and Mick Jagger, who is the business heartbeat and visionary of the Stones enterprise, is that Mick wakes up every morning and thinks about what's going to happen ten days from now, ten weeks from now, ten months from now, ten years from now. Keith gets up every morning and says, "I got up this morning."

Every band needs both.

I have the business moves like Jagger. I have always had the ability to think about what's going to go on ten days from now, ten weeks from now, ten months from now, ten years from now.

Dee being Dee.

I have always been able to operate on multiple levels. Multitasking, I think, is not just something I learned out of necessity, but an innate ability I've always had. I could play guitar and manage the band, but I could also anticipate problems from many sides simultaneously, which was really important. I could foresee booking challenges, I could foresee personnel issues, I could anticipate worst-case scenarios and develop contingency plans. And then I could get up onstage and wail on the guitar.

I'd tell Dee, "You figure out the song lists. You figure out what songs we should cover, because that's too much for me." Dee was more than happy to do that. He loved doing that stuff. He couldn't care less about the business. So I let him do his thing and he let me do mine, and we were fine with that. Dee's strength was in the presentation—the stellar performance and the impact it had on our fans. We all trusted his vision. Our job was to execute without fail,

Signing records in the UK—April 1983.

every time. The pressure would seem enormous to an outsider, but it became second nature to us.

Wisdom helps make the good times better, to be sure. But when everything falls apart, your hard-earned wisdom really pays off by giving you the vision, understanding, and humility to keep going.

Years later, after the first rise and fall of the band, at a time when it was clear to anyone who cared that Twisted Sister was no more, I found myself in bankruptcy court in Bowling Green, New York. The whole thing was blowing my mind and crushing my heart. I am one of these anally perfect credit guys. I pay every bill on time. Having a perfect credit score is really important to me. It always has been. I'm crazily meticulous and protective of my credibility and reputation. I pay people back. I pay people before I take my own money. I pay my road crew before I take my salary.

But there I was, filing bankruptcy. I was also getting divorced from my first wife, who was walking away with a lot of our stuff. I was going to be left with nothing, not one proverbial pot to piss in. Except one thing: I owned the name Twisted Sister. Wisdom whispered to me that one day the name could be worth a lot of money, and I should hold on to it no matter what.

Well, it wasn't quite that mystical. Here's what had happened:

About a month before this, I was in England with the woman who would become my second wife. I was watching a British TV show at her parents' house, and a commercial for Tide detergent came on. The commercial featured this hot guy doing his laundry in a Laundromat. He takes off his shirt and shows off his six-pack, with a hot girl watching him.

That's not what caught my attention, though. The music running under the commercial was "Stand by Me" by Ben E. King. Not a remake, but the original 1961 version of the song. I was thinking, *Wow, that's interesting. Why that song?*

The song added to the message of the commercial, of course. But do you know what that commercial did for the song? It became number one again. A song from 1961 hit number one again because of a TV commercial. Talk about unexpected. It's unbelievable.

When that happened, I thought to myself, *Whoa! TV commercials. Man, that's like a big business. That's huge.*

So a month later, when I was standing in front of the bankruptcy court judge, I was ready when he said to me, "Mr. Segall, your only asset is this name, Twisted Sister. Why shouldn't I just take it from you and give it to the various people you owe money to?"

"Well, you could, Your Honor," I said. "But it's a waste of time."

"What do you mean?" he asked.

"Nothing is as old as yesterday's news," I told him. "And Twisted Sister is as valuable as yesterday's *New York Post.*"

"How are you in bankruptcy court?" asked the judge. "I know your band. You're famous."

"Well, Your Honor," I said. "You know how a movie can cost a hundred million dollars to make, and star the biggest names in Hollywood, and then go on to bomb at the box office?"

"Yeah."

"And a Broadway show with the biggest stars can bomb?"

"Yeah."

"So we made a new album that we thought was gonna be the biggest thing in the world, and we rolled all our money into it. And it bombed. It happens. I didn't want it to happen, but it happened. Now I'm sitting here and I can't pay back this money. The point of Twisted Sister is that we're over. Twisted Sister's dead. It's yesterday's news."

"So . . . ?"

"Right now," I continued, "there's no value to it. But, Your Honor, maybe in ten years I could license one of our songs for a product on TV, and maybe, as a result, I could put the band back together again. But right now, I have nothing left except this name. And right now, this name is worthless to my creditors. But one day, just maybe, I could make it valuable again. And I'd like to have the opportunity to earn some money back should that time come to pass."

"That's pretty compelling," he said, clearly impressed with my vision. "Okay, you can keep the name."

Ten years to the month after that court appearance, Comtrex Nasal Spray licensed "We're Not Gonna Take It" for $100,000 and today our songs are among the most licensed eighties-era anthems in the history of the music business.

Remember, it's not what you know, it's what you *don't* know that's really the most important in business. Keep your eyes and ears open. Keep curious about the business you're in and never stop asking questions. This will help to you to develop your wisdom, to refine your ability to understand and see the full picture, even if—and especially when—all the pieces are not already in place.

I recently thought about a couple of conversations I had with my brother, Jeff, who is ten years older than I am, and with my old friend Victor, whom I had had the great fortune of reestablishing a relationship with recently. Both of them knew me years before I had any success, and both gave me insights into their choices as well as my own decisions.

In both examples, while their respective life choices seem safe, they both went on to have stellar careers in their chosen fields. Both love their jobs and—just as easily as any entrepreneur—could have failed. The difference is that their risks were much closer to the ground, allowing a shorter fall and easier pivot. In other words, and without taking away anything from their respective accomplishments, the decision to go all in was less dangerous in the choices they made.

Jeff became a New York City schoolteacher, a decision he made in part because he felt that a job like that would give him an economically secure future. He's now retired after teaching forty years, and by all accounts, everything worked out financially as planned.

Victor had been a drummer who was following his dream of rock stardom, but when he was twenty-two, he started picking up extra cash by chauffeuring famed theatrical producer Joseph Papp around. This opportunity led him to a stagehand job for Shakespeare in the Park. Victor realized that he loved the backstage theater world, and this is where he established a great career. He told me, "Working in the theater world, days became weeks, weeks became years, and I realized one day that I had a career that I didn't know I had."

Then there's me. My ability to walk away, pivot, and move on probably explains my survival. I take life as it comes, find a different pathway, and move on. My experiences have given me the wisdom to do that.

Around 1995, as I was rebuilding my life after bankruptcy, I took a job at Lyric Hi-Fi, a high-end audio store where I used to buy my stereo equipment back when I was a hot-shot rock star with bucks to burn. They offered me a job as a salesman, and I took it. And for the first time in my life, I felt like Ray Liotta's character in *Goodfellas* when he said, "I'm an average nobody. I get to live the rest of my life like a schnook."

I'd sell stereos during the day, and then at night I'd be vacuuming the store, taking orders from Mike K., the owner. "Jay Jay! There's dirt on this floor! Jay Jay, wipe the dust off the equipment! Jay Jay, go help that customer!"

So, this is where it's wound up, huh? I thought. *My father was a salesman and now I'm a salesman. I'm no different from Lou Segall. It doesn't matter if it's stereos and not jewelry—I'm just a salesman.*

Some people would just drink themselves into oblivion at this point. For me, I had the wisdom to believe it was going to turn around. As I was pushing that vacuum, I couldn't get my head around the fact that this was how my life had worked out. But I also knew there had to be another way. I knew that something else would come— not because of some mystical, help-from-a-benevolent-universe shit, but because in my off hours, I found a way to keep building on my music industry experience—like picking up some extra cash by doing licensing deals for the band's catalog, for example.

As an atheist, I don't believe in divine intervention; I don't believe in that deus ex machina shit. But what happened next was almost enough to make me reconsider my spiritual worldview.

One day, out of nowhere, I got a call from a drummer in an Atlanta band that, years earlier, I used to produce. A band called Sevendust (called Crawlspace at the time) needed a manager, he told me, and they wanted me to do it. So, I signed on, and—just like that— I was back in the business. With Twisted bass player Mark Mendoza, I coproduced Sevendust's debut album, and, under my management, it went on to sell nearly a half million copies. It was on its way to platinum, and it put the band on the map.

As the manager and producer, I made more money than I had ever made with Twisted Sister.

Because they had a drug and alcohol problem that I could tell was going to hurt them, we didn't see eye to eye on the future of the band, and eventually we parted ways—but not before I bought a weekend house on Long Island, socked away a pile of money, and reestablished my credibility in the music industry.

There may be no greater example of wisdom than a meeting I arranged with Dee in February 1996. This meeting led to a cessation of hostilities between us that had been roiling in me since the day I hired him on February 8, 1976. You need to understand that, at this point in our lives and for many years before, Dee and I hated each other. We'd been in business together, and that was it. When the band fell apart and we both went bankrupt, neither of us had any desire to ever see each other again. And we hadn't. Until that February meeting, without which, it turns out, the band would never have come back.

A month before, in January 1996, I had requested an update of domestic record sales of *Stay Hungry* only to learn that we had hit the three million mark. Every million records sold equals one platinum album. So, unbeknownst to us, we had become triple platinum artists. Not bad for a band that no longer even existed. So, I requested that triple platinum album plaques be manufactured for each band member. I gave the record label the addresses of each of the band members, so I didn't have to be the middle man and distribute the awards. At this point, the only members I was talking to were Mark and AJ, so I had no desire to take responsibility for the delivery.

Every plaque was delivered, except Dee's, which was returned to the factory. The label asked me where they should send Dee his award. So here I was in the middle after all, and the last thing I wanted was to connect with Dee. I reached out to a mutual friend for Dee's current mailing address. I never heard back, so I finally decided to bite the bullet and call Dee directly.

I left a short message and my number on his answering machine, and the next day, Dee called. We hadn't spoken since January 1988, at a final meeting in our lawyer's office, which hadn't gone well. Dee had wanted to buy the Twisted Sister trademark from me, and, although this isn't a direct quote, my reaction was something like, "I would rather eat dog food from a toilet bowl in the middle of Times Square then ever sell you the Twisted Sister name." I stormed out, and that was that. Until this moment, eight years later.

"Hey, Jay, it's Dee," he said when I picked up the phone. "I got your message."

"Hey," I said.

"I hear that you had a daughter, Jay. Congratulations!"

He then told me that he had just had his fourth child, and I congratulated him. We were just two dads talking about our kids.

After the niceties were exchanged, Dee explained that he did get the package, but when he asked the postman where it was from, he was told it was from a company called Illegal Records. Not knowing that that was the name of the company that manufactures the plaques, Dee thought it was a demo tape from a band on some indie label, and he refused the package. He then apologized and asked me to have it resent.

At that point I suggested that we talk. We hadn't spoken in eight years, and I suggested that maybe it was time to just say whatever was on our minds and close the door on our history. I invited him to my apartment, and he accepted.

He came into the city on February 16, nearly twenty years to the day from when I hired him to be our singer. When I opened the door, I noticed immediately something had changed. Dee was just a normal guy standing in front of me. I assumed that, as we both had gone through bankruptcy in 1989, we both had to reinvent ourselves. We sat down and started talking about how the bankruptcies had affected our lives.

At this point, the Sevendust album had yet to be released, but I told him the story of how I came to be connected with them after my illustrious stereo sales career. Dee had written a hit song for Celine Dion and was slowly getting his life back together.

Then we started to reflect on the band and our relationship. I didn't tape this conversation, nor did I write down what was said. I can tell you, however, that the conversation was tough to have. Nothing that had happened between us was left unsaid. No grievance from either side was left out. There was no need to be diplomatic. This conversation wasn't about reuniting the band; it was about clearing the air. It was about making amends so we could finally move on and say goodbye, forever.

We sat at my kitchen table for nearly five hours. And, man, we covered a lot of ground. Dee admitted that, as time went on, he saw me as his father. He was very angry at his father for various reasons and I, being older, became a father figure that he needed to destroy along with his relationship with his real dad. I'd represented an authority figure who seemed to tell him that he wasn't good enough. His actions, he admitted, were bent on my destruction.

"I'm really sorry I did that," Dee said, looking me in the eye. "And I hope you can forgive me. I'm not that guy anymore."

I apologized to Dee for ever making him feel that he wasn't good enough.

This very emotional moment was made possible by two men who had been through hell and decided that the world (and the example we set for our children) would be better off if the two of us could make peace.

Around 4:00 p.m., I had to pick up my daughter, Samantha, from preschool, and Dee offered to walk with me to collect her. When she walked up to us, I said, "Sam, meet Dee, the guy who used to sing in the band."

We walked together to the subway station on Ninety-Fourth Street and Broadway. Before Dee turned to head down to the train, we hugged. Dee thanked me for asking him to come.

"You know what, Dee?" I said. "Tomorrow morning, I will wake up not hating you for the first time in twenty years."

"Same here," said Dee, and he headed down to the subway station. I thought that would be the last time we would ever see each other.

Oh, how wrong I was.

Wisdom, I've learned, is seeing the big picture and making daily decisions and working out solutions on that basis. Whether you're in a brainstorming session, drawing up a business proposal, or making a deal, you have to make yourself see that what you're doing is about more than what's going on in this moment. It's knowing that when you're vacuuming a store after business hours, that's not what you'll be doing until you drop dead. It's knowing that everything you do is just a small part of a much larger thing.

If I hadn't been able to see that, I would not have held on to the Twisted Sister trademark. If I hadn't been able to see that, the band would never have reunited and finished our career with our most successful run. If I hadn't had been able to do that, I might still be selling stereo equipment.

It's all connected, and having the wisdom to see the big picture keeps you going, and, just as important, it keeps you inspired along the way.

6

TWISTED

INSPIRATION

IN ORDER TO GET ANYWHERE IN BUSI- ness, you have to be inspired. Inspiration is the fuel that keeps you motivated; without it, you're just going through the motions.

Since I was eleven years old and first started to understand there was a business of music, I wanted to be a part of it. But it wasn't the business side that drew me in. I was obsessed with music, and in addition to playing it, I was always looking for ways to absorb it. Practically every new experience I had having to do with music inspired me and fueled my passion to want to make it in the music business.

And growing up where and when I did in the history of rock gave me the opportunity to have some remarkable experiences.

In the 1960s, there were two small, exclusive clubs getting a lot of attention and attracting big names in the City: Steve Paul's Scene on Eighth Avenue, run by Steve Paul, and Ungano's, an Italian restaurant on Seventieth Street. Those two little establishments had incredible reputations, because all the British rockers would hang out there when they were in New York. Ungano's was a couple blocks from my house.

In July of 1968, my Bermuda-experience buddy David Schiff and I were walking up Seventieth Street and passed Ungano's. The restaurant had a sign in front, and spelled out in those tacky, small plastic letters was:

Tonight. Free & Spooky Tooth.

You have to understand how shocking this was. This was a funky little neighborhood joint. More shocking than that, David said, "We can get in."

"How?" We were underage at the time. They were not going to let us in.

"My mother recently met Free's manager, a guy named Dee Anthony." David's mother was the archetypal hot mom. Free's manager apparently had the hots for her, too.

"He told her any time any of his bands were playing her son was welcome—and to just mention his name to the club owner. So I think we can get in to Ungano's tonight," he said.

Ungano's had all the trappings of a classic mob hangout. When we walked in that night, Nicky Ungano was sitting at a desk with a cigar, a pinkie ring, and a racing form. He looked up at us, two seventeen-year-old Jewish kids from the West Side, and asked, "What do youse want?"

"We're guests of Dee Anthony," David said.

"How the fuck you know Dee Anthony?" Nicky asked.

"My mom's a personal friend."

"We'll see about that," he said and disappeared behind a curtain.

I said to David, "Your mother better know this freaking guy, or you and I are going to be in cement fucking footwear."

A few minutes later, Dee Anthony emerged from the back room. "Who the hell are you?" he demanded.

"My mother," said David, pausing for effect, "is Charlotte Schiff."

And right in front of our eyes, that tough bastard, Mr. Anthony, transformed into that guy from *The Wizard of Oz*: "Well, that's a horse of a different color!"

With a smile on his face and a bounce in his step, he walked the two of us into the legendary den of iniquity.

We were seventeen. And we were in Ungano's.

The room was dark, but I could see some tables and fifteen or so people scattered throughout the room. And, lo and behold, Free, whom I had seen the night before with thousands of other fans at Madison Square Garden, was playing right there on the floor, because the stage hadn't even been set up yet, and they're performing their first album, *Fire and Water*.

Dee Anthony walks us up to the front, right there in front of Paul Kossoff and Paul Rodgers, puts his arms around each of us and he says, "What do you think of my band, Free?"

"We saw them last night at the Garden," I said, astounded and feeling very much out of my body in the moment.

"Well, boys," said Mr. Anthony. "Have a seat and enjoy yourselves."

David and I sat. "Do you believe we're in Ungano's?" I said. "And freaking Free is playing like five feet away?"

After Free's set, Nicky Ungano came out and announced that Spooky Tooth wasn't feeling well, so they wouldn't be performing. And then he said two words that would turn the rest of the evening into a life-altering experience: "Open jam."

Out of the shadows, Jim Keltner from the Delaney and Bonnie Band got up from a table and took a seat behind the drums. Chris Wood from Traffic joined him. Then Ric Grech from Blind Faith strapped on a bass; Steve Winwood got on the organ. Dr. John sat down at the piano, and Eric Clapton picked up a guitar. Then Delaney and Bonnie stepped up.

Just imagine for a moment that you're at a small party, and then, out of nowhere, some of your favorite musicians on the planet get up to play. The impromptu dream team played for three hours to what was, in effect, an exclusive, private party.

"Do you fucking believe what we're seeing?" I asked David. "Do you believe this?"

What could be more inspiring for a young, aspiring musician than this?

Inspiration is the fuel that drives the dream. Inspiration compels you to take the necessary risks to achieve your goals. Inspiration takes away the fear, or at least quiets it down. Why was I *not* afraid to take risks? Why was I *not* afraid to fail?

Every entrepreneur's journey started with inspiration from something that they saw, experienced, read, or heard. And from that point, they had no choice but to pursue their dream. Since I was a kid, rock and roll and R&B have totally inspired and consumed me. I saw the Beatles on TV and said, "That's what I want to be." Then, in a second wave of inspiration, Bowie came along. The Beatles lifted me off the planet, but Bowie shot me into the stratosphere, and I was soon floating in my tin can far above the moon.

Starting from the age of fifteen, I went to see every performer I could, almost every night of the week. I carried a guitar around with me everywhere I went and told people I was going to be a rock star. I practiced my guitar for hours on end and imagined myself playing with the Grateful Dead, the Allman Brothers, Led Zeppelin, Pink Floyd, the Rolling Stones. I also knew one thing for certain: I didn't need a high school diploma or a college degree, which is why I became a high school dropout. I had a crazy dream, which I had absolutely no idea how to accomplish, and I took risk after risk without any safety net. I had no choice. I had to have it so bad, nothing could stop me.

On the back cover of my favorite Paul Butterfield blues album was a picture of Mike Bloomfield playing a Fender Telecaster. So I wanted that one. I crammed a fistful of weed money into my pocket, went down to Forty-Eighth Street, and walked into the famous establishment Manny's Music.

"I want to buy a Fender Telecaster," I said. "I have a hundred and thirty-five bucks."

The clerk said, "It's $147.50."

"I have $135," I repeated.

"Too bad, kid," he said. "Get out."

Undeterred, I walked across the street to a place called Jimmy's. "I just got thrown out of Manny's," I told the clerk. "I've got a hundred and thirty-five bucks and I want to buy a Telecaster," I said, and I laid the cash out on the counter. "Do we have a deal?"

We did.

Now I had a real electric guitar. I was dealing pot for cash and playing music, jamming all night and barely surviving in school. Then I got slammed with mononucleosis and was, once again, pulled out of school and sentenced to my bed to recover.

The last time I was sick and alone, I listened to the radio all day and discovered "Hey Paula." This time I immersed myself in the blues. I absorbed albums by Albert King, John Mayall and the Blues-breakers with Eric Clapton, and Paul Butterfield. I spent eight hours a day listening to those records and playing my Telecaster. I'd pick a song and listen to it over and over and over again. Then I'd play it on my guitar, over and over and over again, for hours and hours a day.

When I returned to school six weeks later, I knew enough to legitimately call myself a guitar player. I understood the positioning, I understood the form, I knew the scales that you needed to play the blues. I had the chord changes. I got it. And I was so excited.

Sometime around the winter of 1968, a kid named Ricky Paul walked up to me in chemistry class at Brandeis High School. "You must be a musician," he told me, looking at my long hair.

"Yeah," I said.

"Do you read *Rolling Stone* magazine?"

"Yeah," I said. Because every real musician did.

"Did you hear about this Johnny Winter guy? He just signed the biggest record deal in the history of Columbia Records."

"Yeah," I said. "He got a $600,000 advance."

"Well, his manager is my brother, Steve Paul. Winter is playing at the Fillmore East this weekend. Do you want to go see him? You'd be my guest."

I'd never been inside the hallowed halls of Fillmore East before, so I said, "Great."

The opening act that fateful evening was Terry Reid, a British bluesman who was purportedly the original choice for lead singer of Led Zeppelin. Then Johnny Winter came out and blew the doors off the place. He was just flat out freaking unbelievable. BB King was the headliner, and it was the first time I'd ever seen him in the flesh.

I was enthralled, mesmerized, gobsmacked, and this place was right down the street from where I lived. I could go there literally any time I wanted. I looked at the billboard of upcoming shows and saw that Iron Butterfly with Canned Heat and the Youngbloods would be playing the next weekend. The following week would be Blood, Sweat & Tears. Tickets were three bucks. Three. Freakin'.

Dollars. I mean, who couldn't go? I started buying tickets and going to the Fillmore every weekend.

But they weren't just concerts; they were training sessions. They continued to feed my inspiration, which fueled my motivation. I'd go see whatever band was playing that weekend, then head home at 3:00 a.m. and stand in front of my mirror with my guitar slung over my shoulder, pretending to be whomever I'd just seen onstage that night. If I saw Iron Butterfly, I'd be Erik Brann in the mirror; Canned Heat turned me into the John Segall version of Henry Vestine. This is the way it went every single weekend, month after month. Rock star in training. On every level.

Then one day, I saw that the Grateful Dead were coming to the Fillmore. The Dead's six-hour concerts were legendary, and you had to be on acid to see them. It was like a prerequisite. I was so excited; this was going to be an unbelievable experience. Not only that, but they'd be opening for Janis Joplin.

On the evening of the concert, I got my ticket, dropped my acid, and waited for what I thought was going to be a typical six-hour Grateful Dead show. My LSD kicked in, everything started to melt, and then, perfectly timed with my burgeoning acid trip, the Dead took the stage. They tuned up, they played one song, then they said good night.

As they exited the stage, I cried, "Everything is melting and you're leaving." I'm pretty sure I didn't perform in front of my mirror that night.

Undeterred, I kept going to the Fillmore every weekend to see all the great bands of the day, but the mythical six-hour Dead concert continued to elude me. When I saw they were coming back to open for Country Joe and the Fish, I, of course, bought a ticket. Obviously, I had learned nothing because, once again, I took all this acid and settled in for the marathon. The Grateful Dead came out and tuned up. They played "China Cat Sunflower," and they said good night.

Then Country Joe stepped up to the mic and said, through his swirling, multicolored face, "You people in New York who have never seen a full Grateful Dead show, you really need to see them. So, tomorrow night, on this stage, *we're* going to open for *them*."

The next night I got my ticket, took my seat, and timed my acid drop so that it would hit just as Jerry Garcia and the crew started their show. Then the Dead came out and played for five hours, and, I kid you not, I thought I saw God. Which is no small thing for an atheist to say.

It was one of the greatest experiences of my life, and it had a profound effect on me. It also taught me a lot about crowd dynamics and the unique relationship that a band can cultivate with its adoring, cultlike fans. They had not only inspired me as musicians but, in the bigger picture, as an act.

Could I ever have imagined at seventeen years old, sitting at the Fillmore East on acid watching the Grateful Dead, that not only would I one day be playing in a band, but that I would be managing the band and trying to figure out survival techniques to keep the business of the band going?

Over the next decades, I would take the inspiration from my Fillmore years and use it to fuel my career. I was twenty when we started Twisted Sister, and, after ten years of struggling and failure after failure, we finally found success in 1983 and rode that wave until we crashed and burned in 1988.

Sevendust was and still are a great band. My issues with them when I managed them from 1996 until 2000 had to do with their substance abuse, which I had zero tolerance for. While many artists can perform under these conditions, I was genuinely concerned for the health and safety of some of the members. This made it impossible (as far as I was concerned) for the band to make good decisions and we parted ways when they wanted to get Creed's manager, Jeff Hansen, to pick up my management contract. I am proud, however, to have co-produced (with Mark Mendoza) their most successful album and to have managed them to their greatest success. Over the years they have asked me to return as manager, but we are better off as friends and I wish them continued success.

Even though the band was dead during my dark times of bankruptcy, divorce, and stereo sales, my inspiration to continue to make music was not. The inspiration that sparked in me during my teen years continued to fuel and motivate me, so I continued to take more chances. I remarried and had a child. I reinvented myself as the producer and manager of Sevendust.

It's all . . . well . . . twisted together: tenacity is the will to keep going; wisdom is the understanding that things will change; inspiration is the fuel that powers your rocket.

I took some very big risks and suffered a number of very big crashes. I had plenty of sleepless nights. I had times when I felt that I was staring down into the abyss. Did I walk away from the music business after the birth of my daughter and assume that I was no longer able to withstand that risk again? Yes, I did. So why did I return, yet again, to the scene of such victory and defeat?

It all comes down to passion fueled by ongoing inspiration. My passion was (and still is) so great that the sheer nature of the intoxicating effects of changing the world through music keeps giving me the faith that I will succeed.

Inspiration is the fuel that drives the dream. The feeling of *I have to do this* triggers your passion, which ignites the fuel that gives you the energy to go pursue your dream, come hell or high water, challenge, crisis, or catastrophe.

Every successful person I've ever met has said that in the beginning, the desire to achieve the dream overrode everything else. But the truth is, there may come a point where your passion runs out, and if you don't succeed by then, you're done.

When I was twenty, I loosely determined that my passion was going to last me five years. I was going to be a rock star at the age of twenty-five, and if I didn't make it, I would start all over again as something else. My passion didn't flounder, though, and by the time I was twenty-nine, the band still had no record deal, despite our success in the bars and clubs.

I remember telling my manager in 1981, after our umpteenth rejection, "You got one more year. If you don't get me a record deal by the time I'm thirty, I'm out." I had never said that out loud before. I'd never officially given myself a deadline to end it. But my passion, the ten years of work and the unrelenting busting of my ass for the love of rock and roll, was about to run out of steam.

Even though we were making a lot of money as a bar band, I saw down the line that wasn't going to continue. The drinking age in New York State was changing, and wisdom told me that would have an impact on our performance success. We were going to lose a huge chunk of our live audience if the drinking age got raised to twenty-one.

Nobody in their right mind thought it could ever happen. The liquor lobby was too strong, and there's no way that New York, Connecticut, and New Jersey were ever going to submit to it. I was looking at this clock ticking and thinking, *It's perfectly coming together, the drinking age and my thirtieth birthday,* which scared the crap out of me.

The photo shoot for *Under the Blade* was at midnight of July 19, 1982, the day I turned thirty. As the clock struck twelve, we were shooting our first album cover, and I thought, *Wow, it happened. We made it.* And that's precisely when the record company went bankrupt.

How many people want to become successful rock stars? Thousands. How many become them? Ten. It's a constant weeding-out process. How many athletes want to win a gold medal at the Olympics? Thousands. How many get the gold medal? One. There's a winner. It's a Ponzi scheme, and your passion takes you through this filtration system over and over and over again.

But, inevitably, there comes a reckoning: your inspiration is either putting food on your table, or it's not. The only difference between those of us who have succeeded and those who haven't is that we just managed to pull it off before the need to survive superseded the inspiration to continue.

The harsh reality is that if the money is not paying for you to pursue your passion, then it's time to find another passion or shift your passion from vocation to avocation. Ninety-nine out of a hundred people who pursue audacious goals will eventually conclude that it's time to do something else. And there's nothing wrong with that. There's great value in a hobby that inspires you because it gives you energy to pursue the activities that pay.

Everybody who's been in a wedding band has had the same dream I did. At some point, their initial dream of stardom had to convert into something else, because they obviously weren't going to become rock stars. So maybe they went back to school, got degrees, and became dentists, or carpenters, or tech giants. Maybe they still played in a wedding band on the weekends, but that was for fun and maybe to make a few extra bucks, and that was good enough.

So, where does that leave you? As an entrepreneur, you've got this idea. You're inspired. You're passionately pursuing it. You've raised money to fuel your business. But you haven't made it yet. You're scrambling to make payroll. And then you come to that moment of truth where you look in the mirror and you realize it's time to fold your tent. Now, there are people that will say you should never give in to that. That you should, in the words of countless motivational speakers, "Never, ever, ever, ever give up!"

But is that really true?

Well . . . yes and no. I believe that you should never give up on your goal to succeed wildly. But you may determine that it's time to give up on the goal of succeeding in a particular way. That'll be your decision at your moment of reckoning—and only you can make it. At the very least, you'll need the inspiration to make it to that moment; quitting before then will leave you with too many unanswered questions and too many regrets.

To put it another way, the problem isn't that people eventually choose to give up; the problem is that they give up too soon.

When we were building Twisted Sister, we had countless opportunities to fold our tent, so why didn't we? There's an inherent conflict between inspiration and tenacity. On the one hand, you could say that tenacity really kicks in when the inspiration wears off; on the other hand, there can come a time when it's a wise move to throw in the proverbial towel and direct your tenacity toward a new pursuit.

The tipping point for us was that TV show in England that saved our careers. If that hadn't happened, then we wouldn't be sitting here talking about Twisted Sister. Because you'd have never heard of us.

On any given day, leaving your house can change your life. On any given day, a seemingly random conversation can be a game changer. While an entrepreneur has to believe that, an entrepreneur also has to look at the reality. My reality was that even as great as we were as a band, we were confronted with bigger issues we could not control, and those issues would have eventually led to our demise.

With one of my guitars in 1984.

Inspiration feeds your spirit and makes you feel happy about what you do. It's not just the pragmatic business decisions that you make, but it's the feeling that you've done something better for this world. Inspiration is that magic pill. And it's always important— whether you continue on your original path or find something else that lights your fire.

I'm still inspired by great musicians and great performances. I still listen to rock bands. I have a phenomenal vinyl collection that inspires me every time I place a record on the turntable. And even though I rarely pick up a guitar anymore, I have a world-class vintage guitar collection that fills me with joy. I can also be inspired by great speakers and by great books or great art. I can be inspired by conversations I have with people. On any given day, any conversation can just light me up.

Inspiration is all around you—you just have to pay attention to it. Try to find the things that fuel your spiritual side, the things that make you want to do something better for this world. And in the process, be curious about everyone and everything.

Curiosity is tied to inspiration; when I'm no longer curious, I think that will mean I'm done with striving. Listen, if you're happy with saying "I'm done," then I have no right to tell you you're wrong.

But if you're reading this book because you're trying to find ways to become successful, I'm going to assume that you're not done. Which means that no matter how rocky the road gets or how choppy the seas—pick your metaphor—you're going to need to summon the ability to stay the course. You're going to need steady legs. Even in the midst of the storm, you're going to need to provide stability.

STABILITY

"THERE IS NOTHING TO KEEPING A BAND TOGETHER. YOU SIMPLY HAVE TO HAVE A GIMMICK, AND THE GIMMICK I USE IS TO PAY THEM MONEY!"

—DUKE ELLINGTON

Every organization needs someone, somewhere in the operation, who's stable enough to control everything when things get out of hand. And things will get out of hand; therefore, without stability, you can't have success.

We went through fourteen lineup changes to get to the band that finally made it. All the guys who were fired were fired for drug and alcohol use. As much of a drug dealer and drug addict as I was between the ages of fifteen and twenty, I became incredibly anti-drug and anti-alcohol because these guys who were getting stoned all the time were destroying my life and preventing me from becoming successful. They weren't living up to the obligation of working hard. So we fired them, one after the other. That was one way we maintained stability for the band.

In the music business, as a band gets more recognized and the power of its image increases, the value of the band rises, too, and, naturally, the issues confronting the band shoot right up alongside their success. As we started to succeed, I saw the choppy waters ahead, so I wanted to hold on to as much power as I could. Fortunately, because of my aforementioned business instincts, I was qualified to take over the management of the enterprise. Not only did my management role guarantee that I could never be fired (unless I wanted to fire myself), but I also bought out the rights to the Twisted Sister trademark. I did this to protect myself against anyone's attempt to damage the band. I was no longer beholden to someone else who could take this away from me. It wasn't about the money; it was about the stability. I never made more money from Twisted than the other guys. I just wanted to make sure that I always was able to steer the ship in a way that was the fairest for everyone involved—including me.

How did I go from being a drug dealer to a super-straight, ultra-pragmatic, steady-as-she-goes stabilizing manager/player of a very successful band? Somewhere, somehow, I must have looked at my life and come to the conclusion that I was one very lucky mother-fucker who could have died a half a dozen times or been thrown in jail. And because I was lucky beyond words, I would build on those fortunate outcomes and become the hardest-working, most respon-sible person in the music business.

Now that I was managing an increasingly valuable band and brand, more and more the inevitable issues began eating away my days.

Did I even know how to hire players and roadies and then fire those who didn't work out? Did I know how to talk to club owners and mob guys? Negotiate with record labels? Studio owners? Pro-ducers? Did I know how to handle budgets? Did I know how to build and sustain a business model that looked after the band members and crews and their wives and/or girlfriends, too?

No! I mean, what do I look like to you? An HR director?

But I did have instincts and a facility with money from my drug dealer days. And as a bonus, I had the "gift of gab," as many people will attest to. My street wisdom served me well in dealing with all this crap.

Early on, I instituted guaranteed salaries for all members. It didn't matter how much they got paid—what mattered was that the guys knew they would be paid whatever amount we all agreed to.

And we always held aside enough money to cover our projects and crises—so no matter what, the guys got paid.

The firings, especially the constant turnover of drummers, became almost comedic. I started to think of myself as the executioner. It became a routine.

So as to not have to lose performing dates, when it was time to fire a drummer (a rather common occurrence) we would already have a new drummer ready to go. I'd then invite the soon-to-be-fired drummer to join me at the diner after the show. Over a late-night meal, I would tell him that things weren't working out, and that in lieu of two weeks' notice, I'd pay him for the next two weeks, but he wouldn't have to show up for the next show. See? Good, solid HR stuff. With a side of fries.

Most of the guys who were replaced were fired due to alcohol or drug issues that impeded their performance abilities. All had been warned about the no drugs/no drinking requirements of the band.

Drummer Tony Petri lasted three and a half years during the very heart of the band's club days from 1976 to 1980. Tony had gotten me the audition to be in Twisted Sister in the first place, so I owed him a lot. But he was fired for making racist and anti-Semitic statements aimed at band and crew members. This was particularly unsettling to me, as we were roommates during that time. Nonetheless, he had to go.

But when Tony went on his racist rant, the humanitarian in me decided that the line had been crossed. The one thing I could control was the ignorance that surrounded me, and we jettisoned him without a second thought.

Stability is generally threatened by what I call the three Cs: challenges, crises, and catastrophes. Trying to differentiate between challenges, crises, and catastrophes became part of the calluses (maybe that's the fourth C) that I developed as I grew into the manager role.

An example of a challenge is having to learn two new songs in a week because the fans demanded new material.

A crisis might be that the truck breaks down on the way to the gig, or having to fire a band member.

An example of a catastrophe is losing a record deal just before signing, or worse, figuring out how to manage the band, internally and externally, when a member suddenly and unexpectedly dies. Before we get to that, it's important to cover how we came out of the catastrophic events of the band breaking up, my subsequent bankruptcy, and the circumstances that brought us back together.

In September 2000, after I had reconciled with Dee, but before the band reunited, Jason Flom, Atlantic Records' soon-to-be chairman and CEO (and the person who had originally wanted to sign us to Atlantic), was being honored by the United Jewish Appeal at Tavern on the Green in New York City. I was having a casual conversation with his assistant one day, who mentioned this event to me.

"Who's going to play for Jason at this thing?" I asked.

"Matchbox 20, Kid Rock, Sebastian Bach from Skid Row, and Blue Man Group. They're all going to perform unplugged for Jason," his assistant told me.

Because of my accumulated wisdom, and, therefore, my ability to see the big picture, I immediately knew that Twisted Sister should appear at that show. Now, that might sound obvious, but given that things were terrible between the members of the band at the time, it shouldn't have seemed like a realistic possibility. To put not too fine a point on it, we all just fucking hated each other. On the other hand, I had just reconciled with Dee.

"What if I could convince the band to make a special appearance and perform for Jason?" I said, musing out loud.

She was fully behind it, so I called the guys up and explained what was going on. "You know, we could show up and it could be really cool," I told each one separately.

Everyone agreed. We hadn't performed together in thirteen years, but we figured a little rehearsal on a few songs and we'd be good as new. The rehearsal never happened, because the day before the performance, Mendoza cracked his ribs in a car accident. But, animal that he is, he didn't want to cancel.

"You do realize," I said to everybody, "that if we do this, we're gonna show up at Tavern on the Green and play in front of that audience for the first time (with AJ) since 1986?" We all agreed with Mark—fuck the rehearsal; we would show up and rock the proverbial house.

We met up at my apartment on the Upper West Side, and, surprisingly, no one acted like they wanted to kill each other. We loaded into a limo and headed down to Tavern on the Green. Since our being there was supposed to be a surprise, the crew led us directly into the kitchen so no one would see us. And while the other bands were playing, we strategized on our three-song set list.

Dee said, "Well, it has to be 'I Wanna Rock,' 'We're Not Gonna Take It,' and 'Rock and Roll.' And we should know those in our sleep, right?"

Of course we should.

When Blue Man Group took the stage, we knew we were next, but we stayed in the kitchen, ready to spring out from behind the utensils to the shock and awe of Jason and the audience.

Think about this. It is sheer craziness. If you had ever said to me that Twisted Sister would re-form thirteen years after breaking up to play at Tavern on the Green in Central Park, I'd have said, "How could you possibly imagine such a profoundly stupid scenario?"

But there we were.

The audience was filled with industry people, many of whom were executives from Atlantic Records and other labels. We were huddling behind the stoves, listening to Blue Man Group and waiting for our cue, which would be a chyron underneath the stage that read:

Ladies and gentleman, in honor of Jason Flom, please welcome . . . for the first time in thirteen years . . . Twisted Sister!

The words flash on the stage, we walk out with our guitars, and the audience is on its feet, screaming in surprise and excitement. We can't believe it! What a reception! Stoked and elated on the adrenaline, we plug in and tear right into "We're Not Gonna Take It."

We sounded awful. Shocked and confused, I looked around at everybody else.

"Wow, what's wrong with you? What's wrong with you?" I mouthed at everyone through the terrible noise. After the first verse,

I looked down at my guitar and had a shocking realization: I was the problem; I was playing in the wrong key. I had hardly picked up a guitar in thirteen years, and I hadn't bothered to even think about these songs. I just thought it would automatically come back. Apparently, I was wrong.

After a quick course correction on my part, we found our groove and blasted through the rest of the song and the two others. At the end of "I Wanna Rock," all the other musicians from the evening joined us onstage. Blue Man Group held up "I Wanna Rock" signs, and the place went completely apeshit crazy.

It was a fantastic show, but that was enough. I wasn't thinking that this gig for Jason was going to lead to anything else. We'd done our part to honor him, and that was totally fine. Still, because we did have the unique experience of playing together without killing each other, I found myself trying to figure out ways to get the band recognized and rebuild the brand.

I approached VH1's *Behind the Music* about doing a piece on Twisted Sister, and they showed no interest.

Seriously? I thought. *Are we that uncool? Have we completely fallen off the face of the earth?* Once upon a time, we had been the biggest band on MTV, and now I couldn't get VH1 to even look at us. It really pissed me off.

Then VH1 got a new executive vice president, a guy by the name of Rick Krim. Rick's first job in the music business had been working on an MTV Twisted Sister project. Twisted and a hundred of our fans were flown to Europe as a promotion for *Come Out and Play*. His job was to usher those kids over. So Rick and I went way back. And look what he'd accomplished.

The minute after he'd been promoted at VH1, Rick received a call from yours truly.

"Mr. Executive Vice President," I said through the phone. "Exactly why is it that Twisted Sister is so persona non grata that you guys won't even do a *Behind the Music* on us?"

"What are you talking about?"

"They told me they're not interested."

At the Jason Flom UJA honoree dinner with Eddie Ojeda, Sebastian Bach, Kid Rock, The Blue Man Group, me, Dee, Mark Mendoza, AJ Pero, and Mark McGrath (Sugar Ray).

"I'll take care of that," said Rick. And the very next day I found myself in a meeting with Rick and the show's production team.

"I understand that Twisted Sister wants to do *Behind the Music*," said the new boss to his minions. "Anybody have a problem with that?"

The answer, of course, was "No. No problem at all."

If you've ever seen an episode of *Behind the Music*, you know they're all very similar: band gets together, band makes a fortune, band gets drunk, someone dies of an overdose, the band loses it all, and everyone hates each other's guts. It's the same story, over and over and over again. Just change the faces and the name of the band, and it's the same story.

The problem with our story was that there were no drugs or alcohol.

"We just hate each other," I'd warned the producers. "No drugs, no alcohol. We just hate each other with a deep, steaming passion."

They brought a director in and filmed us for four months. They interviewed everyone separately, of course, because other than that one evening for Jason's tribute, no one in the band would be caught dead in the same room with the other. Everyone was clear about this when we agreed to do the show. For that reason, I had no idea what anyone was saying about anybody else.

I suppose I should have seen it coming, but because the band didn't have a drug and alcohol past, the editors focused heavily on the hatred. On camera, for the world to see, we all essentially prayed for each other to die in car crashes and for our families to burn in hell. Shit like that.

I was out of the country on vacation when the show aired. A friend of mine called me and told me he'd seen it.

"So? How was it?" I asked.

"Oh my God, Jay Jay," he said. "I wouldn't come back to New York if I were you. I knew you guys hated each other, but I had no idea you hated each other *that much.*"

I arrived back home on September 3, 2001, and my wife and I watched the video together. I don't know how to describe how I felt watching that show, but it wasn't good. I didn't even know what to say.

"Any thought that this band would ever be able to get back together," I said, "has just been completely destroyed."

Tuesday of the following week was September 11, 2001. And we all know what happened on that day.

The next day, I walked down to the Javits Center to volunteer, and there were thirty thousand people in line. I asked a national guardsman, "Do you think I can help?"

"Are you an ironworker, steelworker, paramedic, lawyer, or doctor?" he asked.

"No."

"Then probably not," he said.

I walked up Eleventh Avenue, frustrated that my city just got attacked and I couldn't do a fucking thing. When I got home, I saw an announcement on MTV for a benefit being put on at Madison Square Garden with the Who and Paul McCartney.

And I thought, *Why not us?* I mean, "We're Not Gonna Take It" is *the* rallying cry. And we were New Yorkers, for crying out loud. I'm from Manhattan, AJ is from Staten Island, Eddie is from the Bronx, and Mark and Dee are originally from Queens.

But organizers had no interest in us or any heavy metal band, because they thought we were "too aggressive."

Eddie Trunk, a popular heavy metal radio broadcaster, would have none of that attitude. He called me and said, "I want to do our own heavy metal benefit, Jay Jay. I mean, I don't think you guys probably want to get together for this. But boy, if you could, we'd sell it out. What do you think?"

I knew he was right, so I called each band member in turn and asked if he would participate in a benefit to raise money for the September 11 first responders and their families. And do you know what? No one even hesitated. It was a resounding *yes* all around. We'd all lost people; everybody knew somebody who'd died. That was just the reality in New York. No one was untouched by the tragedy. Friends, relatives, firemen, cops, teachers—everybody knew or knew of someone who'd perished. My daughter's teacher's husband died. We were all connected through the calamity.

We readily agreed to do the benefit, but that would be it. It would be a onetime thing. We would show up, do the show, support our community, take our gear, and go home.

"I'm not doing any press pushing Twisted Sister or our catalog," I told Eddie. "I'll do press supporting the September 11 benefit, but I will not participate in anything that looks remotely like it's a reunion." He agreed.

As you know from our rough start at the Jason Flom tribute, we really needed to rehearse. But I was nervous that once we all occupied the same room, the acrimony created by the *Behind the Music* documentary would lead us into a brawling fistfight.

The event, NY Steel, took place on November 28, 2001, and raised an estimated $90,000.

So, I hired a crew to film our rehearsals. I told the guys that it was because VH1 wanted footage of the rehearsal for promotional purposes. The truth was, I figured if we had a film crew there, everyone would behave. There'd be no histrionics. It was insurance.

The band rehearsed three times, and we all behaved like perfect gentlemen. We showed up at the benefit and did our show, which, of course, was absolutely stellar. At the end, I took my daughter by the hand, walked out the back door of the Hammerstein Ballroom, caught a cab on Eighth Avenue, and went home. That was it.

The next day, Mendoza called and asked me if I'd heard from the other guys in the band. And I told him I hadn't. He was surprised, but I really didn't think anything of it. We did a good thing for the community, and we were done.

But the Twisted genie had escaped from the bottle, and rumors began to spread through the metal world that we had reunited. I started getting calls from big European music festivals. One big Swedish festival called and asked if we'd headline the following May. Not just be on the bill—headline.

As a musician, I thought this could be great, but as a manager I knew that one gig wasn't going to be worth it. The logistics of putting together a company for a major arena show is huge. In order to justify the cost, you'd need to book a series of shows—not just a one-off date.

Still, I was amazed, because even at the peak of our career, we'd never been headliners in Europe. We typically played the seventh or eighth spot in the lineup. So, this was a really compelling opportunity.

I called Dee and Mark, and they readily signed on. But Eddie declined. He had been playing in a wedding band, and he told me they would have a scheduling conflict with the Swedish festival gig.

"Excuse me?" I said.

"We're playing a wedding on that day. I can't lose my gig," he told me.

I know it sounds absurd, but later I understood what Eddie was saying. I was asking him to trade his ongoing gigs for one show. He was concerned about his income source. So, I get it now. But at the time? Not so much.

I was fucking shocked. I looked at my business partner, Sean Sullivan, and, still nonplussed, I told him that Eddie couldn't do it "because he has a wedding gig."

Then I said this:

"Listen to me carefully, Sean. If I ever mention the words *Twisted Sister reunion* again, your job is to punch me right in the mouth. You just knock me out. You'll never hear those words from me ever again."

In hindsight, Eddie was really right. Putting together a crew and rehearsing properly would cost a lot more money than we'd have made on only one show.

But the following year, we were offered another headlining festival gig.

I told our road manager that if he could find three or four more gigs like that, we'd consider it, because then we could come up with a plan for a whole tour. And that would make good business sense.

Call it Duke Ellington's gimmick of paying people money, if you'd like.

We went to work on implementing that idea. Maybe a reunion was in the cards after all—my recent comment to punch me in the mouth notwithstanding.

It took two years to rev up a crew and the gear necessary to actually pull off something of this magnitude. This reunion tour, in my mind, would last five years, tops. In 2003, we headlined Sweden Rock, the biggest metal festival in Sweden. And that kicked off a fourteen-year career of Twisted Sister as a headliner in festivals around the world.

In 2006 we released a Christmas album called *A Twisted Christmas* with an independent record label called Razor & Tie, owned by a personal friend, Cliff Chenfeld. Because of all the contracts I'd read and the lessons I'd learned, we were able to negotiate a deal where we split the profits with the label, and each of us donated money to an autism foundation. The album sold so well, both in the US and Europe, that we made more money from this deal than we did from the initial multiplatinum sales of *Stay Hungry*. Let it snow, let it snow, let it snow.

The pressure to put on big shows in this kind of environment is huge on so many levels. The credibility of every festival rode on our ability to put on a great show. Add to that the constant jet lag from traveling back and forth to Europe, the earsplitting volume of the concerts, and the knowledge that millions of dollars are at stake in every performance, and you'll get the idea of the kind of toll this takes on you after a while.

As much as I liked performing, each year I was getting more tired. Going onstage at midnight (as the headliners do). Getting up early the next day to catch a plane to another festival. Worrying that the crew had stayed up all night loading in the gear from the night before to get to another festival. Showing up and, as a manager, making sure that interviews or press conferences were happening, and never sounding cynical about this whole process. Wondering when disaster would strike again. Concerned that all this was going to crash and burn, just like the club days when the drinking age went up and the big bars went extinct.

And then on Friday, March 20, 2015, catastrophe did strike when AJ Pero died of a heart attack while on tour with another band. On April 8, 2016, we made the official announcement that 2016 would be the last year that Twisted Sister would perform live concerts.

Most businesses are confronted with *challenges* on a day-to-day basis. The problems are basically manageable. It may take a few minutes to get your ducks in a row. You may need to take a deep breath or have a quick meeting. These are small fires that need to be dealt with as quickly as possible.

Coming up with a solution to a *crisis* may take up to a week. Usually, the key is to gather as much information as possible, then, to anticipate questions and, ultimately, articulate a solution to help you get past it. Yes, these are bigger problems, and if you don't handle a crisis well, it could be disastrous to your company and/or your career. But, if you're a good manager, you should be able to get through it.

Catastrophe is the top level of these kinds of events. There are two kinds of real life-changing catastrophes: the first is *proactive* and the second (and much harder to deal with) is *reactive*.

In *proactive* events, you make the decision that will possibly change your life. You have the luxury of having the time to play out all scenarios in your head, like a chess game. You also prepare yourself mentally for what is about to happen. With a proactive catastrophe, you plan the catastrophe in order to save yourself. I call it the nuclear option. Sometimes you have to batten down the freaking hatches and go, "You know what? In order for me to survive, I'm going to take this whole thing down with me. But because I know I'm doing it, I will make all the preparations."

When my bankruptcy happened in 1988, and my wife and I divorced, and the band broke up, I knew it was coming weeks before, and I basically said to myself, "This is going to be a tough stretch."

In reactive catastrophes, you are handed a situation that you couldn't possibly have prepared yourself for, and you have to do go into survival mode.

A *reactive* catastrophe, for example, is like the week my girl-friend left me, the band broke up, and my mom died. I really didn't see much of it coming and it all happened at the same time, and I was devastated by it.

When AJ died, I created a priority list of immediate, short-term, and long-term problems, and right after the funeral, I started to attack each of them, in the order of importance. I never thought that I would have so many issues confront me so quickly. I had been working nonstop, dealing with problem after problem, in an order of importance that I developed instinctively over the years.

A challenge in business is like light turbulence on an airplane. You have to buckle your seat belt. It's an annoyance, but you get through after a few tense moments.

A crisis in business is more like dropping three thousand feet and having to reach for the oxygen mask. It's very scary but recoverable. Terrifying, for sure, but, statistically, nearly always survivable.

And then there is catastrophe. The impending feeling of doom. On planes, catastrophes are frequently fatal, unless the pilot and crew are highly skilled and practiced at responding properly when disaster strikes. For companies, catastrophes can mean the potential end of your company, usually due to circumstances that seemingly come out of nowhere, expose your company's weaknesses, and could relegate your business to the dustbin of history.

Twisted Sister had a summer tour on the schedule. We'd signed contracts for various projects all over the world. Then AJ died.

The best managers of catastrophes have an ability to calmly process effective responses through the haze of confusion sooner rather than later. But they give themselves some moments of breathing room to collect their thoughts before they act.

The first thing we did was have our agent contact the promoters of the festivals and tell them about AJ's death before it hit social media. The reason for this is to protect the promoters from being blindsided by press and to give them the opportunity to form a response when they were asked whether or how the show will go on.

We also needed to establish how much time we had to decide

what we were going to do. When a member of a world-famous band dies suddenly, there is a grace period that is generally extended out of courtesy so that the band can get its affairs in order. We knew that we needed time to think and regroup, but we had to do it quickly.

Furthermore, we also decided to formally announce that 2016 (the fortieth anniversary of me, Dee, and Eddie as the core members of Twisted sister) would mark the end of touring. Not a small decision but one that ironically had been decided just days before AJ's death. My last conversation with AJ, twelve hours before he died, was partly to inform him of the band's vote to make 2015 the final year.

After AJ's death, the rest of the band agreed to extend our touring so we could go out with a final tour to commemorate forty years of Dee, Eddie, and me playing together.

The worst thing you can do after a catastrophic event is to interpret the event as a sign. Everything happens for a reason—but that reason is not preordained. With a strong enough grasp on reality and an unwavering will to survive, one can take the catastrophe, extract its lessons, and put the resulting coincidences, signs, and omens in their place.

We decided within hours of AJ's death, over a conference call, that we would play all the shows booked that year. The next major challenge was to find AJ's replacement. We received calls almost immediately from some of the greatest rock drummers in the world, many of whom were friends with AJ. Most of them called to express their condolences, and many offered their services.

As it happened, the night after AJ died, the legendary drummer Mike Portnoy and I were both asked to perform a tribute song for AJ at a show at the Starland Ballroom in Sayreville, New Jersey. Coincidentally, AJ had recently replaced Mike in the band Adrenaline Mob.

Mike and I knew each other, but we had never really talked. And now, here we were, together in the dressing room, crying over AJ.

Mike said to me, "Jay Jay, if you decide to continue and you need a drummer, I'm free all summer. If you want me, I can play all the Twisted Sister shows." Once I relayed that news to the rest of the band, we knew that that issue was put to bed.

Keeping a business stable through catastrophe and trauma is the key to success. If you freak out, your entire staff will freak out. Sure, you may *be* freaked out, but don't ever let it show. If you've done everything you can do to keep an atmosphere of stability, and if you employ all your tools and skills with calm and rational thinking, you'll more easily develop a strategy and plan to emerge from the trauma intact.

And when your people feel confident that when all hell breaks loose you're going to have the presence of mind to figure out the solution, you know you've established your credibility and trust.

And when all is said and done, nothing happens without trust.

TRUST

TWISTED

IF YOU'RE A LEADER, YOU HAVE TO TRUST your instincts. Not that they're always right, but in the absence of compelling evidence to the contrary, you have to believe that they are. And oftentimes you have to fight off the naysayers. Entrepreneurs understand how important wisdom-informed instincts are in running their companies. I'm a believer in taking in all the information at your disposal and then moving with your gut.

But trusting yourself is only a small part of the story. You also have to earn and maintain the trust of others; in every deal and decision you make, in every action that you take, you need to demonstrate that you're a person of your word. Without that, your credibility is shot, and without credibility, you have nothing.

In research conducted on every continent on the planet for the last forty years, leadership gurus Jim Kouzes and Barry Posner found that, in their words, "Credibility is the foundation of leadership. If people don't believe in the messenger, they won't believe the message."

They describe a trusted, credible person as one who consistently demonstrates a principle they call "DWYSYWD": Do What You Say You Will Do.

It's so simple, and it's so profoundly important in every aspect of life—especially business.

In the late seventies, when we were working five nights a week trying to become more popular, it soon became clear that our little lighting rig (bar bands carried around their own lights in those days) was really inadequate. We needed to make a statement, and a big, impressive light show was very important. But there was a problem: the lights were very expensive, and we didn't have the money.

As fate would have it (fate was always there when we needed it), a guy named Tony Sklarew came to one of our shows and became friends with our lighting tech. Tony worked for one of the biggest lighting companies in the world: Altman Stage Lighting, based in Yonkers, New York. It made all the really huge spotlights and associated gear for the biggest arenas and shows around the world. Tony loved the band and invited me to meet his boss, Ronnie Altman. I went to the factory, a huge complex on the Hudson River in Yonkers. I had never seen anything like this operation.

Ronnie came over to meet me. He was a short man with a huge, bellowing voice. He was brusque and intense. He wore jeans and a work shirt. I got the feeling that he was a hardworking, blue-collar guy who was all business. I was so right, and then some.

Tony told Ronnie about the band and what we needed. Ronnie said that the cost of the light show that Tony described would be around $10,000. Ronnie looked at me and asked if we could afford it. I said that we couldn't.

He took me aside and said, "Tony tells me your band is really good, and that you are a good guy. I'm going to rent you this light show for twenty-five dollars a week. Can you afford that?"

I was blown away. This was exactly what we needed, and it wasn't costing me anything up front. I also knew that the lighting rig would evolve over time, so I wouldn't be burdened with having to resell it.

I readily agreed.

"Good," he replied. "You can pay me that twenty-five dollars every week, whether in person, by mail, or carrier pigeon. But understand this: the week that you miss the payment, you lose me as a friend. The lighting rig that I'm giving you is something that I won't miss. And the ten grand will not make a difference in my life. You, however, will never do business with me again if you miss the payment."

I had never heard anything like this before. Ronnie was, in effect, daring me to be honest—and giving me my own noose with which to hang myself if I wasn't.

I never missed the payment. And, over time, Ronnie's trust in me grew, and he gave us more and more equipment. Every couple of months we got more items, and the lighting system kept growing at no extra charge. I think that he thought of us as a pet project that he could be a part of and tell his friends about. But he wanted to know that I was true to my word. That I was responsible. That he could trust me. This is really old-school stuff where trust is built on an instinct and a handshake. I have run my business with that same sense of responsibility every day since my first meeting with Ronnie.

Ronnie passed away around 1981, as we were leaving the club scene. We didn't need a light show by that time. But Ronnie's lesson really has nothing to do with a lighting rig, the delivery of an album, or appearing onstage at a contracted time. It's about understanding that your word is worth more than anything in a contract. It's about the credibility that you bring to a situation. The more people can count on your commitment, the more opportunity you will have to show your character, and the more you will learn to expect the same accountability from the people that you do business with.

I recently called Altman Stage Lighting to see if it was still in business and wound up speaking to Ronnie's granddaughter. I told her the lesson that Ronnie taught me. She started to cry and said that was the kind of person he was.

The lesson? Fulfill your obligations. Follow through on your promises and commitments. Your credibility matters. When you earn the reputation that your word is gold, actual gold more easily comes your way.

We had the same challenge with a PA system that we'd had with the lighting: we needed one, but we couldn't afford it. In the very

early days, we went to Muscara Music in New Jersey, and Bill Gep-
pner, who was the salesman there, knew and trusted Michael and Mel.

"What do you guys need?" he asked.

They gave him a laundry list.

"Okay. Pick it up next week," he told us.

"With what money?" I asked.

"You just pay me a rental fee, that's all."

I was stunned. First of all, I come from Manhattan. When you
walked into Forty-Eighth Street music stores, you were treated like
a piece of garbage. We were being treated nicely, which was hard to
believe.

Secondly, he trusted Mel and Michael, and he trusted that we
would be good for the weekly payment. And we were. The deal was
done on a handshake. There was no paperwork.

First the lighting, then the PA system. They were deals based on
trust, pure and simple.

Trust forms the foundation of a successful company, and it's not
just about money. No doubt that money issues will break up companies, but the bond of your word is also the most important element
of a productive, professional relationship.

Even if you're a solo entrepreneur and are totally self-reliant,
you're only as good as people's belief that you'll follow through with
what you say. I learned about this the hard way when band members
would say they'd be at a certain place, at a certain time, to do certain
things, and they weren't there. After a while, it gets tedious when
people break that bond. It has nothing to do with the money issues.

In the early days of the band, when I'd ask Mel questions about
the business, he'd act like I was somehow questioning his honesty.
That's bullshit. No one should be made to feel that way. It shows a
significant, deadly lack of trust.

So, when I took over as manager, I decided to be 100 percent
transparent with everyone in the Twisted enterprise. As I saw it,
people were killing themselves and working their asses off every
day. They should be able to look at the books without feeling like
they're offending anyone. And over the years, the guys in Twisted

have been enormously trusting of me. They don't have to be. They're invited to come to every business meeting I have on behalf of the band, but mostly they don't come, because they trust me to make sure that everything we're owed is accounted for. And it is. I check the accounts daily.

It may sound cynical, but the truth is that people who consistently do what they say they will do are exceedingly rare. It's so aggravating to deal with people in business who say yes but don't do yes. How can you run a business when you can't count on people to deliver on their commitments? Yet it is, unfortunately, commonplace.

It sucks to have to anticipate someone else's bullshit. But with business associates, until they've proven otherwise, you have to assume that they won't deliver. Sad but true.

In my band's dealings, I have a lot of guys who work like this. They're not bad people. Some bite off more than they can chew; others are just afraid to say no. They're not inherently dishonest, but they're still damn frustrating to do business with. I like to think I set the right example in the way I conduct myself. I go out of my way to tell people that if I say that I'm going to do something by a particular day, I will do it. Period. And once they see me deliver as promised, they will trust me forever. Because I've earned it.

In a company, trust is the bedrock. It's about your commitment to a project, to its deadlines, to its outcomes, and to all the people who are relying on you to deliver. How can you run a successful business otherwise?

Trust not only comes from the obvious act of doing what you say you're going to do, it also comes from the way you comport yourself. Do people come to expect that you're a decent human being? Do they smile when you walk in the room? Do they enjoy talking with you? Likability and trust are intimately connected. If people like you, and they like doing business with you (because you do what you say you will do), they will trust you to the point where they'll always give you the benefit of the doubt. They will bend over backward to help you if you're having a rough time, if things aren't going so well. They will have your back, because they know that if the situation were reversed, you'd have theirs. But remember, no matter how much they like you to begin with, the minute you screw the pooch by not following through, or by doing something underhanded, or by flat out lying, well, they won't like you so much anymore, will they?

We hired a drummer once who swore up and down in his interview that he was drug-free and that he didn't drink except for an occasional beer or two. At a gig several months later, his playing was speeding up through every song.

At our first break, I pulled him aside and asked him what was going on.

"Oh, I had to do some speed. I didn't get much sleep last night."

"Is this a constant thing?" I asked, doing my best to extend him a bit of trust.

"No, no, no, no. This is just one time," he said.

"You sure?"

"Yeah, yeah. I promise you it is."

I liked him. He was a nice guy. He kept promising me he was clean, and I wanted to believe him, so I kept him on. Then one night during a really important show, in front of a bunch of record executives and radio station guys, he collapsed and had a seizure. When I investigated, I learned that he had done a San Francisco speedball, which is a mixture of heroin and methadone.

You have to understand, this was during the time we were constantly being rejected by record labels. So, when you had guys from a record label come to your show, and you were trying to impress them, you wanted the night to go well. I trusted the drummer to not be an idiot, and he violated that trust in a really big way. So, we fired him.

And then there was our lighting tech/truck driver. Again, I thought he was a really good guy. One day, my assistant manager started noticing that the driver's gas receipts had consecutive numbers from the same gas station. There's no way this could happen when you're filling up once a week. We found out that he'd taken a receipt book and just started submitting fabricated expenses. I confronted him, he pleaded guilty, and I fired him on the spot. It was the dumbest thing he could have done. I mean, he blew his job with us for, what? A few hundred dollars?

And then there was Bobby the roadie. Or, as he came to be known, Bobby the Fuckhead.

One night, we were in the dressing room getting ready to play our show. We were looking for music to listen to while we were psyching ourselves up. We had a boombox, but we couldn't find any tapes.

We knew that Bobby always carried a satchel of cassette tapes, so someone suggested that we open his box and grab a Judas Priest tape. We put it in, cranked up the volume, and instead of *Hell Bent for Leather*, we heard our own voices, our private conversations, blasting out from the boombox.

He had been recording us to collect dirt to use against the band when it suited him. Can you imagine how we all felt in that moment? There's one word that says it all: betrayal.

As you know, I'm a Manhattan kid. I'd been a street hustler and a drug dealer. I'd traveled the world and seen it all. I always had a funny view of life, and a quick mouth to express that view. I could talk my way in and out of anything. I'd talked my way in and out of two drug busts. I'd talked my way out of getting arrested. And, as a result, I'd developed supernaturally thick skin. But getting hustled and lied to like this? That just blew me away.

So that was the end of Bobby's tenure. Fuckhead.

I know this whole thing about your word being your bond sounds incredibly naive in certain ways, especially in the entertainment business. But at the end of the day, when you have vendors that rely on you—T-shirt companies, truck companies, and lighting companies, for example—you have to make pledges. I had to promise, and I had to deliver. And they had to deliver, too. You have no foundation of business whatsoever if you cannot keep your word.

Woody Allen famously said that 90 percent of success is showing up. I'd say 90 percent of success is doing what you say you're going to do. If people can rely on your word, they pass their experience with you to others. If they can't rely on your word, they pass that on, too. You want to know why somebody won't do business with you? Because someone told them you're an idiot, and you don't do what you say you're going to do. You cannot afford to have your word mean squat. As for the guys who seem to succeed in spite of it, I guarantee you that when they start to fall, their business associates will not only run away from them, they'll cheer and celebrate their demise.

And trust just feels good, too. I like people to feel that they can trust me, and I do whatever I can to earn and maintain that trust.

On the occasions when we had trouble drawing crowds, the club owners always helped me out. Sometimes they even gave me extra money to promote the shows. Why? Because they trusted me and, as a bonus, they liked me. I'm a likable guy, and, to be clear, I like people to like me.

Not just the club owners, but the record companies liked and trusted me as well. Tony O'Brien was the COO of Atlantic Records, and over the years he came to be a personal friend of mine. Years after the band stopped playing, I walked into Tony's office and showed him our royalty statements.

"The band broke up and stopped performing in 1988," I said to Tony. "But I keep getting these royalty statements." I spread them out on his desk.

"It says that we owe the record label $450,000. It's a bullshit number! We don't owe Atlantic a penny. What kind of creative accounting is this?" I left it as a rhetorical question and continued with my lecture.

"This is the reason everybody hates record labels and movie companies. How do I sell twenty million records and owe you 450,000 bucks? You gotta help me with this, Tony."

Tony offered to discuss it with Ahmet Ertegun, the chairman of Atlantic at the time. I knew that Ahmet liked the guys in the band, and he liked me.

"Let me see what I can do," said Tony.

Phil Carson, the guy who signed us to Atlantic, was no longer with the company, but he and Ahmet were still very close. Ahmet,

Phil, Tony, and Jason Flom got together, discussed our situation, and unanimously decided that this $450,000 was bullshit.

Tony called me and said, "We're going to wipe it off your sheet. You don't owe us $450,000 anymore."

I thanked him and said, "Hey, Tony. Since you're not releasing our records anymore, why don't you just give me back our masters?"

Let me explain something about the music industry: labels never relinquish the masters. *Never.* Giving up the record masters means giving up all future interest in and ownership of the music. My asking for them was nothing short of ridiculous. It was ballsy for me to even say the words out loud. But since Tony and I were good enough friends, I figured that he wasn't going to throw me out of the office for asking. He wasn't going to accuse me of being a fucking idiot.

"I can't give them back to you," he told me.

No surprise in that answer. But then he offered something almost equally unprecedented, something I never expected.

"But I will license them to you, John. That way you can make deals with other labels and have the control you need to keep making your money, and we'll make a little on the licensing fee. I'll give you a five-year term, and we'll reassess at the end of that period."

He licensed us the masters for our albums. I went off and did deals, and we made a lot of money. After five years, the deal ran out, and Atlantic extended it another five years. Five years later, that deal ran out, and they extended again. This went on for twenty years. For twenty years, I had unfettered access to our masters from Atlantic. I made deals, kept the money, and paid them a small override.

I believe that Twisted Sister may be the only band in the history of Atlantic Records to be offered this kind of a deal, where we—for all intents and purposes—got our masters back. Many times over the years, I've asked other managers, musicians, and various industry types if they've ever gotten their masters back from their label. And, every time, I've gotten the same answer:

"You're kidding, right?"

Then why for me? Simple: because Tony liked doing business with me. He understood the economics of a band's business, so he

Me, Dee, and Eddie. Twisted Sister at its core.

knew how important it was for me to have control of our music. And because he liked me, he wanted me to succeed.

Sometimes like and trust run at odds with each other—and in that case, trust always takes precedence. As you know, we've had long stretches in our band's history when we weren't particularly fond of each other. But on a deeper level, the trust has stayed intact to this day.

Remember, I owned the Twisted Sister brand. *I* did. Not the guys in the band. Now this might sound counterintuitive to some, but because I owned the brand, I felt good about splitting all our revenues evenly among all the guys. And that's what I've always done.

To this day, AJ Pero's estate gets his 20 percent of our money. He was never on the contract, but that was our deal. I promised his kids, and I'd given my word to him, and that was that.

Your partners and your clients have to trust you. They have to trust your vision, and they have to trust you financially, even if they're not liking you so much at the moment. Otherwise, it creates devastating fault lines. Even through all our shit, our band members never stopped trusting me to make the best deals and disburse the resulting money evenly. And from the other side of that coin, I could always trust Dee.

If he said he was going to be ready at a certain time, he'd be ready. And that was true for all the guys. If the band was contracted to be onstage at a certain time, we'd be onstage, as promised.

Trust is about honoring your commitments 100 percent of the time with everyone involved in your enterprise. It's not about perfection; everyone screws up from time to time, and sometimes outside, unexpected circumstances can conspire against your living up to your word. But those situations need to be the rare exceptions to the rule. We experienced that mutual trust every day of our performing career.

Think about it: when you're playing on a one-hundred-foot stage to an audience of a hundred thousand people, you're relying on everyone in your crew—from roadies to sound engineers to lighting techs to bandmates—to do the job they're supposed to be doing that day. The minute you step onstage, you have to have an incredible amount of faith that everyone will do what they have to do.

To put it simply, trust is not a quaint, naive, or old-fashioned idea. It is essential, no matter what business you're in.

And when the trust among your people is deep, your opportunity to achieve excellence is spectacular.

EXCELLENCE

THE DEFINITION OF INSANITY, ACCORD-
ing to Albert Einstein, is doing something over and over again and expecting a different result. This does not sound like insanity to me. In fact, it sounds like my band's business plan. Actually, it sounds like the plan of most successful artists and athletes. It's also the unofficial or unspoken mantra of many successful people. It perfectly melds with Malcolm Gladwell's ten-thousand-hour rule, which is based on a study by Anders Ericsson, a Swedish psychologist, scholar, and professor. In his book *Outliers*, Gladwell says that it takes roughly ten thousand hours of "deliberate practice" to achieve mastery in any field.

I added up all the hours we spent playing in the bars during the first ten years of our history and found that just in playing time and rehearsing alone, we spent about ninety-six hundred hours from 1973 to 1982. Once all the travel and performance prep time was added up, I was amazed to discover that we actually spent 50 percent of our waking hours of every day working toward our goal of a record deal.

I thought about that for a moment and what it really means. Talk about endless repetition becoming a habit. I thought about the ability we all have to actually rewire our brain's synapses, so the real results of repetition become an automatic and almost perfect replication of a defined goal. It's the ability to call up the delivery of that habit, like having it on demand, whether it's performing a piano solo or gymnastic exercise.

Twisted Sister was one of the greatest live bands on the planet. And we played mostly the same songs every night. The same songs. Over and over and over again. We were like the heavy metal version of *Cats*. Except a few of us were Jewish, so it'd be spelled Katz.

Many people balk at the idea of repetition because they associate it with punishment—like that time your teacher made you write "I will not chew gum in class" a hundred times. But in this context, repetition is not punitive; it leads to excellence.

At this point in my life, I have played more shows than the Grateful Dead. More than Springsteen. More than any other rocker, living or dead. And I have the evidence to prove it. (See our list of concert dates in the back of this book.)

In the bar days, we'd play our set and then debrief it afterward. If there'd been a problem that night, if we hadn't nailed the transitions between songs or if we'd missed the lighting cues, we would correct it and ensure that we didn't repeat the same mistakes at the next show. We continued to make mistakes, but not the same ones over and over. That would be the wrong kind of repetition.

Over time, each repetition you do may expose just a sliver of imperfection. And you learn from those slivers. Ask any musician and they'll tell you they play the same chords and scales, over and over and over again, for hours and hours, because the synapses in your brain have to connect to your fingers. And those fingers then eventually react to the synapses of your brain. The same thing happens with any habit. Excellence is achieved through methodical boredom. And it can be a lonely process, too.

Just ask the ice skater who gets up at five in the morning to spend hours and hours alone on the ice; ask the skier who is on the slopes when everyone else is still tucked in their warm beds; ask the artist who paints in the studio late into the night after everyone in their family has gone to sleep. And what are they all doing? Honing their routine, practicing their skills, perfecting their craft, over and over and over again. Because that's what you do if you want to be great. If you want to reach for the stars, then you'd better be prepared to practice your stretching.

Over and over and over again.

We played about seven thousand performances before we got signed. The repetition of playing five or six nights a week, four or five shows per night—day after day, week after week, year after year—was very boring at times. But that's what it took back then, and that's what it takes today. Monotony is the downside to becoming excellent at anything. The problem is that it can feel like a waste of time; however, if it's to achieve your goals, what seems like mindless, endless repetition, is, in fact, time well spent.

From the earliest days of the band, we were prepared for the monotony of excellence.

Back in our club days, most of the summer bars in the Hamptons already had a house band. That was always a very coveted position because it was a steady gig and it gave a band an opportunity to build a strong and loyal fan base. We auditioned and beat out several other bands for the privilege to play Mad Hatter in the Hamptons on Long Island in the summer of 1973.

There we were, a bunch of twenty-year-old kids, dressed in drag, playing rock 'n' roll for fifteen weeks in a row (Memorial Day to Labor Day), four fifty-minute shows, five nights a week.

That's why whenever any current twenty-year-old musician asks me for advice (which happens a lot), the conversation goes something like this:

MUSICIAN: Hey, Jay Jay, you gotta come and see my band.

ME: How long have you been together?

MUSICIAN: About two years.

ME: How many shows have you played over that two-year period?

MUSICIAN: A lot! About fifty shows!

ME: How long are your performances?

MUSICIAN: Twenty to forty-five minutes, depending on our time slot.

ME: Tell me when you get to five hundred shows, then I'll come down and see your band.

MUSICIAN: Five hundred shows? That will take years!

ME: Well, then, I probably won't be seeing your band.

I'm not trying to be an ass; I'm telling it like it is. Or like it needs to be. Twisted Sister didn't achieve excellence in our art because we played a few shows—we achieved it because we played a shit ton.

To be specific, this is what 1973 and 1974 (our first two years) looked like for us:

TOTAL NIGHTS PERFORMING AT A CLUB: 396

TOTAL PERFORMANCES: 1,972 (mostly five forty-minute shows each night, with only a couple of single one-hour performances)

TOTAL PERFORMANCE HOURS: 5,916, with an average of three hours of actual performances each night.

REHEARSAL DAYS: Approximately 150

REHEARSAL HOURS: Approximately 750

TOTAL HOURS PERFORMING AND REHEARSING: Approximately 6,600

Many people think that a band makes it because of having some kind of fairy dust sprinkled upon the tops of their heads. The real truth of it is that in the first two years, with so much daily interaction among the band members, I learned everything I needed to know to build the very (solid) foundation of what it takes to really succeed in business.

We worked hard every hour of every day in an unrelenting quest to be the best. Under all the pressure, none of the guys in the first iteration of Twisted Sister could ultimately stand it except for me. But I was relentless, and I kept pushing. I eventually found the right

Early days on the bar scene.

guys who could handle it as well—Dee, Eddie, Mark, and then finally AJ, who joined us just before the record deal in 1982.

Live shows have always been our bread and butter, the core product of our business. We have had to perform many times in the face of really depressing business news, but we have learned to shrug it off, put on the game face, get into a zone—a zone created by all that practice and performance time—and carry the fuck on.

That practice, and the performance muscle memory it created, was never more evident than in the months after AJ died.

We played our first show with a new drummer, Mike Portnoy (a legend, and we couldn't have asked for a better replacement), at the Joint in the Hard Rock Hotel and Casino in Las Vegas, in June. It was, of course, a bittersweet experience and very emotional for everyone. But our longtime fans told us we played with more passion than they had ever seen. Like we were totally in control.

Twisted Sister with new drummer, Mike Portnoy (right).

That's not how I felt. Not at all.

The truth is, in those final days of the band, we only played about a dozen shows a year, almost always between May and August. We were off doing other things the other nine months of the year.

We'd usually only run over the songs once at a rehearsal. I was always feeling just a little queasy and unsure. That's why, before we'd go into our first rehearsals, sometime in April, I'd be gripped with anxiety. But this time, going on without AJ, I was also anxious about a new drummer who had only three rehearsals to learn not just the music but also the pacing of the show; the fact that we were doing a live recording for DVD; multiple bands being on the same bill with us (their equipment changes can always cause problems); and special effects, flames, sparklers, and explosions that could light you on fire if you stood in the wrong place. Plus, because I was the manager and not just a guitar player, I had a long mental checklist. More important, I was really sad that AJ wasn't up there with us.

Here is my confession: there were just too many unknowns this time. Too many potential areas of disruption. Too much emotion. Because it was the first show of the year, I just couldn't get lost in the performance. My mind was overwhelmed by the confluence of information. And I was still dealing with my own emotions about this first show without AJ.

So what did I do? I consciously let go. I set my brain on autopilot and let the songs flow out. I kept in the back of my mind an idea of what I would need to do if something really went out of control. But I tried not to think about it, and instead, I relied on my ability to do something I'd done for more than ten thousand hours.

And . . . nothing bad happened. The show went on about as smoothly as I could have hoped.

This is what separates the big boys from the also-rans. The confidence—in our case, forged in the fires of the live club circuit—that we could always deliver, no matter what was thrown at us, is burned into our DNA. As long as we want to do it, it will be done at the highest levels.

Because we've done it over and over and over again.

The same is true for companies and entrepreneurs. For you or your company to be great, nothing can ever present an obstacle to excellence. You need to practice until you've got muscle memory. You can't stop Twisted Sister. And you can't stop a great company when you have a great foundation.

There's another aspect to excellence that, I believe, is a wonderful opportunity given to those who have achieved it for themselves. I call it "elevation"—the act of creating excellence in others, of making other people greater than yourself.

I always help and advise people in their business pursuits—especially in the music industry. And I do that for one simple reason: I want to help them succeed in their careers by coaching them to achieve higher levels of excellence. Whether I'm managing a band or an artist or simply giving informal counsel to someone, I strive to educate them, teach them about the business, and help them get a vision of what they have to look forward to. Those things will look different for each person and situation, but my goal is always the same: I want them to be stellar at what they do.

Why? Simply because it feels right. I get great satisfaction from it. I love the fact that I'm excellent at helping to make others excellent. And, besides, I've always appreciated when others have done that for me.

When Steve Farber first encouraged me to be a speaker, I felt that I could do it, but I had my doubts. How would I structure it? Should I have a theme or just tell a bunch of stories? And how would I even get on a stage to try it? I had no idea where to begin.

Farber told me that he would give me my debut speaking opportunity at his upcoming Extreme Leadership event in San Diego.

"As for the structure," he said, "don't worry about it. I'll sit on the side of the stage and shoot questions to you, interview style. You answer with your amazing stories and insights—do what you do naturally—and I'll guide the flow through my questions. You'll be the only one on camera, so you'll have great video clips to use in marketing your speaking services."

When Twisted Sister is onstage, I'm the banter guy. I'm the one who talks to the audience between songs. Which means I've spent a lot of years speaking to audiences of up to a hundred thousand people. But speaking to Farber's audience of 120 business leaders on that day in 2012? That scared the living shit out of me. I was in new territory.

But as soon as I stepped up on that stage, I felt right at home. The presentation was a phenomenal success. And I was hooked.

And why did Farber create that elevation for me? For the same reason I do it for others:

Because.

As time went on, the more I committed myself to keynoting, the more I watched other speakers. I would play their videos, observe what they were doing and set the intention of being the best speaker on the circuit. And then it was back to . . . you guessed it . . . practice, practice, repetition, repetition—over and over and over again.

The more I did it, the more I worked to make my stories interesting and sexy and funny. Now I'm told that I'm as effective and entertaining as the best speakers out there. And ask Farber how he feels about that. (I'll give you a hint: this book.)

My advice to you is this: strive for excellence in yourself and others. Share what you know freely, because by helping others to be better at what they do, you will rise up as well. Coach and advise the people you love just because you want to help them. If you take money out of the equation, it frees you up to be a true mentor. When I tell people I believe in, "Don't doubt for a minute how good you are," it makes me really happy to see them light up and rise to the occasion.

Ask yourself if there's a part of you that would benefit from giving your time and wisdom, just because. I suspect that you'll enjoy sharing what you've learned with others.

Along the way, learn everything you can about your craft. Study the greats in your art, field, or industry. Know what's going on in the world. Read novels and biographies. Watch documentaries. Be a student of human nature.

I hated school and didn't go to college, but, starting when I was ten, my parents encouraged me to read the *New York Times* from cover to cover every day. As a result, I could talk to anyone about anything. I had a greater capability to dream and plan how I'd achieve that dream. Which led to my ability to visualize excellence and figure out exactly what I needed to do . . .

Over and over and over again.

DISCIPLINE

EXCELLENCE IS ACHIEVED THROUGH repetition, but it takes discipline to keep you coming back. Discipline is about getting clear on your priorities, defining your own rules about how you're going to achieve your goals, and then sticking to those rules no matter what. Throughout the years, I wrote my own rules, and then I stuck to them. Especially when chaos rained down on me. It's easy to follow your rules and do the work when everything is rosy, but can you remain disciplined when all hell is breaking loose? That's the true test of your discipline level. Do you give up when your practice becomes challenging or inconvenient, or do you redouble your resolve to do what's necessary even when—especially when—the world is crashing down around you?

I know that "discipline" and "heavy metal band" may not seem to go hand in hand, but by now you understand that I don't give a fuck about how other bands do things.

I have a rule: no drugs. So, I hired Dee Snider because he hated drugs and he hated alcohol, and he was just ferocious in wanting to be successful. One by one, we fired every damn guy in the band who drank and did drugs—no matter how talented they were—until we had a clean band.

Mark Mendoza also shared that passion and disdain for drugs and alcohol. Eddie and I picked Mark and Dee not only because of their disdain for drugs but also because they both showed us how badly they wanted to succeed. That's our winning combination.

Of course the irony is, I'm in the only business where being clean is actually the worst thing that could possibly happen to your reputation and career. Think about it. A politician gets caught with a young girl and cocaine, and he's done. An athlete gets caught with a young girl and cocaine, and he's done. What happens when a musician gets caught with a young girl and cocaine? "Hey, good for you, man." You write a song about it.

As rock stars, we're essentially given a license to do bad things. To remain kids. We have carte blanche to be crazy and to wing it with a "who gives a fuck" attitude. But that doesn't work if you want to be successful in the business of rock and roll.

So, we had a rule: be responsible adults in our finances and in our dealings with others. But that was our internal rule; it was not our brand image.

Because Twisted Sister was so clean, we had to seem crazier than we were. We called ourselves Twisted Fucking Sister, and our motto was, "Look like women, talk like men, play like motherfuckers." Our fan club became the Sick Motherfucking Friends of Twisted Sister. Why? Because we had to appear like we were out of our minds.

But we were not.

While we were acting crazy onstage, I was looking out to the screaming crowd of fans and thinking, *Let's see, what do we have? Like 1,350 people in here tonight, times $7.85?* I stuck to my responsible-finance rule, even in the context of pretending to do otherwise, even with every temptation to be as wacko and irresponsible as we appeared. Discipline.

Early in our bar phase, our pay was determined by how many people came to our shows, and I wasn't getting straight answers from the owners about audience numbers. I realized if I knew what the drink averages were, I could figure out how many people were there.

I hired a guy who hid in the corner with a clicker and counted the number of people entering the club. Then I pretended to drink with the bartenders. I've had five beers in my life. I really hate the taste of beer. But I would pretend to drink with them, and over time, the bartender would tell me what his sales averages were. When I started to know the bar averages, I started to understand how many people were really coming. I knew that the club owners were lying to the agents to keep our money down. So, I told our agent, "I know how many people are coming. If the guy's not giving me a raise, tell him, 'Fine, guess what? We're going to leave.'" Knowledge is power, and that's how we operated our business.

I don't mean to be cynical or make you think that I believe all musicians are dummies, or that other heavy metal bands have no discipline. Obviously, they do. Iron Maiden, Metallica, and KISS are extremely successful. These bands aren't stupid; they didn't get there by accident. But I can tell you that Twisted Sister ran our band like a business from day one, because we knew our rules and practices, and we stuck to them. And that's really the key to all of it.

Tenacity and discipline have similar qualities, but there are things that set them apart. Tenacity may be the never-ending desire to want something and to keep going after it, to keep attacking the hill through all the flak and bullets. You know you want it; you really gotta have it; you're gonna keep pushing.

But discipline's a rules-based system—something I've been living by for as long as I can remember. I didn't even understand it until I looked back at my life and consciously realized that I had been instinctually holding myself accountable to rules that I'd created for myself.

Tenacity is wonderful from an energy perspective, but discipline is where the rubber meets the road. When the shit hits the fan and people are freaking out and running around like chickens with their heads cut off, you need to be able to stand in the middle of the tsunami and declare, "We can survive, but we've gotta do it like this." And, therefore, you need to be clear about and committed to your rules and practices.

Pilots follow a set of rules for dealing with turbulence. While terrified passengers are screaming, "Oh my God! We're gonna die, we're gonna die!" a seasoned pilot will calmly sit and chant, "Check one, check two, check three." The pilot knows that if she does things in the order she's been taught, there's a 99 percent chance she'll get everyone out of this disaster. But if you're the pilot and you just start flailing and hitting every switch in the cockpit, you can kiss your ass goodbye.

Since my days as a drug-dealing teenager, I've instinctively had the discipline and presence of mind to stay focused in the midst of chaos. The purpose of my drug deals was to get enough money to pursue music. My rule was to invest half of my earnings in the tools of the rock trade: if I got to $2,000, I'd spend $1,000 to buy some gear or go to a concert. Even back then, I had a strong sense of discipline.

After I had that particularly nuts LSD trip that turned my parents into hogs, I decided that either I had to stop dealing acid, or I had to learn how to take it effectively. And I committed myself to that endeavor. I know it sounds nuts, but that commitment represents the very discipline I would eventually practice in my career.

Here's what it looked like back then:

About a week after the aforementioned acid trip, I took just a quarter of a tab and had a couple little hallucinations. I did that for about a week straight. Then, methodically working my way up, I took half a tab. Then I worked my way up to an advanced maneuver.

I started to take walks in the park. I'd sit on a rock and look at the horizon of the East Side. I learned to make the buildings do things. I could make gargoyles get up and move. I could make animals appear out of rooftops. I was totally in control of my own mind-bending experience.

I worked myself up to one or two tabs, and soon I could function perfectly well on acid, so I took it all the time. I was a high-functioning acid head. I was able to go to Grateful Dead concerts and make everything melt, then I'd turn around and do a drug deal. I was multitasking while on acid.

But it wasn't normal. And it was dangerous and destructive, so I stopped all that shit. But it did reveal something significant and essential that would later serve me in running our business: I had the ability to stay focused, even while the world was literally melting around me.

Throughout my life, I was always able to stay focused and stay out of trouble, even when I was surrounded by it.

Let me give you an example of how I stayed focused and disciplined even in the face of one of the most surreal events of my younger life.

In the Upper West Side building where I grew up, the same apartment building I live in today, there were several interesting characters. Especially my friend John Belleau.

John's mother, unlike every political lefty in the building, was a right-wing Republican Nixon supporter. John wasn't the most political guy, but if you pushed him, he'd lean more toward his mother's views and say he was more of a Republican than a Democrat.

Now, I don't know what it is about New York City, but unlike Texas or Oklahoma, where lots of young men were getting drafted to fight in the Vietnam War, no New Yorkers seemed to be going over there. We didn't get drafted; we got deferments. I didn't know anyone who had enlisted or was forced to soldier up. But John Belleau volunteered. Right smack in the middle of 1968 New York City hippiedom, John up and joined the army.

One year later, in the spring of '69, I heard from John's mom that he was busted for having a tenth of a gram of marijuana and two melted dexamyls, which are prescription uppers. It was nothing, really. But not as far as the army was concerned. He was court martialed and given a sentence of eight years of hard labor in Leavenworth penitentiary, which his counsel bargained down to a year.

One afternoon, I walked out of George Washington High School on to 191st Street and there, standing right in front of me, was John Belleau in the flesh. "John!" I said. "What happened, man? Did you cut a deal?"

"No," he said. "I escaped from prison in Fort Riley, Kansas, yesterday."

"What?"

"I escaped, man."

Now, remember, at this point in my career, I'm not a professional guitar player; I'm a drug dealer. This guy had just escaped from Fort Riley. Every MP on the planet was probably searching for him. As much as he was my friend, John Belleau and I didn't need to be seen together right then.

"You've got to help me, man," he said. "Your mother has to know people in Canada, right? She has to get me out of here."

This right-leaning guy wanted to use my mother's left-leaning connections to do what the draft dodgers did: flee to Canada. Which is more than a little ironic. But my mother was a principled lefty, and she always liked John. She saw him as a harmless, sad-sack kind of guy. So, I brought John home and told Mom the story.

She didn't judge him. She didn't ask any details about how he escaped from Fort Riley. But she fully understood.

"I will get you to Canada," she said.

Moving quickly, my mother hit the phones and made arrangements for our fugitive. Then he disappeared. We didn't know what happened. He could have made it across the border, or he could have been nabbed by the police. Either way, as quickly as he'd appeared in front of George Washington High School, he was gone. And that was the end of that.

Or so I thought.

Several months later, during the summer of 1969, I was dealing drugs like a motherfucker. I was selling, getting wasted, dropping acid, and jamming with bands during the day and going to rock concerts every night. Day in, day out. Full-on, überhippie drug mode.

One afternoon, I was, as per usual, doing a drug deal in my bedroom. These customers, however, were not my typical clientele. They were all in their early twenties, but they looked pretty hard. It was a mixed group of black and white, men and women. They looked like a movie set version of a radical revolutionary group, but they were buying dope from me, and that was all that really mattered.

The guy who brought them to me said, "By the way, these are serious revolutionaries."

To this day, I still don't know if that was true, but this was the scene at the time: I'm in my apartment doing a drug deal with the people who may have blown up a bank. And we're smoking so much dope that my room looks like Chernobyl. Sitting there, I was thinking, *Wow, man. These guys are hard-core criminals.* But I didn't really give a fuck. I was just trying to make a sale.

My mother came in (yeah, she was more or less used to this kind of scene by then) and told me I had a phone call from Betty Belleau, John's mother. I rarely, if ever, spoke with Betty, so I had no idea why she'd be calling me, but I took the call.

"Listen," said Betty. "I'm not home. I'm at our house on the Jersey Shore. I just got a call from John. He's in our apartment."

I said, "What do you mean? He's here? In the building?"

"Yes," she said. "He wasn't feeling well, so he's been staying in the apartment for a few days."

"I haven't seen him in months and now he's been here in the building for the last couple of days and he didn't tell me?"

"Yeah," she said. "Anyway, he says that someone's knocking at the front door, and he thinks it's the dry cleaner. He doesn't want to answer it, for obvious reasons. You think you can go over and see what's up?"

So, I left my room, which, you will remember, was full of revolutionary, criminal, drug-dealing weirdos, and I was wasted.

I headed downstairs and crossed the lobby to the other tower, then took the elevator up to the eighth floor, where the Belleaus lived. The door opened, and I saw three MPs with rifles standing there at John's door. They saw me and shouted, "That's him!"

I shouted, "Oh shit!" and slammed frantically on the "door close" button until the elevator door shut. I descended to the lobby, but these guys ran down the stairs and got there first. They pulled me out of the elevator, threw me up against the wall, and forced my arms up like you've seen in every Hollywood cop show.

While they were frisking me, my mother, coincidentally, had come down to get the mail. She walked into the lobby, saw these cops, who had her son flayed out all akimbo, and, having no idea about the current John Belleau situation, thought I was finally, after all this time dealing dope in my bedroom, getting my ass busted.

My dear sweet mom sprinted across the lobby, flew through the air, landed on the back of the cop who was on top of me, and screamed, "You fucking pig, get off my son!"

She pounded her fists on the guy's back, and then the building superintendent walked out. "What's going on here?" he shouted.

"We're arresting John Belleau," said one of the MPs.

"That's not John Belleau," the super said. "That's John Segall."

"Oh, wrong guy," said one of the cops, and they left me—just like that—and raced back up to find Belleau.

Meanwhile, the building was crawling with federal agents, alarms were blaring, police were running down the street to our building, and I had got a gang of Weathermen wannabes sitting in a reefer haze upstairs in my bedroom.

I had to keep my head on straight.

I got back to the apartment and walked into my room, where everyone was, understandably, freaked out. They thought the man was coming for them. My mom thought the cops were coming for me. And I thought that all this had to end in my getting busted for some fucking thing.

I took a breath. I needed the discipline to stay focused and figure a way out of this mess. I looked around the room and came up with a very simple plan.

"Listen people," I said, and explained what was going on. "Let's just calm down, sit tight, and this should all blow over."

Everyone agreed and settled down a little. I then walked down the hall to call John on the phone. "Dude," I said. "That's not the dry cleaner out there. There are three guys with M16s aimed at your door. You have to give up."

I headed back down to the lobby just in time to see John in handcuffs being walked out of the building and into a paddy wagon.

The sirens stopped. All the police left. Things quickly returned to normal, and, with a sigh, I realized I'd probably never see John Belleau again.

But what a day, man. Calmer heads prevailed, and everybody (except John) got what they came for that day.

The next September, I was back at George Washington High. One afternoon I walked out onto 191st Street and there, standing right in front of me, was John Belleau in the flesh. Déjà vu.

"Oh no!" I started to say. "Don't tell me . . . "

"Wait," he said. "It's all cool. I'm out of the army. Everything is fine."

They arrested John in New York and brought him back to Fort Riley; meanwhile, a local congressman was reviewing drug sentences for army guys and looked at John's case. He felt that John's sentence was more than a little harsh, and the congressman successfully made his case to the powers that be in Washington.

The army gave John three choices: he could stay in the local jail and get out in one year with an honorable discharge; he could stay in jail for six months and get out with a general discharge; or he could get out immediately with a dishonorable discharge.

"Give me a pen," John had said.

Here's another of my rules: learn from setbacks and mistakes. It's a challenging one. When you're lying flat on your back, the last thing you're likely to say to yourself is "What did I learn from that punch?"

Yet that's exactly what you need to do. And that takes discipline.

Legendary boxer Joe Louis purportedly once said, "Sometimes you have to take the ten count."

When you have a setback in business—when you've been knocked down—instead of trying to jump right back up on your feet, take the ten count. It gives you a little breathing room and allows you to shake the cobwebs out of your head. That ten count gives you the focus you need to keep going.

And while you're still lying there in a pool of your own blood and sweat, reflect on what happened. The reflection is the most brutal aspect of all this, because you have to really, seriously take a look at why something didn't work. And you may not be happy. It may have happened because of a bad idea that you had enthusiastically acted upon, and your ego doesn't want to admit that a genius like you could ever have made such a boneheaded move. Many entrepreneurs are overly self-confident by nature, and they believe that the world revolves around them. That's not necessarily a bad thing, unless that attitude causes them to overlook their own mistakes.

The biggest mistake Twisted Sister made, and the one that led to the eventual demise of the band and my subsequent bankruptcy in 1988, was the release of the song "Leader of the Pack" as the first single from our album *Come Out and Play*. There were plenty of other good songs on that album that would have reinforced the heavy metal image of the band, but "Leader of the Pack" was a terrible choice because it conveyed the wrong idea about who we were. It lumped us squarely in the buffoon rock world. And it absolutely crushed us.

We were in the goofball era of MTV. "Walk Like an Egyptian," Devo, the B52's, and other shit like that was plastered all over the station's programming. If you look for the "Leader of the Pack" video on YouTube now, you'll see that it has nearly three million views. So . . . was "Leader of the Pack" really all that bad? Yes, it was. We abruptly followed that up by sinking all that was left of our credibility into the video for "Be Chrool to Your Scuel," in which Alice Cooper, Lainie Kazan, and Bobcat Goldthwait made cameo appearances. And that sealed it.

We went from this really heavy grit rock band to being interpreted as a goofball band. If we had used our previous album, *Stay Hungry*, which had gone triple platinum in the US and quintuple platinum in Canada, as a launching point to the next level of our career, we would not have crashed and burned. But crash and burn we did, and we never recovered. We didn't have a plan to come out of a knockout like that.

There was no plan from me because I had checked out emotionally at that point. I've had a lot of years to reflect and ruminate on this, and I've looked at it from so many perspectives. It's been a very long, slow ten count.

Sometimes super successful bands (and businesses) focus so much of their energy to prove to the world that they can create a better mousetrap, they end up turning on themselves. There is a very fine line between reinvention and annihilation. Reinvention is always important, but you also need to hold on to the essence of what makes you great. Once you compromise that core, the end is near.

A few talented artists have overcome the "overnight sensation" label and gone on to deliver a consistently good product and remain viable for years—even decades. It is true, however, that as hard as it is to make it the first time, it is even harder to continually replicate that success. This fear of failure was deeply ingrained in our psyche, yet we didn't see the danger markers approaching. I dismissed the warning signs, I think, because I was just feeling jealous of all the media attention Dee was getting. But that wasn't the problem.

The cracks in the band's enormous success started to show in ways that were completely unexpected. And it started with our fans.

The first time I was aware that a fan backlash was coming was when I went to a Mets-Phillies game in Philadelphia in the summer of 1984, just months into our MTV explosion, and while our two videos, "We're Not Gonna Take It" and "I Wanna Rock," seemed to be playing every ten minutes. As I sat in the stands, incognito under sunglasses and a hat, two kids, an eighteen-year-old and an eight-year-old, were walking up the stairs to their seats carrying hot dogs. The younger one was singing "We're Not Gonna Take It," and the older one responded with these fateful, ominous words:

"Shut up. I hate that song."

I was horrified. An eighteen-year-old, our *core* fan base, was sick of our song because his little brother was singing it. In my mind, we went from hip to over in a nanosecond. Little kids were singing our song. I'm sure they weren't singing songs by Motörhead or Iron Maiden or Mötley Crüe. Those bands still had badass reputations.

We became, it seemed, a cartoon. An over-the-top corporate representation of a "hair band" that was soon to become a punch line.

That was the problem. In reality, Twisted Sister was a tough-ass bar band. We made it by looking almost like a cartoon, and then instead of being able to move away from the cartoon, and looking like a tougher band, we just looked dumber. In pursuit of a higher level of accomplishment, we'd lost the discipline of holding on to our bar-forged, heavy metal soul.

The Beatles were one of the most disciplined bands of all time, and because of that, they built a strong fan base. From 1964 to 1969, they delivered nine studio albums, three soundtracks, and twenty-four singles. In McCartney's interviews, he's very matter-of-fact about their approach: "We just wrote for business, like we know how to do it."

When I visited the Beatles Museum in Liverpool, I understood why Brian Epstein was such a damn good manager. Before the world knew who the Beatles were, Epstein spent three years laying the groundwork in England. I don't believe any band ever did that before. They played consistently. They played on Sundays on the BBC. When they heard that fans couldn't make it to a show, they'd write those fans a letter. This incredible connection with their fan base sustained them. When things took off, they already had the foundation.

But here's the thing: years later, if the Beatles hadn't released the White Album and *Abbey Road*, they might have forever been remembered in their cartoonish Sergeant Pepper's suits. The Beatles could have looked like a joke had they stayed psychedelic, but they didn't. They walked away from it. They were disciplined enough to know that to stay true to their Beatles-ness, they had to get away from the psychedelic thing. The White Album legitimized them as a rock band again. And then, of course, *Abbey Road* was one of the greatest albums ever made.

We did not have that same discipline, and as a result, we weren't able to escape the buffoon era.

Before our demise, we had developed the same type of loyal following from our fans as the Beatles had from theirs. Don't get me wrong. I don't equate us to the Beatles. That's not what I'm saying. They learned by playing in the bars; we developed our sense of discipline in the same way. That's where we became ultra-professional.

But if we had remained truly disciplined, we would not have released the single that destroyed our career.

We lost the vision. We lost our discipline, and we learned a tough lesson from that. We tried to retool and reapply, but I had no control at that point. I had lost it all, so I went with the nuclear option and blew up the whole fucking enterprise.

But today, after our resurrection and all the lessons we've learned, I keep control of the business, and I make damn sure we ain't a goofball band anymore. And our fans love us more than ever. And maybe that's the greatest lesson of all.

Every successful business has to have a loyal base to get you through the tough times. If you lose the faith that your loyal base has with your brand, you'll lose it all. A successful business runs on consistency. No matter what business you're in, you have to be consistent. You have to be consistent in how the public perceives the product you're delivering. Be true to who you are. Be true to your message. Be true to your clients and customers—and stay disciplined to always strive to maintain that connection.

Thankfully, Twisted Sister returned, and we were given one more shot to get it right.

Through the process of reinvention, I've developed the insight to understand and appreciate all the hard work, pain, and joy of being in a world-class band.

I am grateful to all our fans around the world. And I'm grateful to Dee, Eddie, Mark, AJ, and Mike for the last fourteen-year run. And I'm forever thankful to our crew, Danny, Duane, George, Matt, Mehtis, Keith, Russel, Peter, and Rick. They always delivered by getting to the shows and turning around stages in forty-five minutes. They made us look good . . . every time.

Having said all that, here's my advice to you:

Stay true to your core. Be consistent. Write your own rules and develop the discipline to stick to them, come what may. When you get clocked (which you will), stay down and take the ten count. Learn your lessons, and then, with tenacity, wisdom, inspiration, stability, trust, excellence, and discipline, leap back on your feet and reclaim what is yours for the taking.

EPILOGUE

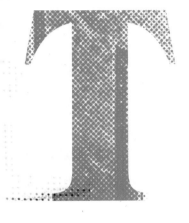

HE VERY LAST SHOW TWISTED SISTER played was on November 16, 2016, in Monterrey, Mexico, with KISS closing the show. Before the show I called a meeting of the band and crew in our dressing room. I got pretty emotional. Not because we wouldn't play again, but because I wasn't going to see our crew again. I said my piece, which was video-taped and may be released someday.

As the set wound down to our last number, I was pretty numb. After the final encore, we all walked to the front, bowed, and left the stage. I thought that we would regroup back at the hotel for last goodbyes but, as everyone had different departure schedules the next day, that didn't happen. Mark Mendoza, my wife, Sharon, and I flew home the next day with some of the crew. We had carried on our luggage, so we got off the plane without anyone saying goodbye.

That was it.

I knew what was next for me. I was writing for several online publications, and my public speaking career was gearing up, thanks in large part to my coauthor, Steve Farber. I speak about twice a month, and my goal is to do fifty dates a year.

The business of Twisted Sister, however, is and will always remain a top priority.

Over the last thirty years, I have had a vision of where things needed to go. After our first deal with Atlantic, almost

Celebrating at my sixtieth birthday party with our former TS soundman Charlie "sixth Sister" Barreca—2012.

every subsequent recording contract was set to sunset at the same time so that all rights to our masters reverted back to us. We have re-recorded our songs and we own the masters to our biggest hits, which we license.

"We're Not Gonna Take It" and "I Wanna Rock" are among the most licensed heavy metal songs in history. They appear in more TV shows, commercials, movies, video games, and online promotions than any other song from any heavy metal band on the planet.

This visibility, as well as the control of the Twisted Sister trademark, remains a gold standard in the industry.

I have lived a crazy life as a hippie, drug dealer, high school revolutionary, musician, band leader, band manager, producer, stereo salesman, father, and survivor of two heart procedures and prostate cancer.

Although Sharon will say, "In the heart of it, you do love each other," I will say that there was an amazing amount of energy that went into becoming successful. I will say that we were audacious enough to believe we could be one of the biggest bands in the world, and we became one of the biggest bands in the world. The proof is that we've sold millions of records. I have thirty-seven gold and platinum albums on my wall as a guitarist, producer, executive producer, and manager.

People always ask me, "What's the crowning glory of Twisted Sister?" Is it the success of our music? Is it the experience of having played in front of hundreds of thousands of people?

Well, that was all great, of course. But our crowning glory, the end-all and be-all of our existence, the undeniable proof of our remarkable legacy, happened in 1988, when the legendary fashion maven Mr. Blackwell named us on his list of the top ten worst-dressed women!

I guess that says it all.

JAY JAY FRENCH'S ACKNOWLEDGMENTS

Thank you to Jeff Segall, Ricky Lulov Segall, Sharon Gitelle, Samantha French Blackwell, Mike Kagan, Mike Meeropol, Mike Bloomfield, Eric Clapton, Albert King, John, Paul, George, and Ringo, the Grateful Dead, David Bowie, Lou Reed, Mott The Hoople, Kenny Neill, Eddie, Mark, Dee, AJ (RIP), Charlie Barreca (RIP), Joe Gerber, Kevin Brenner (RIP), Danny Stanton, Phil Carson, Mark Puma, Sevendust, Jimmy Maceda, Lenny Belleza, Rebecca Wallace Segall/Jeremy Wallace & Writopia, Eric Schurenberg (Inc.com), Janice Lombardo (Inc.com), Maureen Errico, Jane Raab, Jodie Glickman, Janice Brock, David Schiff, David Perry, Victor Weiss (RIP), Andrew Horn (RIP), Tommy Spaulding, Norm and Elaine Brodsky, Pat Prince (Goldmine), Jim Levine, Bill Leebens (Copper), the entire crew at RosettaBooks, Francine LaSala, and Kim Dower (Our GeeDubs crew didn't do so bad after all, did it?).

And to my cowriter, Steve Farber. If you didn't push me, this book never would have happened. You have my eternal gratitude.

STEVE FARBER'S ACKNOWLEDGMENTS

First, I'll start with the obvious: my love and gratitude to John "Jay Jay" French for inviting me in on this fantastic project. It was such a thrill to help capture his unique speaking voice in the written word. I'm proud of the work we've done together, and, even more so, the way he's reinvented himself, yet again, as an author, phenomenal speaker, consultant, podcast host, and all-around Yoda-like luminary. I'm honored to call him a close friend. And I admit that I lust after his voluptuous vintage guitar collection.

Thanks to Patrick Gillam and Stephen Caldwell for their heroic editorial help when pages and pages of transcripts piled up around me as various deadlines loomed and threatened. Much gratitude to Francine LaSala for her immense help in organizing and sequencing the phenomenal stories and lessons in this book, and to eagle-eyed Sara Brady for catching the persistent little mistakes and making them right.

My eternal gratitude to my friends, readers, and fans in the Extreme Leadership community who have always encouraged me to bring inspiring work to the world.

And finally, thanks to my wife, Veronica, for, well, just everything, every day.

THE TWISTED
COLLECTION

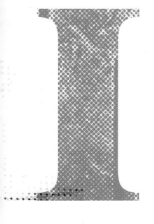**N MAY OF 1978, A FRIEND OF OURS, STEVE** Bramberg, who managed Media Sound, a major recording studio on West Fifty-Seventh Street, invited us to record some demos. He let us record for free, with no strings attached—just to see and feel the experience. It was a Sunday night, and we set up our amps and drums and blazed through about ten songs that we were playing live at the time. All were recorded in a single take. We finished at sunrise, then loaded up our gear and returned to Long Island. These tracks eventually appeared on an album called *Club Daze 2*:

- **"Pay the Price"**
- **"Under the Blade"**
- **"Come Back"**
- **"You Know I Cry"**
- **"Lady's Boy"**
- **"Follow Me"**
- **"Plastic Money"**
- **"Honey, Look 3 Times"**
- **"Can't Stand Still"**
- **"Without You"**

After that summer, we recorded more demos at a studio called Monkey Hill in Queens, but it wasn't until the summer of 1979, after selling out the Palladium Theater (the only unsigned band in history to ever do this), that we'd get any recognition from a label or producer. That July, world-renowned producer Eddie Kramer saw us play at a club called Detroit located in Port Chester, New York. Thanks to the gas crisis at the time, we were having trouble filling the room, but even though there were only about three hundred at the club that night, Eddie was impressed. We signed a production deal with him and recorded four songs in the newly refurbished Electric Lady Studios (originally built by and for Jimi Hendrix) that November:

- **"I'll Never Grow Up, Now!"**
- **"Under the Blade"**
- **"Leader of the Pack" (cover)**
- **"Lady's Boy"**

These Kramer demos proved unsuccessful in getting us a record deal, and Eddie Kramer was shocked at the number of rejections we got. It made no sense to any of us. It seemed like we were being blackballed by the record industry. How could a band like ours, who drew thousands of fans nightly to bars around the tristate area, be rejected time and time again? Even if a label didn't like our music, couldn't they see the almost-religious fanaticism that surrounded us, with bars packed night after night—bars that held up to five thousand people!

We had two of the songs ("I'll Never Grow Up, Now!" and "Under the Blade") pressed into a 45 RPM single with a pink cover and a leather-style logo, which we made for our fans and distributed for free at our shows to give our fans a feeling of forward momentum.

Bad boys in 1980. Extra glammed up.

BAD BOYS (OF ROCK 'N' ROLL)

In the winter of 1980, the band sent me and our newly hired manager, Mark Puma, to the Midem Conference in Nice, France. Apparently, more international record deals, historically, have been signed during that four-day conference than all the deals worldwide combined. That's where we met Freddy Cannon, who promised we were as good as signed, but who ultimately let us down. I also met with a couple from Holland, who had a label called Handshake Records, who were about to open an American office, and the German producer who owned X Records, Peter Hauke, who died of a heart attack on his flight back to Germany.

We went back to the studio, this time to Minot in White Plains, to record what would become our summer of 1980 theme song, "Bad

Boys (of Rock 'n' Roll)." We pressed a new 45, with "Bad Boys" on the A side and "Lady's Boy" on the B side. Rob Freeman, who had been the engineer for the Kramer demos, was the producer. The single again was distributed to fans for free at our shows, and all we could do was hope that we'd get a break soon.

RUFF CUTTS (FOUR-SONG EP)

In April 1981, we found out that one of the main writers of British rock newspaper *Sounds* had featured one of our singles on his recommended playlist. *Sounds* sent over journalist Garry Bushell, who wrote an incredible review for the next issue, titled "Sister Sledgehammer."

That review caught the eye of Martin Hooker, who had just started a punk label called Secret Records. He contacted us and said that he wanted to sign us if we were as good as Garry said we were. He attended one of our sold-out shows and afterward came to our dressing room to tell us how great we were and to let us know he was going to offer us a record deal.

During the winter of 1981, we recorded two more songs at a Long Island studio called Bolognese:

- "Shoot 'Em Down"
- "What You Don't Know (Sure Can Hurt You)"

UNDER THE BLADE

Our debut album, *Under the Blade*, was composed mostly of songs we'd been playing since 1976. It was recorded from July 5 to July 26, 1982, in various locations around the UK. I believe we kept moving studios to take advantage of the cheapest daily rates.

The basic tracks were recorded in a barn with a mobile recording studio attached to it. It was a working farm. I don't remember how we wound up there, but we had an argument with a local studio owner and had to leave. The barn was at the bottom of a hill in Hastings, where the famous battle of Hastings was fought in 1066. We all stayed in a hotel that was built around 1300. Nothing like New York, that was for sure.

TOP: Recording *Under the Blade* in the barn in Hastings, UK, where the Battle of Hastings was fought. **LEFT:** Surrounded by hay bales to keep noise down—July 1982.

At midnight on July 19, we took the photo that wound up on the back of the album. It was my thirtieth birthday. On my twenty-ninth, I had given myself exactly one more year, and if we didn't have a deal by the time I was thirty, I was going to end the band. I just made it under the wire, and it felt great.

That summer, *Sounds* sent Ross Halfin down to take some shots for a cover story for the magazine. After a series of band photos, Dee suggested some solo shots be taken of him. When the issue came out the following week with only Dee's photo on the cover, I sensed trouble brewing. At least the album cover had all five members of the band on it, front and back.

Under the Blade was released in September, and we were supposed to go to the UK for our first tour to promote it. The tour got pushed and then got canceled when the label went bankrupt. By the end of October, we were back to square one once again.

YOU CAN'T STOP ROCK 'N' ROLL

This album was our first official album recorded for Atlantic Records. The budget was $60,000 for all, including making a promotional video, which was a new concept at the time.

In order to make this record as cheaply as possible, Phil Carson, the music executive who signed the band and who also was the former tour manager for Led Zeppelin, arranged to have us record at a studio called the Sol. The Sol was owned by Led Zeppelin's Jimmy Page, who bought it from Elton John's producer, Gus Dudgeon. Jimmy gave Phil a very cheap daily rate and allowed the band to actually also live at the studio, which had an adjoining house. The studio was located in one of the most conservative towns in the UK, called Cookham, which was populated mostly by former members of Parliament. Everything shut down after 3:00 p.m. I mean everything.

We probably brought the average age of the town down to eighty-five!

Every morning, Dee and I would go for a run and pass some old guy walking his sheepdog and smoking a pipe. This was right out of Monty Python.

One of the best things about this experience was that our producer, Stu Epps, who was the caretaker and engineer of the studio, was working on the remastering of classic Led Zeppelin music for an album called *CODA*. This meant that all the two-inch master tapes that contained all the classic Led Zeppelin songs were on the shelves at the studio.

Here we were, a band from Long Island that used to play Zep songs, in the same room with all the master tapes of one of the greatest bands in the world. This was only two years since Zeppelin had decided to retire after the death of their drummer, John Bonham.

Not only that, Phil and Stu told us that Jimmy would probably visit us at some point. This was really great for me, as I had been in the first row of Zep's first-ever New York City concert at the Fillmore East on January 28, 1969, and had seen them many times since then.

Jimmy never came.

Dee had written most of the songs for the album while we were recording *Under the Blade* the previous summer. We were all getting along really well as a band, and we decided early on that the song "You Can't Stop Rock 'n' Roll" was the perfect title for the album.

We arrived at Heathrow on February 2, and Stu Epps picked us up in a van. He drove us down to the studio in Cookham, then to the M&L rentals, where the Who stored their stuff, and picked out the amps and drums for the recording sessions.

On February 3, we began preproduction (rehearsing) on the first two songs: "I Am, I'm Me" and "We're Gonna Make It."

Because of contractual issues with Secret Records that had to be sorted out before the actual recording began, it took two weeks before the recording session started. The drum and bass for "The Kids Are Back" and "You're Not Alone" commenced on February 16.

On March 17, Secret Records agreed to release us, freeing us to sign the Atlantic deal. We wrapped recording on March 18.

On March 22, our first single, "I Am, I'm Me," entered the national charts at number forty-five. On April 7, we made our first appearance on *Top of the Pops*. The next day, we started the UK tour to support the album.

On set, shooting the video for You Can't Stop Rock 'n' Roll—1983.

STAY HUNGRY

Hot on the heels of the commercially successful release of *You Can't Stop Rock 'n' Roll*, Doug Morris, the president of Atlantic, who had hated us up to this point, said that if we gave him the right record, he was going to make us "the world's biggest band." I told my brother the whole story that night and he was happy for me, but I told him not to get too excited, as Doug seemed to have a reputation for being full of shit.

The first week of January, Tom Werman came to New York to meet us and hear the songs planned for the album. He didn't seem too excited about any of them and even suggested we record some songs by Saxon. This really didn't go down well with Dee. From that point on, Tom and Dee never got along, which caused a great deal of friction during the recording process.

We started recording in New York City, at the Record Plant, but Tom wanted us to record in Los Angeles at Cherokee Sound, the studio he was comfortable with.

As the album-making process continued through March 1984, the only song I really loved was "Don't Let Me Down." The ones that would be the biggest hits, "We're Not Gonna Take It" and "I Wanna Rock," were not obvious hits to me at the time. They were great, but like the other singles we'd recorded, they all had the same kind of anthem theme.

Our engineer, Geoff Workman, did most of the heavy lifting as Tom stayed away a lot because of the friction with Dee. He did, however, put his stamp on the album in the way that it sounded.

During the sessions, I went to his house in Laurel Canyon to listen to some rough mixes. I thought we'd be listening to the music on a huge stereo, but instead, Tom played a cassette of the mixes on a tape deck in his kitchen. I asked him why we weren't listening on the big system. He explained, "Look, ninety-five percent of your fans are going to listen to the album on a ninety-nine-dollar cassette deck. It has to sound good on this, and if it sounds good on this, it will also sound good on the radio."

Say what you will about the fact that the album wasn't anywhere near as heavy as we were as a band, the album was a smash, due in no small part to the way the songs sounded on radio and the constant exposure of our groundbreaking videos on MTV.

One thing, however, brought a cloud of disharmony to the band. The cover shot. Intended or not, the solo shot of Dee picked for the cover cemented the image that the band was just about Dee. The two videos Dee created with director Marty Callner, "We're Not Gonna Take It" and "I Wanna Rock," further enforced that narrative.

The album was released May 10, 1984. It went gold (five hundred thousand copies sold) on August 9 and hit platinum (one million copies sold) on October 21. The album was selling so fast that in one week in July of 1984, it was the second-biggest album on the entire Warner Music roster, second only to the *Purple Rain* soundtrack by Prince.

Sadly, October 21, 1984, was also the day that my father passed away. He had been sick with cancer the previous six weeks and was deteriorating quickly. Also taking away from the joy of our success was that the band was slowly coming apart due to jealousy. My first marriage was also falling apart, and AJ's dad died that December.

Things couldn't have been worse . . . and then New Year's Eve happened. The band had been invited to the MTV New Year's Eve bash at the Manhattan Center. When we got there, only Dee and his wife, Suzette, were allowed on the main floor. The rest of us were forced to stay upstairs on the balcony.

The *Stay Hungry* tour went on until May of 1985, and we became one of the biggest bands in the world. To date, *Stay Hungry* has sold six million copies worldwide.

My dad holding a platinum album one week before he died— October 1984.

COME OUT AND PLAY

Come Out and Play, the much-anticipated follow-up to *Stay Hungry*, was recorded primarily at the Record Plant in Los Angeles from September through November 1985.

Before anyone knew us, back when we were struggling in the bars, we'd make mistakes, but since no one really knew or cared about us beyond the tristate area, any errors usually went unnoticed and were easily remedied. Not so after *Stay Hungry*, when the whole world was watching. The errors and miscalculations of timing and song choices now directly led to the beginning of the end of the album/video era of the band's history.

We should have toured longer. We should have gone to the UK and Europe for one more round of touring on the back of *Stay Hungry*, but we basically abandoned the UK, which was a very big mistake. Then, when we were deciding on a producer for the album, Dee defied Doug Morris, who wanted us to work with Tom Werman again because he felt it was a winning combination. Dee didn't want Tom back, we said no, and Doug never liked our choice of German producer Dieter Dierks.

When it came to the song choices, I was concerned that the band was becoming like a bubblegum pop-metal band. No one else seemed to feel that way, and Dee always held Alice Cooper up as an example of a hard rock/metal band that also had hit records. You have to be very careful when choosing what to promote—meaning you have to be heavy enough to keep the older fans, but commercial enough to get on the radio. It was a tough balance to navigate, and choosing "Leader of the Pack" as the first song to release from the new album was, perhaps, the biggest error of our career.

Despite success we'd had playing it live, the song flopped right out of the gate on the rock radio stations. We were still successful on MTV, however, and we became the first band ever to do an international record promotion, sponsored by MTV, where the winners (one hundred from all over the US) were flown to England to watch us perform a concert. Also seemingly unaware of our decline in popularity, Winterland, who created merchandise for acts like Bruce Springsteen and Madonna, gave us the first million-dollar advance in merchandise history.

We quickly pivoted to the next song, "You Want What We Got," which kind of sounded like "We're Not Gonna Take It." This one also failed on radio, and we never even got around to making a video for it.

We had one more shot with "Be Chrool to your Scuel." Dee had an idea for a video that would be so outrageous, it would somehow bring back all our hard-earned credibility. The song featured guest appearances by Billy Joel on piano, Clarence Clemons on sax, Brian Setzer on guitar, and Alice Cooper on vocals. We spent over $300,000 of our own money (with the expectation that our record label would reimburse us) to hire legendary horror makeup artist Tom Savini to transform the hundred or so extras into zombies walking around a horror high school. We even got Bobcat Goldthwait to play a school-teacher, and Lainie Kazan to play a lunch lady in the video.

The video was incredibly directed by Marty Callner and took two days to shoot. When it was finished and shown to the Atlantic Records staff, Doug Morris walked out of the room and declared it revolting. He said he would not only not support it, but he basically shut down promotion for the album. Our only hope was that the public would come to our rescue. They didn't. The video was also banned in over one hundred countries.

Our touring stage set was huge and very expensive. Only big-ticket concert sales could save it. Again, that didn't happen. A world tour that should have lasted at least a year and a half (through mid-1987) ground to a halt by the end of January 1986.

In hindsight, we should have released "The Fire Still Burns" as the first single. That probably would have given us the best shot at success. "Leader of the Pack" should have never even been on the album.

Still, *Come Out and Play* hit platinum in the US and several other European countries, but it never came close to the success of *Stay Hungry*.

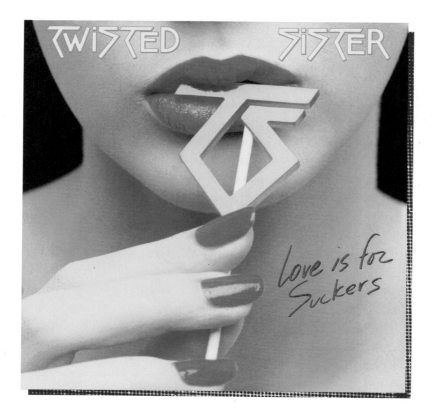

LOVE IS FOR SUCKERS

In a last-ditch effort to save the band, we recorded *Love Is for Suckers* during the summer of 1987 in Atlantic Records' own studios. This album had originally been slated to be a Dee Snider solo album, but we were advised by management that Doug Morris would only get back on board if we agreed to make it a Twisted Sister album, and to use his handpicked choice of producer. In this case, his choice was Beau Hill, who had lots of success with Ratt.

AJ had quit the band after our last live shows in Europe in 1986 and was replaced by Joey "Seven" Franco, so named because he was the seventh drummer to hold that position. Ironically, Joey didn't actually play drums on the album. He programmed a drum machine, but I believe he did hit live cymbals. Most if not all the guitar parts were played by Reb Beach, who was the go-to guitar guy for Beau Hill. Reb either played or re-recorded many of the guitar parts on the album.

The end of this part of the history of the band came shortly after the release of this album. For the first time, we recorded songs that Dee didn't write, including the title cut. We made one video for the song "Hot Love" and embarked on a tour in the fall of 1987 that was supposed to last two to three months. It ended within three weeks.

Dee submitted his official resignation on March 15, 1988.

THE REUNION ALBUMS 2004/2006

STILL HUNGRY

In 2004, the band decided to package an updated version of *Stay Hungry* to go along with a DVD of a live concert filmed in Germany. When postproduction video problems hit the project (all the live audio was lost), the band decided to record more songs and release a music-only package comprised of seven additional tracks—among them two songs originally recorded for the *Stay Hungry* album, which Werman had rejected. The cuts, "Never Say Never & Blastin'

Fast & Loud" and "Heroes Are Hard to Find," were originally recorded in 1999 for the soundtrack to Dee's movie *Strangeland*. The
new collection also featured newly recorded songs from our old bar
days: "Come Back," "Plastic Money," "You Know I Cry," and "Rock
'n' Roll Saviors."

The purpose behind the re-record of *Stay Hungry* was twofold:

1. The band had never liked how the original album sounded
   and wanted to update it to sound more like we really
   played.

2. We wanted to license our own better-sounding versions
   of the songs for movies, TV shows, and commercials.
   We pioneered this movement to re-record and control
   100 percent of the masters and all the licensing money—
   cutting out the record company's version (and half the
   fees). This has been one of the best things we've ever done,
   as our songs are among the most licensed songs in the
   history of heavy metal.

A TWISTED CHRISTMAS

In 2006 we came up with the idea of *A Twisted Christmas*. It was all about marketing and taking all the lessons we'd learned about making deals to the max. We partnered with a label called Razor & Tie and made deals with VH1 for a major marketing push during Christmas 2006. The thinking was that, instead of downloads, people would want to give an actual gift for Christmas.

We kept the idea simple: make heavy metal versions of some of the most popular Christmas songs. It didn't hurt that the classic "O Come, All Ye Faithful" was strangely similar to "We're Not Gonna Take It." Along with a classic video and lots of VH1 and broadcast TV promotion (*The Tonight Show, The Late Late Show with Craig*

Ferguson, plus local morning shows), the album, against all odds, became a hit.

Our CD sales soared. We performed Christmas shows live on Broadway and did a week at the Hilton in Las Vegas. Along with the CD, we also released two DVDs of the Christmas show. Now, every year, another metal band releases Christmas music . . . thanks to our vision!

TWISTED SISTER CONCERT DATES

3.20.73 (FIRST SHOW), 3.21.73, 3.23.73, 3.24.73, 3.25.73: Satellite Lounge, Cookstone, NJ

3.30.73: Wreck Room, Shamsburg, PA

3.31.73, 4.3.73, 4.4.73, 4.5.73, 4.6.73, 4.7.73, 4.8.73: Satellite Lounge, Cookstone, NJ

4.12.73, 4.13.73, 4.14.73, 4.15.73: Spruce Goose, Passaic, NJ

4.20.73, 4.21.73: Unknown, Greenwoodlake, NY

4.27.73, 4.28.73: Unknown, Adams, MA

5.2.73, 5.3.73, 5.4.73, 5.5.73, 5.9.73, 5.10.73, 5.11.73, 5.12.73: Colony III, Nutley, NJ

5.18.73, 5.19.73, 5.25.73, 5.26.73, 5.27.73, 5.30.73, 5.31.73, 6.1.73, 6.2.73, 6.3.73, 6.6.73, 6.7.73, 6.8.73, 6.9.73, 6.10.73, 6.13.73, 6.14.73, 6.15.73, 6.17.73, 6.20.73, 6.21.73, 6.22.73, 6.23.73, 6.24.73, 6.27.73, 6.28.73, 6.29.73, 6.30.73, 7.1.73, 7.4.73, 7.5.73, 7.6.73, 7.7.73, 7.8.73, 7.11.73, 7.12.73, 7.13.73, 7.14.73, 7.15.73, 7.18.73, 7.19.73, 7.20.73, 7.21.73, 7.22.73, 7.25.73, 7.26.73, 7.27.73, 7.28.73, 7.29.73, 8.1.73, 8.3.73, 8.4.73, 8.5.73, 8.6.73, 8.8.73, 8.10.73, 8.11.73: Mad Hatter (EQ), East Quogue, NY

8.12.73: The Sunshine in Ashbury Park w/Mott the Hoople

8.13.73, 8.15.73, 8.16.73, 8.17.73, 8.18.73, 8.19.73, 8.22.73, 8.23.73, 8.24.73, 8.25.73, 8.26.73, 8.29.73, 8.30.73, 8.31.73, 9.1.73, 9.2.73, 9.3.73, 9.7.73, 9.8.73, 9.9.73: Mad Hatter (EQ), East Quogue, NY

9.14.73, 9.15.73: T.G.'s, Greenwood Lake, NY

9.19.73, 9.20.73, 9.21.73, 9.22.73: Colony III, Nutley, NJ

9.25.73: Searchlite Netcong, NJ CANCELED

9.26.73, 9.27.73, 9.28.73, 9.29.73, 10.3.73, 10.4.73, 10.5.73, 10.6.73: Searchlite, Netcong, NJ

10.7.73: Rush Disco, Glen Cove, NY

10.10.73, 10.11.73, 10.12.73, 10.13.73, 10.14.73: Capricorn, Hasbrouck Heights, NJ

10.17.73, 10.18.73, 10.19.73, 10.20.73: Colony III, Nutley, NJ

10.25.73: Richochete Slick

10.26.73, 10.27.73: Searchlite, Netcong, NJ

11.2.73, 11.3.73: Sahara, Adams, MA

11.4.73: Searchlite, Netcong, NJ

11.7.73, 11.8.73: Hunter Village Inn, Hunter Mtn, NY

8.13.73, 8.15.73, 8.16.73, 8.17.73, 8.18.73, 8.19.73, 8.22.73, 8.23.73, 8.24.73, 8.25.73, 8.26.73, 8.29.73, 8.30.73, 8.31.73, 9.1.73, 9.2.73, 9.3.73, 9.7.73, 9.8.73, 9.9.73: Mad Hatter (EQ), East Quogue, NY

9.14.73, 9.15.73: T.G.'s, Greenwood Lake, NY

9.19.73, 9.20.73, 9.21.73, 9.22.73: Colony III, Nutley, NJ

9.25.73: Searchlite Netcong, NJ CANCELED

9.26.73, 9.27.73, 9.28.73, 9.29.73, 10.3.73, 10.4.73, 10.5.73, 10.6.73: Searchlite, Netcong, NJ

10.7.73: Rush Disco, Glen Cove, NY

10.10.73, 10.11.73, 10.12.73, 10.13.73, 10.14.73: Capricorn, Hasbrouck Heights, NJ

10.17.73, 10.18.73, 10.19.73, 10.20.73: Colony III, Nutley, NJ

10.25.73: Richochete Slick

10.26.73, 10.27.73: Searchlite, Netcong, NJ

11.2.73, 11.3.73: Sahara, Adams, MA

11.4.73: Searchlite, Netcong, NJ

11.7.73, 11.8.73, 11.9.73, 11.10.73: Hunter Village Inn, Hunter Mtn, NY

11.14.73, 11.16.73, 11.17.73, 11.18.73: Capricorn, Hasbrouck Heights, NJ

11.22.73, 11.23.73: Joker II, Passiac, NJ

11.28.73, 11.30.73, 12.1.73, 12.2.73: Searchlite, Netcong, NJ

12.6.73, 12.7.73, 12.8.73, 12.9.73: George Inn, Great Gorge, NJ

12.12.73: Richochete Slick

12.14.73, 12.15.73, 12.16.73: Popeye's Spinach Factory, Sheepshead Bay, NY

12.22.73, 12.23.73: Sahara, Adams, MA

12.25.73: Dodds, Orange, NJ

12.28.73, 12.29.73, 12.31.73: Sahara, Adams, MA

1.3.74: Dodds, Orange, NJ

1.4.74, 1.5.74, 1.6.74: Hunter Village Inn, Hunter Mtn, NY

1.9.74: Joker II, Passiac, NJ

1.10.74: Doddscrest, West Orange, NJ

1.11.74, 1.12.74: Caspers, New Brunswick, NJ

1.16.74: Joker, Passiac, NJ

1.17.74: Doddscrest, West Orange, NJ

1.18.74, 1.19.74: Sahara, Adams, MA

1.23.74: Joker, Passiac, NJ

1.24.74: Doddscrest, West Orange, NJ

1.25.74, 1.26.74, 1.27.74, 1.30.74: Joker, Passaic,NJ

1.31.74: Doddscrest, West Orange, NJ

2.1.74, 2.2.74: Searchlite, Netcong, NJ

2.9.74, 2.10.74: Caspers, New Brunswick, NJ

2.13.74, 2.15.74, 2.16.74, 2.17.74: Mr. T's, Wantagh, NY

2.21.74: Showboat, Newport, RI

2.22.74, 2.23.74, 2.24.74: Hunter Village Inn, Hunter Mtn, NY

2.25.74: College Concert, NJ State Univ

2.26.74, 2.27.74: Mr. T's, Wantagh, NY

2.28.74: Colonial Theatre, Pompyon Lakes—w/Another Pretty Face

3.1.74, 3.2.74, 3.3.74: Mr. T's, Wantagh, NY

3.7.74, 3.8.74, 3.9.74, 3.10.74: Liberty Bell, Philadelphia,PA

3.13.74, 3.14.74, 3.15.74, 3.16.74, 3.17.74: Mr. T's, Wantagh, NY

3.20.74, 3.21.74, 3.22.74, 3.23.74, 3.24.74: Joker II, Passiac, NJ

3.27.74, 3.28.74, 3.29.74, 3.30.74, 3.31.74: Dodds, Orange, NJ

4.3.74: Mr. T's, Wantagh, NY

4.5.74, 4.6.74: Sahara, Adams, MA

4.10.74: Mr. T's, Wantagh, NY

4.11.74: Pourhouse, Bronx, NY

4.12.74, 4.13.74: Sahara Adams, MA

4.17.74: Mr. T's, Wantagh, NY

4.18.74: Pourhouse, Bronx, NY

4.19.74, 4.20.74, 4.21.74: Capricorn, Hasbrouck Height, NJ

4.23.74, 4.24.74, 4.25.74, 4.26.74, 4.27.74: Dodds, Orange, NJ

4.28.74, 4.30.74: Mr. T's, Wantagh, NY

5.1.74, 5.2.74, 5.3.74, 5.4.74, 5.5.74: Joker II, Passiac, NJ

5.6.74: Dodds, Orange, NJ

5.7.74, 5.8.74, 5.9.74, 5.10.74, 5.11.74, 5.12.74: Mr. T's, Wantagh, NY

5.15.74: Montclair State, Montclair, NJ

5.16.74, 5.17.74, 5.18.74, 5.19.74: Liberty Bell, Philadelphia, PA

5.20.74: Christopher St., Glen Cove, NY

5.22.74: Mr. T's, Wantagh, NY

5.23.74, 5.24.74, 5.25.74, 5.26.74, 5.27.74, 5.29.74, 5.30.74, 5.31.74, 6.1.74, 6.2.74, 6.5.74, 6.6.74, 6.7.74, 6.8.74, 6.9.74, 6.12.74, 6.13.74, 6.14.74, 6.15.74, 6.16.74, 6.19.74, 6.20.74, 6.21.74, 6.22.74, 6.23.74, 6.26.74, 6.27.74, 6.28.74, 6.29.74, 6.30.74: Mad Hatter (EQ), East Quogue, NY

7.1.74: Mr. T's, Wantagh, NY

7.3.74: Dodds, Orange, NJ

7.5.74, 7.6.74: Sahara, Adams, MA

7.10.74: Dodds, Orange, NJ

7.11.74, 7.12.74, 7.13.74, 7.14.74: Joker II, Passiac, NJ

7.15.74: Mr. T's, Wantgh, NY

7.17.74: Dodds, Orange, NJ

7.19.74, 7.20.74: Sahara, Adams, MA

7.22.74, 7.24.74, 7.25.74, 7.26.74, 7.27.74, 7.28.74, 7.29.74: Mr. T's, Wantagh, NY

8.1.74, 8.2.74, 8.3.74: OBI East, Hamptons Bays, NY

8.4.74, 8.5.74: Electric Elephant, Newport, RI

8.8.74, 8.9.74, 8.10.74: OBI East, Hamptons Bays, NY

8.11.74, 8.12.74: Mr. T's, Wantagh, NY

8.15.74, 8.16.74, 8.17.74, 8.22.74, 8.23.74, 8.24.74, 8.30.74, 8.31.74, 9.1.74: OBI East, Hamptons Bays, NY

9.8.74, 9.9.74: Electric Elephant, Newport, RI

9.13.74, 9.14.74, 9.17.74: Rumbottoms, Masapequa, NY

9.20.74, 9.21.74: Emmit's, Jamesberg, NJ

9.27.74, 9.28.74, 10.8.74: Rumbottoms, Masapequa, NY

10.11.74, 10.12.74: Sahara, Adams, MA

10.15.74: Rumbottoms, Masapequa, NY

10.18.74, 10.19.74: Mr. D's, Jersey City, NJ

10.22.74: Rumbottoms, Masapequa, NY

10.23.74: Silver Schooner, Long Island—*Show player w/o Jay Jay*

10.25.74, 10.26.74, 10.29.74: Rumbottoms, Masapequa, NY

10.30.74, 10.31.74, 11.1.74, 11.2.74, 11.3.74: Electric Elephant, Newport, RI

11.5.74: Rumbottoms, Masapequa, NY

11.6.74: Silver Schooner, Long Island, NY

11.8.74, 11.9.74, 11.12.74: Ubie's O.T.J's, West Islip, NY

11.14.74, 11.15.74, 11.16.74, 11.17.74: Dodds, Orange, NJ

11.19.74: Ubie's O.T.J's, West Islip, NY

11.21.74: Pourhouse, Bronx, NY

11.22.74, 11.23.74: Sahara, Adams, MA

11.26.74: Ubie's O.T.J's West Islip, NY

11.28.74: Pourhouse, Bronx, NY

11.29.74, 11.30.74, 12.1.74: Hunter Village Inn, Hunter Mtn, NY

12.3.74, 12.4.74: Ubie's O.T.J's, West Islip, NY

12.6.74, 12.7.74: Inner Circle, Long Island

12.8.74: Searchlite, Netcong, NJ

12.10.74, 12.13.74, 12.14.74: Ubie's O.T.J's, West Islip, NY

12.15.74: Searchlite, Netcong, NJ

12.18.74, 12.19.74, 12.20.74, 12.21.74, 12.22.74: Electric Elephant, Newport, RI

12.26.74, 12.27.74, 12.28.74, 12.29.74: Dodds, Orange, NJ

12.31.74: Inner Circle, Long Island, NY

1.1.75, 1.2.75, 1.3.75, 1.4.75, 1.5.75: Joker II, Passiac, NJ—*Last date of original lineup*

1.7.75, 1.8.75, 1.9.75, 1.10.75, 1.11.75, 1.12.75: Rehearsal, Queen's, NY—*Rehearsals for new lineup*

1.15.75: *Debut of new lineup*

1.16.75, 1.17.75: Caspers, New Brunswick, NJ

1.24.75, 1.25.75: Ubie's O.T.J's, West Islip, NY

1.26.75: Beggar's Banque, Queen's, NY

1.28.75: Ubie's O.T.J's, West Islip, NY

1.29.75: Beggar's Banque, Queen's, NY

1.30.75: Joker II, Passiac, NJ—*Original lineup subs for new lineup*

2.2.75: Beggar's Banque, Queen's, NY

2.4.75: Ubie's O.T.J's, West Islip, NY

2.7.75, 2.8.75: Rumbottoms, Masapequa, NY

2.9.75: Beggar's Banque, Queen's, NY

2.11.75: Ubie's O.T.J's, West Islip, NY

2.13.75, 2.14.75, 2.15.75: Electic Elephant, Newport, RI

2.16.75: Beggar's Banque, Queen's, NY

2.18.75 Ubie's O.T.J's, West Islip, NY

2.19.75: Rumbottoms, Masapequa, NY

2.21.75, 2.22.75: Maxi's, Wantagh, NY

2.23.75: Beggar's Banque, Queen's, NY

2.25.75: Ubie's O.T.J's, West Islip, NY

2.26.75: Maxi's, Wantagh, NY

3.2.75: Beggar's Banque, Queen's, NY

3.5.75: Maxi's, Wantagh, NY

3.7.75, 3.8.75: Rumbottoms, Masapequa, NY

3.9.75: Beggar's Banque Queen's, NY

3.11.75: Ubie's O.T.J's, West Islip, NY

3.12.75: Maxi's, Wantagh, NY

3.14.75, 3.15.75: Ubie's O.T.J's, West Islip, NY

3.16.75: Beggar's Banque, Queen's, NY

3.18.75: Ubie's O.T.J's, West Islip, NY—*Lead singer Rick Price fired and band performs for the first timeas a 4-piece with Jay Jay singing*

3.19.75: Maxi's, Wantagh, NY

3.21.75, 3.22.75: Sahara, Adams, MA

3.23.75: Beggar's Banque, Queen's, NY

3.25.75: *Relationship formally ended with Frank Richard's Management*

3.28.75, 3.29.75: Maxi's, Wantagh, NY

3.30.75: Beggar's Banque, Queen's, NY

4.2.75: Maxi's, Wantagh, NY

4.4.75, 4.5.75: Rumbottoms, Masapequa, NY

4.6.75: Beggar's Banque, Queen's, NY

4.9.75: Maxi's, Wantagh, NY

4.11.75, 4.12.75: Ubie's O.T.J's, West Islip, NY

4.13.75: Beggar's Banque, Queen's, NY

4.16.75, 4.18.75, 4.19.75: Maxi's, Wantagh, NY

4.20.75: Beggar's Banque, Queen's, NY

4.23.75: Maxi's, Wantagh, NY

4.25.75, 4.26.75: Sahara, Adams, MA

4.27.75: Beggar's Banque, Queen's, NY
4.30.75: Maxi's, Wantagh, NY
5.2.75, 5.3.75: The Dunes, Atlantic City, NJ
5.4.75: Beggar's Banque, Queen's, NY
5.7.75: Maxi's, Wantagh, NY
5.9.75, 5.10.75: Chaucer's Ale House, Oakdale, NY
5.11.75: Beggar's Banque Queen's, NY
5.14.75: Maxi's, Wantagh, NY
5.16.75, 5.17.75: OBI East, Hampton Bays, NY
5.18.75: Beggar's Banque, Queen's, NY
5.21.75: Maxi's, Wantagh, NY
5.22.75: 1890's, Baldwin, NY
5.23.75, 5.24.75, 5.25.75: OBI East, Hampton Bays, NY
5.27.75: G.G.'s North, Armonk, NY
5.28.75: Maxi's, Wantagh, NY
5.30.75, 5.31.75: OBI East, Hampton Bays, NY
6.1.75: Beggar's Banque Queen's, NY
6.3.75: G.G.'s North, Armonk, NY
6.4.75: Maxi's, Wantagh, NY
6.5.75: Chaucer's Ale House, Oakdale, NY
6.6.75, 6.7.75: OBI East, Hampton Bays, NY
6.10.75: G.G.'s North, Armonk, NY
6.11.75: Maxi's, Wantagh, NY
6.12.75: Chaucer's Ale House, Oakdale, NY
6.13.75, 6.14.75: OBI East, Hampton Bays, NY
6.17.75: G.G.'s North, Armonk, NY
6.18.75: Maxi's, Wantagh, NY
6.19.75: Chaucer's Ale House, Oakdale, NY
6.20.75, 6.21.75: OBI East, Hampton Bays, NY
6.22.75: Dodds, Orange, NJ
6.24.75: G.G.'s North, Armonk, NY
6.25.75: Maxi's, Wantagh, NY
6.26.75: Chaucer's Ale House, Oakdale, NY
6.27.75, 6.28.75: OBI North, Smithtown, NY
6.29.75: Dodds, Orange, NJ
7.1.75: 1890's, Baldwin, NY
7.2.75: Maxi's, Wantagh, NY
7.3.75: Chaucer's Ale House, Oakdale, NY
7.4.75, 7.5.75, 7.6.75: Final Exam, Randolph Township, NJ
7.9.75: Maxi's, Wantagh, NY
7.10.75: Chaucer's Ale House, Oakdale, NY
7.11.75, 7.12.75: Casablanca, Queen's, NY
7.16.75: Maxi's,Wantagh, NY
7.17.75: Chaucer's Ale House, Oakdale, NY
7.18.75, 7.19.75: Marshmallows, New Jersey
7.21.75, 7.22.75, 7.23.75, 7.24.75: Electric Elephant, Newport, RI
7.25.75, 7.26.75: Peaches, Hampton Bays—Formerly OBI East
7.30.75: Maxi's, Wantagh, NY
8.1.75, 8.2.75, 8.3.75: Dodds, Orange, NJ
8.6.75: Maxi's, Wantagh, NY
8.8.75, 8.9.75: Ubie's O.T.J's, West Islip, NY
8.13.75: Maxi's, Wantagh, NY
8.15.75, 8.16.75, 8.17.75, 8.18.75: Electric Elephant Newport, RI
8.20.75, 8.27.75: Maxi's, Wantagh, NY
8.29.75, 8.30.75: Rock Palace, Lake Carmel, NY—Final show

of TS Version #2. Final show of John, Kenny, Mell and Keith
10.31.75, 11.1.75: Grandma's, Brooklyn, NY
11.7.75, 11.8.75: Goodtime Charlie's
11.12.75: Ubie's O.T.J's, West Islip, NY
11.14.75, 11.15.75: Dodds, Orange, NJ
11.19.75: Ubie's O.T.J's, West Islip, NY
11.21.75, 11.22.75: Pine Crest CC, Shelton, CT
11.26.75: Hound & Hare, ???, NJ
11.28.75, 11.29.75: Grandma's, Brooklyn, NY
12.3.75: Ubie's O.T.J's, West Islip, NY
12.5.75, 12.6.75: Dino's CANCELED
12.10.75: Ubie's O.T.J's, West Islip, NY
12.12.75, 12.13.75: Final Exam, Randolph Township, NJ
12.17.75: Ubie's O.T.J's, West Islip, NY
12.19.75, 12.20.75: Red Fox Inn, New Brunswick, NJ
12.24.75: Julio's, ???, NJ
12.26.75, 1 2.27.75: Beau Brummels Mineola, NY
12.31.75: Pine Crest CC, Shelton, CT
1.1.76: Dodds, Orange, NJ
1.2.76, 1.3.76: Chaucer's Ale House, Oakdale, NY
1.5.76: Julio's, ???, NJ
1.7.76: Hound & Hare, Hamburg, NJ
1.9.76, 1.10.76: Dodds, Orange, NJ
1.16.76, 1.17.76: TG's, Greenwood Lake, NY
1.22.76: 1890's, Baldwin, NY
1.23.76, 1.24.76: Turtleneck Inn, Hunter Village, NY
1.25.76: Squire's Lounge Newburgh, NY
1.30.76, 1.31.76: Final Exam, Randolph Township, NJ
2.2.76, 2.3.76, 2.4.76, 2.5.76, 2.6.76, 2.7.76, 2.8.76: Turtleneck Inn Hunter Village, Ny—Dee Snider Audtion Week
2.11.76: The Beach House, ?
2.12.76, 2.13.76, 2.14.76: Grandma's, Brooklyn, NY
2.15.76: Squire's Lounge, Newburgh, NY
2.19.76: Rising Sun, Yonkers, NY
2.20.76, 2.21.76: Red Fox, New Brunswick, NJ
2.26.76: D'Place, Dover, NJ
2.27.76, 2.28.76, 2.29.76, 3.3.76: Hammerheads, Levittown, NY
3.4.76: Maxi's, Wantagh, NY
3.5.76, 3.6.76: 1890's, Baldwin, NY
3.7.76: Squire's Lounge, Newburgh, NY
3.10.76: Hammerheads, Levittown, NY
3.11.76: Rising Sun, Yonkers, NY
3.12.76, 3.13.76: Hammerheads, Levittown, NY
3.14.76: Squire's Lounge, Newburgh, NY
3.17.76: Hammerheads, Levittown, NY
3.18.76: Maxi's Wantagh, NY
3.19.76, 3.20.76: Rock Palace, Lake Carmel, NY
3.21.76: Squire's Lounge, Newburgh, NY
3.24.76: Hammerheads, Levittown, NY
3.25.76, 3.26.76, 3.27.76: Grandma's, Oneonta, NY
3.28.76: Squire's Lounge, Newburgh, NY
3.31.76: Hammerheads, Levittown, NY
4.1.76: Maxi's, Wantagh, NY
4.2.76, 4.3.76: 1890's, Baldwin, NY
4.7.76: Squire's Lounge, Newburgh, NY
4.8.76: Maxi's, Wantagh, NY

4.9.76, 4.10.76: Rising Sun, Yonkers, NY
4.14.76: 1890's, Baldwin, NY
4.15.76: Maxi's, Wantagh, NY
4.1 6.76, 4.17.76: Hammerheads, Levittown, NY
4.21.76: 1890's, Baldwin, NY
4.22.76, 4.23.76, 4.24.76: Maxi's, Wantagh, NY
4.28.76: Squire's Lounge, Newburgh, NY
4.29.76: Maxi's, Wantagh, NY
4.30.76, 5.1.76: Rock Palace, Lake Carmel, NY
5.6.76: Maxi's, Wantagh, NY
5.7.76, 5.8.76: 1890's, Baldwin, NY
5.13.76, 5.13.76, 5.14.76, 5.15.76, 5.20.76: Maxi's, Wantagh, NY
5.21.76, 5.22.76: Mad Hatter (SB), Stony Brook, NY
5.26.76: 1890's, Baldwin, NY
5.27.76: Maxi's, Wantagh, NY
5.28.76, 5.29.76: Hammerheads, Levittown, NY
6.1.76: Mad Hatter (SB), Stony Brook, NY
6.3.76: Maxi's, Wantagh, NY
6.4.76, 6.5.76: Rising Sun, Yonkers, NY
6.8.76, 6.9.76: Mad Hatter (SB), Stony Brook, NY
6.10.76: Maxi's, Wantagh, NY
6.11.76, 6.12.76: Rock Palace, Lake Carmel, NY
6.15.76: Mad Hatter (EQ), East Quogue, NY
6.16.76: Mad Hatter (SB), Stony Brook, NY
6.17.76, 6.18.76, 6.19.76: Maxi's, Wantagh, NY
6.22.76: Glen Island Casino, City Island, NY
6.23.76: Mad Hatter (SB), Stony Brook, NY
6.24.76: Maxi's, Wantagh, NY
6.25.76, 6.26.76: Mad Hatter (EQ), East Quogue, NY
6.30.76: Mad Hatter (SB), Stony Brook, NY
7.1.76: Maxi's, Wantagh, NY
7.2.76, 7.3.76: 1980's, Baldwin, NY
7.6.76: Mad Hatter (EQ), East Quogue, NY
7.7.76: Mad Hatter (SB), Stony Brook, NY
7.8.76, 7.9.76, 7.10.76: Maxi's, Wantagh, NY
7.13.76: Mad Hatter (EQ), East Quogue, NY
7.14.76: Mad Hatter (SB), Stony Brook, NY
7.15.76: Maxi's, Wantagh, NY
7.16.76, 7.17.76: Rock Palace, Lake Carmel, NY
7.20.76: Mad Hatter (EQ), East Quogue, NY
7.21.76: Mad Hatter (SB), Stony Brook, NY
7.22.76: Maxi's, Wantagh, NY
7.23.76, 7.24.76: Mad Hatter (SB), Stony Brook, NY
7.27.76: Mad Hatter (EQ), East Quogue, NY
7.28.76: Mad Hatter (SB), Stony Brook, NY
7.29.76: Maxi's, Wantagh, NY
7.30.76, 7.31.76: Mad Hatter (SB), Stony Brook, NY
8.3.76: Mad Hatter (EQ), East Quogue, NY
8.4.76: Sonny's Lounge, Staten Island, NY
8.5.76: Maxi's, Wantagh, NY
8.6.76, 8.7.76: 1980's, Baldwin, NY
8.10.76: Mad Hatter (EQ), East Quogue, NY
8.11.76: Sonny's Lounge, Staten Island, NY
8.12.76: Maxi's, Wantagh, NY
8.13.76, 8.14.76: Hammerheads, Levittown, NY
8.17.76: Mad Hatter (EQ), East Quogue, NY

8.18.76: Sonny's Lounge, Staten Island, NY
8.19.76: Maxi's, Wantagh, NY
8.20.76, 8.21.76: Mad Hatter (EQ), East Quogue, NY
8.24.76: Mad Hatter (SB), Stony Brook, NY
8.25.76: Sonny's Lounge, Staten Island, NY
8.26.76, 8.27.76, 8.28.76: Maxi's, Wantagh, NY
8.31.76: Mad Hatter (EQ), East Quogue, NY
9.1.76: Mad Hatter (SB), Stony Brook, NY
9.2.76: Maxi's, Wantagh, NY
9.3.76, 9.4.76, 9.5.76: Rock Palace, Lake Carmel, NY
9.7.76: Mad Hatter (EQ), East Quogue, NY
9.8.76: Mad Hatter (SB), Stony Brook, NY
9.9.76: Maxi's, Wantagh, NY
9.10.76, 9.11.76, 9.15.76: Mad Hatter (SB), Stony Brook, NY
9.16.76: Maxi's, Wantagh, NY
9.17.76, 9.18.76: Hammerheads, Levittown, NY
9.22.76: Mad Hatter (SB), Stony Brook, NY
9.23.76: Maxi's, Wantagh, NY
9.24.76, 9.25.76, 9.29.76: Mad Hatter (SB), Stony Brook, NY
9.30.76, 10.7.76: Maxi's, Wantagh, NY
10.8.76, 10.9.76: Hammerheads, Levittown, NY
10.12.76: Mother's, Wayne, NJ
10.13.76: Mad Hatter (SB), Stony Brook, NY
10.14.76: Maxi's, Wantagh, NY
10.15.76, 10.16.76: Hammerheads, Levittown, NY
10.19.76: Mother's, Wayne, NJ
10.20.76: Mad Hatter (SB), Stony Brook, NY
10.21.76, 10.22.76, 10.23.76: Maxi's, Wantagh, NY
10.27.76: Mad Hatter (SB), Stony Brook, NY
10.28.76: Maxi's, Wantagh, NY
10.29.76, 10.30.76, 10.31.76: Rock Palace, Lake Carmel, NY
11.2.76: Mad Hatter (SB), Stony Brook, NY
11.3.76: Fore 'n' Aft, White Plains, NY
11.4.76: Maxi's, Wantagh, NY
11.5.76, 11.6.76: Brendan's, East Quogue, NY
11.9.76: Mad Hatter (SB), Stony Brook, NY
11.10.76: Fore 'n' Aft, White Plains, NY
11.11.76: Maxi's, Wantagh, NY
11.12.76, 11.13.76: Hammerheads II Baldwin, NY
11.14.76: Dodds, Orange, NJ
11.16.76: Mad Hatter (SB), Stony Brook, NY
11.17.76: Fore 'n' Aft, White Plains, NY
11.18.76: Maxi's, Wantagh, NY
11.19.76, 11.20.76, 11.23.76: Mad Hatter (SB), Stony Brook, NY
11.24.76: Commack Arena, Commack, NY
11.25.76, 11 .26.76, 11.27.76: Maxi's, Wantagh, NY
11.30.76: Mad Hatter (SB), Stony Brook, NY
12.1.76: Fore 'n' Aft, White Plains, NY
12.2.76: Maxi's, Wantagh, NY
12.3.76, 12.4.76: Hammerheads, Levittown, NY
12.7.76: Mad Hatter (SB), Stony Brook, NY
12.8.76: Fore 'n' Aft, White Plains, NY
12.9.76: Maxi's, Wantagh, NY
12.10.76, 12.11.76: Brendan's, East Quogue, NY
12.14.76: Mad Hatter (SB), Stony Brook, NY
12.15.76: Fore 'n' Aft, White Plains, NY

12.16.76: Maxi's, Wantagh, NY
12.17.76, 12.18.76, 12.19.76: Rock Palace, Lake Carmel, NY
12.21.76: Mad Hatter (SB), Stony Brook, NY
12.22.76: Fore 'n' Aft, White Plains, NY
12.23.76, 12.24.76, 12.25.76: Maxi's, Wantagh, NY
12.26.76, 12.27.76: Beau Brummel's, Mineola, NY
12.28.76: Mad Hatter (SB), Stony Brook, NY
12.29.76: Fore 'n' Aft, White Plains, NY
12.30.76: Maxi's, Wantagh, NY
12.31.76: Brendan's, East Quogue, NY
1.5.77: Mad Hatter (SB), Stony Brook, NY
1.6.77: Fore 'n' Aft, White Plains, NY
1.7.77: Maxi's, Wantagh, NY
1.8.77, 1.9.77: Hammerheads, Levittown, NY
1.12.77: Mad Hatter (SB), Stony Brook, NY
1.13.77: Fore 'n' Aft, White Plains, NY
1.14.77: Maxi's, Wantagh, NY
1.15.77, 1.16.77, 1.19.77: Mad Hatter (SB), Stony Brook, NY
1.20.77: Fore 'n' Aft, White Plains, NY
1.21.77: Maxi's, Wantagh, NY
1.22.77, 1.23.77: Brendan's, East Quogue, NY
1.26.77: Mad Hatter (SB), Stony Brook, NY
1.27.77: Fore 'n' Aft, White Plains, NY
1.28.77: Maxi's, Wantagh, NY
1.29.77, 1.30.77: Fore 'n' Aft, White Plains, NY
2.2.77: Mad Hatter (SB), Stony Brook, NY
2.3.77: Fore 'n' Aft, White Plains, NY
2.4.77: Maxi's, Wantagh, NY
2.5.77, 2.6.77: Hammerheads, Levittown, NY
2.9.77: Mad Hatter (SB), Stony Brook, NY
2.10.77: Fore 'n' Aft, White Plains, NY
2.11.77, 2.12.77, 2.13.77: Maxi's, Wantagh, NY
2.16.77: Mad Hatter (SB), Stony Brook, NY
2.17.77: Fore 'n' Aft, White Plains, NY
2.18.77: Maxi's, Wantagh, NY
2.19.77, 2.20.77: Rock Palace, Lake Carmel, NY
2.23.77: Mad Hatter (SB), Stony Brook, NY
2.24.77: Fore 'n' Aft, White Plains, NY
2.25.77: Maxi's, Wantagh, NY
2.26.77, 2.27.77, 3.2.77: Mad Hatter (SB), Stony Brook, NY
3.5.77, 3.6.77: Hammerheads, Levittown, NY
3.9.77: Mad Hatter (SB), Stony Brook, NY
3.10.77: Fore 'n' Aft, White Plains, NY
3.11.77, 3.12.77, 3.13.77: Maxi's, Wantagh, NY
3.16.77: Mad Hatter (SB), Stony Brook, NY
3.17.77: Fore 'n' Aft, White Plains, NY
3.18.77: Maxi's, Wantagh, NY
3.19.77, 3.20.77: Rock Palace, Lake Carmel, NY
3.23.77: Mad Hatter (SB), Stony Brook, NY
3.24.77: Fore 'n' Aft, White Plains, NY
3.25.77: Maxi's, Wantagh, NY
3.26.77, 3.27.77, 3.30.77: Mad Hatter (SB), Stony Brook, NY
3.31.77: Fore 'n' Aft, White Plains, NY
4.1.77: Maxi's, Wantagh, NY
4.2.77, 4.3.77, 5.24.77: Hammerheads, Levittown, NY
5.25.77: Fore 'n' Aft, White Plains, NY

5.26.77: Mad Hatter (SB), Stony Brook, NY
5.27.77, 5.28.77: Mad Hatter (EQ), East Quogue, NY
5.30.77: Mad Hatter (SB), Stony Brook, NY
5.31.77: Hammerheads, Levittown, NY
6.1.77: Fore 'n' Aft, White Plains, NY
6.2.77: Mad Hatter (SB), Stony Brook, NY
6.3.77, 6.4.77, 6.7.77: Hammerheads, Levittown, NY
6.8.77: Fore 'n' Aft, White Plains, NY
6.9.77, 6.10.77, 6.11.77: Mad Hatter (SB), Stony Brook, NY
6.14.77: Hammerheads, Levittown, NY
6.15.77: Fore 'n' Aft, White Plains, NY
6.16.77: Mad Hatter (SB), Stony Brook, NY
6.17.77, 6.18.77: Brendan's, East Quogue, NY
6.21.77: Hammerheads, Levittown, NY
6.22.77: Fore 'n' Aft, White Plains, NY
6.23.77: Mad Hatter (SB), Stony Brook, NY
6.24.77, 6.25.77: Fore 'n' Aft, White Plains, NY
6.28.77: Hammerheads, Levittown, NY
6.29.77: Fore 'n' Aft, White Plains, NY
6.30.77: Mad Hatter (SB), Stony Brook, NY
7.1.77, 7.2.77: Maxi's, Wantagh, NY
7.6.77: Mad Hatter (SB), Stony Brook, NY
7.7.77: Mad Hatter (EQ), East Quogue, NY
7.8.77, 7.9.77, 7.12.77: Hammerheads, Levittown, NY
7.13.77: Mad Hatter (SB), Stony Brook, NY
7.14.77: Mad Hatter (EQ), East Quogue, NY
7.15.77, 7.16.77: Brendan's, East Quogue, NY
7.1 9.77: Hammerheads, Levittown, NY
7.20.77: Mad Hatter (SB), Stony Brook, NY
7.21.77: Mad Hatter (EQ), East Quogue, NY
7.22.77, 7.23.77: Fore 'n' Aft, White Plains, NY
7.26.77: Hammerheads, Levittown, NY
7.27.77: Mad Hatter (SB), Stony Brook, NY
7.28.77: Mad Hatter (EQ), East Quogue, NY
7.29.77, 7.30.77: Mad Hatter (SB), Stony Brook, NY
8.2.77: Hammerheads, Levittown, NY
8.3.77: Mad Hatter (SB), Stony Brook, NY
8.4.77: Mad Hatter (EQ), East Quogue, NY
8.5.77, 8.6.77: Maxi's, Wantagh, NY
8.9.77: Hammerheads, Levittown, NY
8.10.77: Mad Hatter (SB), Stony Brook, NY
8.11.77: Mad Hatter (EQ), East Quogue, NY
8.12.77, 8.13.77, 8.16.77: Hammerheads, Levittown, NY
8.17.77: Mad Hatter (SB), Stony Brook, NY
8.18.77: Mad Hatter (EQ), East Quogue, NY
8.19.77, 8.20.77: Speaks, Island Park, NY
8.23.77: Hammerheads, Levittown, NY
8.24.77: Mad Hatter (SB), Stony Brook, NY
8.25.77: Mad Hatter (EQ), East Quogue, NY
8.26.77, 8.27.77: Hammerheads, Levittown, NY
8.28.77: Mad Hatter (EQ), East Quogue, NY
8.30.77: Hammerheads, Levittown, NY—*First SMF Party*
8.31.77: Mad Hatter (SB), Stony Brook, NY
9.1.77: Mad Hatter (EQ), East Quogue, NY
9.2.77, 9.3.77, 9.4.77: Brendan's, East Quogue, NY
9.7.77: Mad Hatter (SB), Stony Brook, NY

9.8.77: Speaks, Island Park, NY
9.9.77, 9.10.77: Mad Hatter (EQ), East Quogue, NY
9.13.77: Gemini II, Yorktown Heights, NY
9.14.77: Mad Hatter (SB), Stony Brook, NY
9.15.77: Speaks, Island Park, NY
9.16.77, 9.17.77: Mad Hatter (SB), Stony Brook, NY
10.5.77: Fore 'n' Aft North Brewster, NY
10.6.77, 10.7.77, 10.8.77: Speaks, Island Park, NY
10.11.77, 10.12.77: Fore 'n' Aft North Brewster, NY
10.13.77: Speaks, Island Park, NY
10.14.77, 10.15.77, 10.18.77: Fore 'n' Aft, White Plains, NY
10.19.77: Fore 'n' Aft North Brewster, NY
10.20.77: Speaks, Island Park, NY
10.21.77, 10.22.77: Gemini II, Yorktown Heights, NY
10.25.77: Fore 'n' Aft, White Plains, NY
10.26.77: Fore 'n' Aft North Brewster, NY
10.27.77: Speaks, Island Park, NY
10.28.77, 10.29.77: Fore 'n' Aft, Westport, CT
11.1.77: Chaucer's Ale House, Oakdale, NY
11.2.77: Fore 'n' Aft North Brewster, NY
11.3.77: Speaks, Island Park, NY
11.4.77, 11.5.77: Chaucer's Ale House, Oakdale, NY
11.9.77: Fore 'n' Aft North Brewster, NY
11.10.77: Speaks, Island Park, NY
11.11.77: Fore 'n' Aft, White Plains, NY
11.12.77, 11.16.77: Fore 'n' Aft North Brewster, NY
11.17.77, 11.18.77, 11.19.77: Speaks, Island Park, NY
11.23.77: Fore 'n' Aft, North Brewster, NY
2.1.77: Speaks, Island Park, NY
12.2.77, 12.3.77: Klondike, Hunter Mountain, NY
12.7.77: Fore 'n' Aft, North Brewster, NY
12.8.77: Speaks, Island Park, NY
12.9.77: Fore 'n' Aft, White Plains, NY
12.10.77, 12.14.77: Fore 'n' Aft, North Brewster, NY
12.15.77: Speaks, Island Park, NY
12.16.77: Rock Palace, Lake Carmel, NY
12.17.77: Fore 'n' Aft, Westport, CT
12.22.77: Speaks, Island Park, NY
12.23.77: Gemini II, Yorktown Heights, NY
12.27.77: Fore 'n' Aft, Westport, CT
12.28.77: Fore 'n' Aft, North Brewster, NY
12.29.77: Speaks, Island Park, NY
12.30.77: Mad Hatter (SB), Stony Brook, NY
12.31.77: Niteclub, East Quogue, NY
1.4.78: Gemini II, Yorktown Heights, NY
1.5.78: Speaks, Island Park, NY
1.6.78, 1.7.78: Zaffe's, Piscataway, NJ
1.11.78: Gemini II, Yorktown Heights, NY
1.12.78: Speaks, Island Park, NY
3.17.78: Chaucer's Ale House, Oakdale, NY
1.14.78: Cheers, Deer Park, NY
1.18.78: Gemini II, Yorktown Heights, NY
1.19.78: Speaks, Island Park, NY
1.20.78: Speaks, Island Park, NY CANCELED due to snow
1.21.78: Speaks, Island Park, NY
1.25.78: Gemini II, Yorktown Heights, NY

1.26.78: Speaks, Island Park, NY
1.27.78, 1.28.78: Rock Palace, Lake Carmel, NY
2.1.78: Gemini II, Yorktown Heights, NY
2.2.78: Speaks, Island Park, NY
2.3.78: Mad Hatter (SB), Stony Brook, NY
2.4.78: The Nite Club, East Quogue, NY
2.8.78: Gemini II, Yorktown Heights, NY
2.9.78: Speaks, Island Park, NY
2.10.78, 2.11.78: Zaffe's, Piscataway, NJ
2.15.78: Gemini II, Yorktown Heights, NY
2.16.78: Speaks, Island Park, NY
2.17.78: Chaucer's Ale House, Oakdale, NY
2.18.78: Cheers, Deer Park, NY
2.20.78: Rocky Horror Convention, Hempstead, NY—Calderone concert Hall First Rocky Horror Show Convention
2.22.78: Gemini II, Yorktown Heights, NY
2.23.78: Speaks, Island Park, NY
2.24.78, 2.25.78: Beggars Opera, Queens Village, NY
3.1.78: Gemini II, Yorktown Heights, NY
3.2.78: Speaks, Island Park, NY
3.3.78: Red Fox, New Brunswick CANCELED due to snow
3.4.78: Red Fox, New Brunswick, NJ
3.8.78: Gemini II, Yorktown Heights, NY
3.9.78: Speaks, Island Park, NY
3.10.78: Mad Hatter (SB), Stony Brook, NY
3.11.78: The Nite Club, East Quogue, NY
3.15.78: Gemini II, Yorktown Heights, NY
3.16.78: Speaks, Island Park, NY
3.17.78: Chaucer's Ale House, Oakdale, NY
3.18.78: Cheers, Deer Park, NY
3.22.78: Gemini II, Yorktown Heights, NY
3.23.78, 3.24.78, 3.25.78: Speaks, Island Park, NY
3.28.78: Happy Daze, Port Chester, NY
3.29.78: Gemini II, Yorktown Heights, NY
3.30.78: Speaks, Island Park, NY
3.31.78, 4.1.78: Zaffe's, Piscataway, NJ
4.6.78: Good Times, Poughkeepsie, NY
4.7.78, 4.8.78: Emmits, Jamesburg, NY
4.13.78: Fore 'n' Aft, Westport, CT
4.14.78, 4.15.78: Mad Hatter (SB), Stony Brook, NY
4.20.78: Rolling Stone, Bronx, NY
4.21.78: Fore 'n' Aft, Westport, CT
4.22.78: Rising Sun, Yonkers, NY
4.28.78, 4.29.78: Red Fox, New Brunswick, NJ
4.30.78: Gemini II, Yorktown Heights, NY
5.5.78, 5.6.78: Emmits, Jamesburg, NY
5.10.78: Good Times, Poughkeepsie, N:
5.11.78: Rolling Stone, Bronx, NY
5.12.78:, 5.13.78: Zaffe's, Piscataway, NJ
5.18.78: Fore 'n' Aft, Westport, CT
5.19.78, 5.20.78: Sgt Pepper, Hazlet, NJ
5.24.78: Cheers, Deer Park, NY
5.25.78: Speaks, Island Park, NY
5.26.78, 5.27.78, 5.28.78: The Nite Club, East Quogue, NY
5.31.78: Cheers, Deer Park, NY
6.1.78: Speaks, Island Park, NY
6.2.78, 6.3.78, 6.5.78: Beggars Opera, Queens Village, NY

6.7.78: Cheers, Deer Park, NY
6.8.78, 6.9.78, 6.10.78: Speaks, Island Park, NY
6.13.78: Happy Daze, Port Chester, NY
6.14.78: Cheers, Deer Park, NY
6.15.78: Speaks, Island Park, NY
6.16.78, 6.17.78: Mad Hatter (SB), Stony Brook, NY
6.20.78: Happy Daze, Port Chester, NY
6.21.78: Cheers, Deer Park, NY
6.22.78: Speaks, Island Park, NY
6.23.78, 6.24.78: Red Fox, New Brunswick, NJ
6.25.78: Speaks, Island Park, NY—Benefit for Good Times Magazine
6.29.78: Speaks, Island Park, NY
6.30.78, 7.1.78, 7.2.78: The Nite Club, East Quogue, NY
7.3.78: Gemini II, Yorktown Heights, NY
7.5.78: Cheers, Deer Park, NY
7.6.78: Speaks, Island Park, NY
7.7.78: Zaffe's, Piscataway, NJ
7.8.78: Fore 'n' Aft, White Plains, NY
7.11.78: Happy Daze, Port Chester, NY
7.12.78: Cheers, Deer Park, NY
7.13.78: Speaks, Island Park, NY
7.14.78, 7.15.78: Emmits, Jamesburg, NY
7.18.78: Happy Daze, Port Chester, NY
7.19.78: Cheers, Deer Park, NY
7.20.78: Speaks, Island Park, NY
7.21.78, 7.22.78: Mad Hatter (SB), Stony Brook, NY
7.25.78: Happy Daze, Port Chester, NY
7.26.78: Cheers, Deer Park, NY
7.27.78: Speaks, Island Park, NY
7.28.78: Zaffe's, Piscataway, NJ
7.29.78: Rising Sun, Yonkers, NY
8.1.78: Happy Daze, Port Chester, NY CANCELED
8.2.78: Cheers, Deer Park, NY
8.3.78: Speaks, Island Park, NY
8.4.78, 8.5.78: The Nite Club, East Quogue, NY
8.7.78: Gemini II, Yorktown Heights, NY
8.9.78: Cheers, Deer Park, NY
8.10.78: Speaks, Island Park, NY
8.11.78, 8.12.78: Hammerheads, Levittown, NY
8.15.78: Fore 'n' Aft, Brewster, NY
8.16.78: Cheers, Deer Park, NY
8.17.78: Speaks, Island Park, NY
8.18.78, 8.19.78: Mad Hatter (SB), Stony Brook, NY
8.22.78: Fore 'n' Aft, Brewster, NY
8.23.78: Gemini North, Newburgh, NY
8.24.78: Speaks, Island Park, NY
8.25.78: Zaffe's, Piscataway, NJ
8.26.78: Rising Sun, Yonkers, NY
8.29.78: Fore 'n' Aft, Brewster, NY
8.30.78: Cheers, Deer Park, NY
8.31.78: Speaks, Island Park, NY
9.1.78, 9.2.78:, 9.3.78: The Nite Club, East Quogue, NY
10.3.78: Emmits, Jamesburg, NY
10.4.78: Zaffe's, Piscataway, NJ
10.5.78: Gemini II, Yorktown Heights, NY
10.6.78, 10.7.78, 10.10.78: Emmits, Jamesburg, NY

10.11.78: Zaffe's, Piscataway, NJ
10.12.78: Gemini II, Yorktown Heights, NY
10.13.78: Zaffe's, Piscataway, NJ
10.14.78: Zaffe's, Piscataway, NJ
10.17.78: Emmits, Jamesburg, NY
10.18.78: Zaffe's, Piscataway, NJ
10.19.78, 10.20.78: Gemini North, Newburgh, NY
10.22.78: Gemini II, Yorktown Heights, NY
10.24.78: Emmits, Jamesburg, NY
10.25.78: Zaffe's, Piscataway, NJ
10.26.78: Gemini II, Yorktown Height CANCELED
10.27.78: Rising Sun, Yonkers, NY CANCELED
10.28.78: Calderone Theat Hempstead, NY
10.29.78: Fore 'n' Aft, White Plains, NY
10.31.78: Emmits, Jamesburg, NY
11.1.78: Zaffe's, Piscataway, NJ
11.2.78: Gemini II, Yorktown Heights, NY
11.3.78, 11.4.78: The Factory, Staten Island, NY
11.7.78: Emmits, Jamesburg, NY
11.8.78: Zaffe's, Piscataway, NJ
11.9.78: Gemini II, Yorktown Heights, NY
11.12.78: Speaks, Island Park, NY
11.15.78: Speaks, Island Park, NY CANCELED
11.16.78: Gemini II, Yorktown Height CANCELED
11.17.78: Fore 'n' Aft, White Plains, NY CANCELED
11.18.78: Fore 'n' Aft, White Plains, NY
11.19.78: Fore 'n' Aft, Brewster, NY
11.21.78: Roxy Music Hall, Huntington, NY
11.22.78: The Nite Club, East Quogue, NY
11.24.78, 11.25.78: Mad Hatter (SB), Stony Brook, NY
11.29.78: Zaffe's, Piscataway, NJ
11.30.78: Gemini II, Yorktown Heights, NY
12.1.78, 12.2.78: Rising Sun, Yonkers, NY
12.3.78: Gemini II, Yorktown Heights, NY
12.6.78: Zaffe's, Piscataway, NJ
12.7.78: Gemini North, Newburgh, NY
12.8.78, 12.9.78: Zaffe's, Piscataway, NJ
12.12.78: Gemini II, Yorktown Heights, NY
12.13.78: Zaffe's, Piscataway, NJ
12.14.78, 12.15.78: Gemini North, Newburgh, NY
12.16.78: Fore 'n' Aft, White Plains, NY
12.17.78: Fore 'n' Aft, Brewster, NY—Kenny's last show
12.20.78: Zaffe's, Piscataway, NJ—Mark Mendoza's first show
12.21.78: Gemini North, Newburgh, NY
12.22.78: Mad Hatter (SB), Stony Brook, NY
12.23.78: Mad Hatter (SB), Stony Brook, NY
12.27.78: Mad Hatter (SB), Stony Brook, NY
12.28.78: Detroit, Port Chester, NY
12.29.78: Speaks, Island Park, NY
12.30.78: Speaks, Island Park, NY
12.31.78: Mad Hatter (SB), Stony Brook, NY
1.2.79: Detroit, Port Chester, NY
1.3.79: Mad Hatter (SB), Stony Brook, NY CANCELED
1.4.79: Speaks, Island Park, NY
1.5.79: Emmits, Jamesburg, NY
1.6.79: Emmits, Jamesburg, NY

1.9.79: Detroit, Port Chester, NY
1.10.79: , Mad Hatter (SB), Stony Brook, NY
1.11.79: Speaks, Island Park, NY
1.12.79: Gemini II, Yorktown Heights, NY
1.13.79: Gemini II, Yorktown Heights, NY
1.16.79: Detroit, Port Chester, NY
1.17.79: Mad Hatter (SB), Stony Brook, NY
1.18.79: Speaks, Island Park, NY
1.19.79: Gemini North, Newburgh, NY
1.20.79: Gemini North, Newburgh, NY
1.23.79: Detroit, Port Chester, NY
1.24.79:, Mad Hatter (SB), Stony Brook, NY
1.25.79: Speaks, Island Park, NY
1.26.79: The Factory, Staten Island, NY
1.27.79: The Factory, Staten Island, NY
1.30.79: Detroit, Port Chester, NY CANCELED
1.31.79: Mad Hatter (SB), Stony Brook, NY
2.1.79: Speaks, Island Park, NY
2.2.79: Cheers, Deer Park, NY
2.3.79: Cheers, Deer Park, NY
2.8.79, 2.9.79, 2.10.79, 2.15.79: Speaks, Island Park, NY
2.16.79, 2.17.79: Roxy Music Hall Bayshore, NY
2.18.79: Detroit, Port Chester, NY
2.22.79: Speaks, Island Park, NY
2.23.79, 2.24.79: Zaffe's, Piscataway, NJ
3.1.79, 3.2.79, 3.3.79: Gemini North, Newburgh, NY
3.4.79: Fore 'n' Aft, Brewster, NY
3.5.79: Farmingdale College, Farmingdale, NY
3.9.79, 3.10.79: Mad Hatter (SB), Stony Brook, NY
3.16.79: The Palladium, New York, NY CANCELED
3.17.79: Emmits, Jamesburg, NY CANCELED
3.29.79: Good Times, Poughkeepsie, NY
3.30.79, 3.31.79: Gemini North, Newburgh, NY
4.6.79: The Palladium, New York, NY
4.7.79: Cheers, Deer Park, NY
4.8.79: Fore 'n' Aft, Brewster, NY
4.11.79: Detroit, Port Chester, NY
4.12.79: Speaks, Island Park, NY
4.13.79: Emmits, Jamesburg, NY
4.14.79: Rising Sun, Yonkers, NY
4.18.79: Detroit, Port Chester, NY
4.19.79: Mad Hatter (SB), Stony Brook, NY
4.20.79, 4.21.79: Gemini II, Yorktown Heights, NY
4.25.79: Detroit, Port Chester, NY
4.26.79: Good Times, Poughkeepsie, NY
4.27.79, 4.28.79: The Factory, Staten Island, NY
5.2.79: Detroit, Port Chester, NY
5.3.79: Creation, West Orange. NJ
5.4.79, 5.5.79: Speaks, Island Park, NY
5.9.79: Detroit, Port Chester, NY
5.11.79, 5.12.79: Zaffe's, Piscataway, NJ
5.13.79: Fore 'n' Aft, Brewster, NY
5.17.79: Arcadia Ballroom, New Haven, CT
5.18.79: Zappas, Brooklyn, NY
5.19.79: Roxy Music Hall, Huntington, NY
5.23.79: Detroit, Port Chester, NY

5.24.79: Speaks, Island Park, NY
5.25.79: Cheers, Deer Park, NY
5.26.79, 5.27.79: Gemini II, Yorktown Heights, NY
5.30.79: Detroit, Port Chester, NY
5.31.79: Speaks, Island Park, NY
6.1.79, 6.2.79: Beggars Opera, Queens Village, NY
6.6.79: Detroit, Port Chester, NY
6.7.79: Speaks, Island Park, NY
6.8.79, 6.9.79: Emmits, Jamesburg, NY
6.13.79: Detroit, Port Chester, NY
6.14.79: Speaks, Island Park, NY
6.15.79: The Factory, Staten Island, NY
6.16.79: Dizzy Duncan's, Morris Plains, NJ
6.19.79: Arcadia Ballroom, New Haven, CT
6.20.79: Detroit, Port Chester, NY
6.21.79: Speaks, Island Park, NY
6.22.79: Mad Hatter (SB), Stony Brook, NY CANCELED
6.2 3.79: Mad Hatter (SB), Stony Brook, NY
6.26.79: Arcadia Ballroom, New Haven, CT
6.27.79: Detroit, Port Chester, NY
6.28.79: Alfredo's, Waterbury, CT
6.29.79: Cheers, Deer Park, NY
6.30.79: Gemini North, Newburgh, NY
7.3.79: Mother's, Wayne, NJ
7.4.79: Detroit, Port Chester, NY
7.5.79: Speaks, Island Park, NY
7.6.79: Soap Factory, Pallisades Park, NJ
7.7.79: Mad Hatter (SB), Stony Brook, NY
7.11.79: Detroit, Port Chester, NY
7.12.79: Speaks, Island Park, NY
7.13.79: The Factory, Staten Island, NY
7.14.79: Gemini North, Newburgh, NY
7.18.79: Detroit, Port Chester, NY
7.19.79: Speaks, Staten Island, NY
7.20.79: Soap Factory, Pallisades Park, NJ
7.21.79: Zaffe's, Piscataway, NJ
7.24.79: Adventure Land, Farmingdale, NY
7.25.79: Detroit, Port Chester, NY
7.26.79: Speaks, Island Park, NY
7.27.79, 7.28.79: Silver Dollar, Jersey Shore, NJ
7.31.79: Mother's, Wayne, NJ
8.1.79: Detroit, Port Chester, NY
8.2.79: Speaks, Island Park, NY
8.4.79: Mad Hatter (SB), Stony Brook, NY
8.5.79: The Nite Club, East Quogue, NY
8.7.79: Good Times, Poughkeepsie, NY
8.8.79: Detroit, Port Chester, NY
8.9.79: Alfredo's, Waterbury, CT
8.10.79: Emmits, Jamesburg, NY
8.11.79: Gemini North, Newburgh, NY
8.14.79: Arcadia Ballroom, New Haven, CT
8.15.79: Detroit, Port Chester, NY
8.16.79: Speaks, Island Park, NY
8.17.79, 8.18.79: Dizzy Duncan's Morris Plains, NJ
8.21.79: Arcadia Ballroom, New Haven, CT
8.22.79: Detroit, Port Chester, NY

8.23.79: Speaks, Island Park, NY
8.24.79: Soap Factory, Pallisades Park, NJ
8.26.79: Trade Winds, Seabright, NJ
8.28.79: Good Times, Poughkeepsie, NY
8.30.79: Speaks, Island Park, NY
8.31.79, 9.1.79: Silver Dollar, Jersey Shore, NJ
9.2.79: Gemini II, Yorktown Heights, NY
9.6.79: Alfredo's, Waterbury, CT
9.7.79: The Factory, Staten Island, NY
9.8.79: Convention Center, Asbury Park, NJ—w/Judas Priest
9.9.79: Fore 'n' Aft, Brewster, NY
9.11.79: Mother's, Wayne, NJ
9.12.79: Brave Bull, Windsor CT
9.13.79: Arcadia Ballroom, New Haven, CT
9.14.79: Cheers, Deer Park, NY
9.15.79: Beggars Opera, Queens Village, NY
9.16.79: Mad Hatter (SB), Stony Brook, NY
10.6.79: Soap Factory, Pallisades Park, NJ
10.11.79: Arcadia Ballroom, New Haven, CT
10.12.79, 10.13.79: Detroit, Port Chester, NY
10.18.79: Arcadia Ballroom, New Haven, CT
10.19.79, 10.20.79: Dolly Dimples, Freehold NJ
10.25.79: Arcadia Ballroom, New Haven, CT
10.26.79, 10.27.79: Zaffe's, Piscataway, NJ
10.31.79: Detroit, Port Chester, NY
11.1.79: Arcadia Ballroom, New Haven, CT
11.2.79: Soap Factory, Pallisades Park, NJ
11.8.79: Zaffe's, Piscataway, NJ
11.9.79, 11.10.79: The Factory, Staten Island, NY
11.15.79: Hole in The Wall, Rochelle Park, NJ—Molly Cribb Benefit
11.21.79, 11.23.79, 11.24.79: Detroit, Port Chester, NY
11.29.79: Zaffe's, Piscataway, NJ
11.30.79: Soap Factory, Pallisades Park, NJ
12.1.79: Great American, New Haven, CT w/Good Rat
12.5.79: Great American, New Haven, CT
12.6.79: Circus, Bergenfield, NJ
12.7.79, 12.8.79: The Factory, Staten Island, NY
12.13.79: Hole in The Wall, Rochelle Park, NJ
12.14.79, 12.15.79: Dolly Dimples, Freehold NJ
12.20.79: Zaffe's, Piscataway, NJ
12.21.79, 12.22.79: Hole in The Wall, Rochelle Park, NJ
12.27.79: Zaffe's, Piscataway, NJ
12.28.79, 12.29.79: Detroit, Port Chester, NY
12.30.79: Calderone, Hempstead, NY—Rehearsal
12.31.79: Calderone, Hempstead, NY
1.2.80, 1.3.80: Zaffe's, Piscataway, NJ
1.4.80, 1.5.80: Beggars Opera, Queens Village, NY
1.9.80: Zaffe's, Piscataway, NJ
1.11.80, 1.12.80: Speaks, Island Park, NY
1.18.80, 1.19.80: Soap Factory, Pallisades Park, NJ
1.23.80: Zaffe's, Piscataway, NJ
1.25.80, 1.26.80: Mad Hatter (SB), Stony Brook, NY
1.30.80: Zaffe's, Piscataway, NJ
2.1.80, 2.2.80: Detroit, Port Chester, NY
2.8.80: Nassau Coliseun Uniondale, NY, w/Blue Oster Cult
2.9.80: Hole in The Wall, Rochelle Park, NJ

2.15.80, 2.16.80: Beggars Opera, Queens Village, NY
2.17.80, 2.22.80, 2.23.80: Gemini II, Yorktown Heights, NY
2.29.80, 3.1.80: Emmits, Jamesburg, NY
3.7.80, 3.8.80: Hammerheads, West Islip, NY
3.14.80, 3.15.80: Soap Factory, Pallisades Park, NJ
3.21.80, 3.22.80: Beggars Opera, Queens Village, NY
3.23.80: Fore 'n' Aft, Brewster, NY
3.28.80: Zaffe's, Piscataway, NJ
4.4.80, 4.5.80: Detroit, Port Chester, NY
4.11.80, 4.12.80: Speaks, Island Park, NY
4.17.80: Recorded first, Al Falcone Studios
4.18.80: Soap Factory, Pallisades Park, NJ
4.19.80: Rock Palace, Staten Island, NY
4.25.80: Gemini II, Yorktown Heights, NY CANCELED
4.26.80: Gemini II, Yorktown Heights, NY
4.27.80: Hofstra University, Hempstead, NY
5.2.80, 5.3.80: Speaks, Island Park, NY
5.12.80: Speaks, Island Park, NY—Benefit for the hand Samantha w/Whiplash, Zebra, Lady & Dennis Mann, Tattoo
5.16.80: The Factory, Staten Island, NY
5.17.80: Zaffe's, Piscataway, NJ
5.23.80: Detroit, Port Chester, NY—Recorded show for Broadcast on 6.3
5.24.80: Detroit, Port Chester, NY
5.25.80: Gemini II, Yorktown Heights, NY
5.27.80: Glen Island Casino, New Rochelle, NY
5.30.80, 5.31.80: Mad Hatter (SB), Stony Brook, NY
6.1.80: Fore 'n' Aft, Brewster, NY
6.5.80: Circus Circus, Bergensfield, NJ
6.6.80, 6.7.80: Speaks, Island Park, NY
6.8.80: Final Exam, Randolph, NJ
6.10.80: Glen Island Casino, New Rochelle, NY
6.12.80: Fountain Casino, Aberdeen, NJ
6.13.80: Good Times, Poughkeepsie, NY
6.14.80: Main Event, New Brunswick, NJ
6.15.80: Good Times, Poughkeepsie, NY
6.18.80: 2001, Brooklyn, NY
6.19.80: Night Owl II, Norwalk, CT
6.20.80, 6.21.80: Hammerheads, West Islip, NY
6.26.80: Hole in The Wall, Rochelle Park, NJ
6.27.80, 6.28.80: Mad Hatter (EQ), East Quogue, NY
7.2.80: Speaks, Island Park, NY
7.3.80: Gemini II, Yorktown Heights, NY
7.4.80: Buccaneer, Wall Township, NJ
7.10.80: Circus Circus, Bergenfield, NJ
7.11.80: Zaffe's, Piscataway, NJ
7.12.80: Detroit, Port Chester, NY
7.13.80: Fore 'n' Aft, Brewster, NY
7.17.80: Fountain Casino, Aberdeen, NJ
7.18.80, 7.19.80: Speaks, Island Park, NY
7.20.80: Good Times, Poughkeepsie, NY
7.23.80: Detroit, Port Chester, NY
7.24.80: Night Owl II, Norwalk, CT
7.25.80: Soap Factory, Pallisades Park, NJ
7.29.80: Glen Island Casino, New Rochelle, NY
7.31.80: Hole in The Wall, Rochelle Park, NJ
8.1.80, 8.2.80: Mad Hatter (EQ), East Quogue, NY

8.6.80: Speaks, Island Park, NY
8.7.80: Good Times, Poughkeepsie, NY
8.8.80, 8.9.80: Hammerheads, West Islip, NY
8.14.80: Night Owl II, Norwalk, CT
8.15.80: Soap Factory, Pallisades Park, NJ
8.16.80: Rock Palace, Staten Island, NY
8.21.80: Fountain Casino, Aberdeen, NJ
8.22.80: Zaffe's, Piscataway, NJ
8.23.80: Detroit, Port Chester, NY
8.24.80: Fore 'n' Aft, Brewster, NY
8.25.80: Speaks, Island Park, NY—SMF End of Summer Party
8.28.80: Gemini II, Yorktown Heights, NY
8.29.80, 8.30.80: Mad Hatter (SB), Stony Brook, NY
8.31.80: Paramount Theatre, Asbury Park, NJ
9.5.80, 9.6.80: Beggar's Opera, Queens Village, NY
9.11.80: Night Owl II, Norwalk, CT
9.12.80, 9.13.80: Rock Palace, Staten Island, NY
9.19.80: Circus Circus, Bergensfield, NJ
9.20.80: Final Exam, Randolph, NJ
9.26.80: Detroit, Port Chester, NY
9.27.80: Rumours, Middletown, NY
10.2.80: Good Times, Poughkeepsie, NY
10.3.80, 10.4.80: Hammerheads, West Islip, NY
10.9.80: Night Owl II, Norwalk, CT
10.10.80: Gemini II, Yorktown Heights, NY
10.13.80: Malibu, Lido Beach, NY
10.16.80: SUNY New Paltz, New Paltz, NY
10.17.80: Main Event, New Brunswick, NJ
10.18.80: Mad Hatter (SB), Stony Brook, NY
10.21.80: Arcadia Ballroom, New Haven, CT
10.23.80: L'Armour, Brooklyn, NY
10.24.80: Final Exam, Randolph, NJ
10.25.80: Fast Lane, Asbury Park, NJ
10.29.80, 10.30.80: Fountain Casino, Aberdeen, NJ
10.31.80: Detroit, Port Chester, NY
11.1.80: Soap Factory, Pallisades Park, NJ
11.4.80: El Greco's, Queens, NY
11.6.80: Night Owl II, Norwalk, CT CANCELED
11.7.80, 11.8.80: El Greco's, Queens, NY
11.9.80: Final Exam, Randolph, NJ
11.11.80: El Greco's, Queens, NY
11.13.80: Good Times, Poughkeepsie, NY
11.14.80: Rumours, Middletown, NY
11.15.80: The Long Run, Greenwood Lake, NY
11.18.80: El Greco's, Queens, NY
11.20.80: L'Armour, Brooklyn, NY
11.21.80: El Greco's, Queens, NY
11.22.80: Circus Circus, Bergensfield, NJ
11.23.80: Gemini II, Yorktown Heights, NY
11.26.80: Hammerheads, West Islip, NY
11.28.80, 11.29.80: Detroit, Poughkeepsie, NY
12.5.80: Hole in The Wall, Rochelle Park, NJ
12.7.80: Final Exam, Randolph, NJ
12.11.80: Night Owl II, Norwalk, CT
12.12.80, 12.13.80: Hammerheads, West Islip, NY
12.15.80, 12.16.80, 12.17.80, 12.1 8.80: Rehearse, SRS

12.19.80: Soap Factory, Pallisades Park, NJ
12.20.80: Rock Palace, Staten Island, NY
12.21.80: Fore 'n' Aft, Brewster, NY
12.26.80: Rumours, Middletown, NY
12.28.80: Good Times, Poughkeepsie, NY
12.30.80: Soap Factory, Pallisades Park, NJ
12.31.80: Detroit, Port Chester, NY
1.3.81: Palladium, New York, NY
1.8.81: Fountain Casino, Aberdeen, NJ
1.9.81: Mad Hatter (SB), Stony Brook, NY
1.10.81: Gemini II, Yorktown Height—One 90min show due to Dee Illness
1.11.81: Gemini II, Yorktown Height CANCELED
1.15.81: Rockaway, Queens, NY
1.16.81, 1.17.81: Hammerheads, West Islip, NY
1.18.81: Final Exam, Randolph, NJ
1.22.81: L'Armour, Brooklyn, NY
1.23.81: Rock Palace, Staten Island, NY
1.24.81: Beggar's Opera, Queens Village, NY
2.15.81: Gemini II, Yorktown Heights, NY
2.16.81: Hammerheads, West Islip, NY
2.18.81: Rehearsal, Marks House—First Time
2.19.81: Nile Owl, Westport, CT
2.20.81, 2.21.81: Hammerheads, West Islip, NY
2.27.81: Detroit, Port Chester, NY
2.28.81: Final Exam, Randolph, NJ
3.1.81: Fore 'n' Aft, Brewster, NY
3.4.81: Rehearsal, With Joey Brightc—First
3.6.81: Hole in The Wall, Rochelle Park, NJ
3.7.81: Gemini II, Yorktown Heights, NY
3.13.81: Beggar's Opera Queens Village, NY
3.14.81: Rumours, Middletown, NY
3.17.81: Emmits, Jamesburg, NY
3.19.81: Detroit, Port Chester, NY
3.20.81: Soap Factory, Pallisades Park, NJ
3.21.81: Main Event, New Brunswick, NJ
3.26.81: Rock Palace, Staten Island, NY
3.27.81: Circus Circus, Bergenfield, NJ
3.28.81: Rockaway, Queens, NY
3.29.81: Good Times Cafe, Poughkeepsie, NY
4.2.81: Nite Owl, Norwalk, CT
4.3.81, 4.4.81: Hammerheads, West Islip, NY
4.9.81: Main Event, New Brunswick, NJ
4.10.81: Snoopy's, Staten Island, NY
4.17.81: Hole in The Wall, Rochelle Park, NJ
4.23.81: Fountain Casino, Aberdeen, NJ
4.24.81: Gemini II, Yorktown Heights, NY
4.25.81: Soap Factory, Pallisades Park, NJ
4.30.81: Nite Owl, Norwalk, CT
5.1.81: Osprey Hotel, Manasqan, NJ
5.2.81: Mad Hatter (SB), Stony Brook, NY
5.7.81: L'Armour, Brooklyn, NY
5.14.81: Final Exam, Randolph, NJ
5.15.81: Circus Circus, Bergenfield, NJ
5.16.81: Main Event, New Brunswick, NJ
5.21.81: Fountain Casino, Aberdeen, NJ
5.22.81: Gemini II, Yorktown Heights, NY

5.23.81: Final Exam, Randolph, NJ
5.24.81: El Greco's, Queens, NY
5.28.81: The Surrey, Rosendale, NY
5.29.81: Rumours, Middletown, NY
5.30.81: Good Times Cafe, Poughkeepsie, NY
6.4.81: Nite Owl II, Norwalk, CT
6.5.81: Mad Hatter (SB), Stony Brook, NY
6.6.81: Mad Hatter (EQ), East Quogue, NY
6.9.81: Emmets Inn, Jamesburg, NY
6.10.81: Rock Palace, Staten Island, NY
6.12.81: Hammerheads, West Islip, NY
6.13.81: El Greco's, Queens, NY
6.18.81: Fountain Casino, Aberdeen, NJ
6.19.81: Soap Factory, Fort Lee, NJ
6.20.81: Park Place, Asbury Park, NJ
6.25.81: L'Armour, Brooklyn, NY
6.26.81: Main Event, New Brunswick, NJ
6.27.81: Osprey Hotel, Manasqan, NJ
7.2.81: Nite Owl II, Norwalk, CT
7.3.81, 7.4.81: Mad Hatter (EQ), East Quogue, NY
7.9.81: Gemini II, Yorktown Heights, NY
7.10.81: Mad Hatter (SB), Stony Brook, NY
7.11.81: Final Exam, Randolph, NJ
7.16.81: Fountain Casino, Aberdeen, NJ
7.17.81: Hammerheads, West Islip, NY
7.18.81: Agora Ballroom, New Haven, CT
7.23.81: Good Times CafE Poughkeepsie, NY
7.24.81: Rumours, Middletown, NY
7.25.81: Gemini II, Yorktown Heights, NY
7.30.81: Nite Owl II, Norwalk, CT
7.31.81: Snoopy's, Staten Island, NY
8.1.81: Rock Palace, Asbury Park, NJ
8.6.81: L'Armour, Brooklyn, NY
8.7.81: Mad Hatter (EQ), East Quogue, NY
8.8.81: Mad Hatter (EQ), East Quogue, NY
8.13.81: Gemini II, Yorktown Heights, NY
8.14.81: Hole in The Wall, Rochelle Park, NJ
8.15.81: El Greco's, Queens, NY
8.19.81: Rock Palace, Staten Island, NY
8.20.81: Fountain Casino, Aberdeen, NJ
8.21.81: Mad Hatter (SB), Stony Brook, NY
8.27.81: Nite Owl II, Norwalk, CT
8.28.81: Main Event, Osprey Hotel
8.29.81: New Brunswick, NJ Manasqan, NJ
8.31.81: Fountain Casino Aberdeen, NJ—SMF Summer Party
9.3.81: L'Armour, Brooklyn, NY
9.4.81: Final Exam, Randolph, NJ
9.5.81, 9.6.81: Mad Hatter (EQ), East Quogue, NY
9.30.81: Zaffe's, Piscataway, NJ
10.1.81: The Fields, Queens, NY
10.2.81: Hammerheads, West Islip, NY
10.3.81: Rockaway, Queens, NY
10.7.81: Fore 'n' Aft, Brewster, NY
10.8.81: Nite Owl II, Norwalk, CT
10.9.81: Agora Ballroom, New Haven, CT
10.10.81: Final Exam, Randolph, NJ

10.15.81: L'Armour, Brooklyn, NY
10.16.81: Snoopy's, Staten Island, NY
10.17.81: Beggar's Opera, Queens, NY
10.30.81: Main Event, New Brunswick, NJ
10.31.81: Gemini II, Yorktown Heights, NY
11.5.81: Rock Palace, Staten Island, NY
11.6.81: Tradewinds, Seabright, NJ
11.7.81: Rockaway, Queens, NY
11.12.81: Fountain Casino, Aberdeen, NJ
11.13.81: Final Exam, Randolph, NJ
11.14.81: Hole in The Wall, Rochelle Park, NJ
11.19.81: Nite Owl II, Norwalk, CT
11.20.81: Agora Ballroom, New Haven, CT
11.21.81: Hammerheads, West Islip, NY
11.25.81: Snoopy's, Staten Island, NY
11.27.81: L'Armour, Brooklyn, NY
11.28.81: Beggar's Opera, Queens, NY
12.3.81: The Surrey, Rosendale, NY
12.4.81: Rumours, Middletown, NY
12.5.81: Ace in the Hole, Fishkill, NY
12.10.81: Tradewinds, Seabright, NJ
12.11.81: Emmets Inn, Jamesburg, NY
12.12.81: Gemini II, Yorktown Heights, NY
12.17.81: Fountain Casino, Aberdeen, NJ
12.18.81: Agora Ballroom, New Haven, CT
12.19.81: Snoopy's, Staten Island, NY
12.26.81: Soap Factory, Pallisades Park, NJ
12.27.81: Final Exam, Randolph, NJ
12.28.81: Mid Hudson Civi, Poughkeepsie, NY—*Martin Hooker from Secret Records offers the band a deal at this show*
12.29.81: Ace in the Hole, Fishkill, NY
12.31.81: L'Armour, Brooklyn, NY
1.2.82: Hammerheads, West Islip, NY
1.6.82: Rock Palace, Staten Island, NY
1.7.82: Gemini II, Yorktown Heights, NY
1.8.82: Soap Factory, Palisades, NJ
1.9.82: Tradewinds, Seabright, NJ
1.13.82: Fore n' Aft North Brewster, NY
1.14.82: L'Armour, Brooklyn, NY
1.15.82: Agora Ballroom, New Haven, CT
1.16.82: Pebbles, Rochelle Park, NJ—*CBS TV Studios, New York, NY*
1.21.82: Fountain Casino, Aberdeen, NJ
1.22.82: Mad Hatter (SB), Stony Brook, NY
1.23.82: Rockaway, Queens, NY
1.28.82: L'Amour, Brooklyn, NY
1.29.82: Final Exam, Randolf, NJ
1.30.82: The Circus, Bergenfield, NJ
2.5.82: Ace in the Hole, Fishkill, NY
2.6.82: Rumours, Middletown, NY
2.11.82: L'Amour, Brooklyn, NY
2.12.82: Snoopy's, Staten Island, NY
2.13.82: Beggar's Opera, Queens, NY
2.14.82: Gemini II, Yorktown Heights, NY
2.17.82: Fore n' Aft North, Brewster, NY
2.18.82: Hammerheads, West Islip, NY, WPLJ Night

2.19.82: Agora Ballroom, New Haven, CT

2.20.82: Soap Factory, Palisades, NJ

2.26.82: Mad Hatter (SB), Stony Brook, NY CANCELED

2.27.82: Ace in the Hole, Fishkill, NY

3.5.82: Final Exam, Randolf, NJ

3.5.82: Hammerheads, West Islip, NY

3.11.82: Fountain Casino, Aberdeen, NJ

3.12.82: Agora Ballroom Hartford, CT

3.13.82: Gemini II, Yorktown Heights, NY

3.17.82: Emmentt's Inn, Jamesburg, NJ

3.19.82: Pebbles, Rochelle Park, NJ

3.20.82: Hammerheads, West Islip, NY

3.25.82: The Nook, Hackettstown, NJ

3.26.82: Agora Ballroom, New Haven, CT

3.27.82: Creation, West Orange, NJ

4.1.82: L'Amour, Brooklyn, NY—AJ First Show

4.2.82: Tradewinds, Seabright, NJ

4.3.82: Gemini II, Yorktown Heights, NY—Video Party for Flo + Eddie

4.8.82: L'Amour, Brooklyn, NY

4.9.82: Beggar's Opera, Queens, NY

4.10.82: Snoopy's, Staten Island, NY

4.13.82: USA Roller Rink, Centereach, NY

4.15.82: Fountain Casino, Aberdeen, NJ

4.16.82: Soap Factory, Palisades, NJ

4.17.82: Rockaway, Queens, NY

4.22.82: Gemini II, Yorktown Heights, NY

4.23.82: Hammerheads, West Islip, NY

4.24.82: Final Exam, Randolf, NJ

4.29.82: Gemini II, Yorktown Heights, NY

4.30.82: Creation, West Orange, NJ

5.1.82: Ace in the Hole, Fishkill, NY

5.2.82: Hammerheads, West Islip, NY

5.6.82: The Nook, Hackettstown, NJ

5.7.82: Agora Ballroom, New Haven, CT

5.8.82: Tradewinds, Seabright, NJ

5.13.82: L'Amour, Brooklyn, NY

5.14.82: Beggar's Opera, Queens, NY

5.15.82: Snoopy's, Staten Island, NY

5.20.82: Gemini II, Yorktown Heights, NY

5.21.82: Emmentt's Inn, Jamesburg, NJ

5.22.82: Hammerheads, West Islip, NY

5.27.82: Fountain Casino, Aberdeen, NJ

5.28.82: Soap Factory, Palisades, NJ

5.29.82: Final Exam, Randolf, NJ

5.30.82: Rockaway, Queens, NY

6.3.82: The Chance, Poughkeepsie, NY

6.4.82: Pebbles, Rochelle Park, NJ

6.5.82: Creation, West Orange, NJ

6.8.82: Hammerheads, West Islip, NY—w/Zebra & Cintron

6.11.82: Emmentt's Inn, Jamesburg, NJ

6.12.82: Fast Lane, Asbury Park, NJ

6.16.82: Gemini II, Yorktown Heights, NY

6.17.82, 6.18.82: Agora Ballroom, New Haven, CT

6.19.82: Ace in the Hole, Fishkill, NY

6.23.82: Northstage, Glen Cove, NY

6.24.82: L'Amour, Brooklyn, NY

6.25.82: Snoopy's, Staten Island, NY

6.26.82: Chatterbox, Seaside Heights, NJ

7.24.82: Wrexham, Wales, UK

8.2.82, 8.3.82: Marquee Club, London, UK

8.11.82: Mid Hudson Civic Poughkeepsie, NY

8.12.82: Fountain Casino, Aberdeen, NJ

8.13.82: L'Amour, Brooklyn, NY

8.14.82: Gemini II, Yorktown Heights, NY

8.19.82: Agora Ballroom, New Haven, CT

8.20.82: Soap Factory, Palisades, NJ

8.21.82: Hammerheads, West Islip, NY

8.29.82: Reading Festival, Reading, UK

9.2.82: Fountain Casino, Aberdeen, NJ

9.3.82: L'Amour, Brooklyn, NY

9.4.82: Gemini II, Yorktown Heights, NY

9.5.82: Emmentt's Inn, Jamesburg, NJ

9.17.82: Final Exam, Randolf, NJ

9.25.82: The Factory, Staten Island, NY

10.8.82: Ace in the Hole, Fishkill, NY

10.9.82: Hammerheads, West Islip, NY

10.14.82: Fountain Casino, Aberdeen, NJ

10.15.82: Pebbles, Rochelle Park, NJ

10.16.82: L'Amour, Brooklyn, NY

11.24.82: Paramount Theatre, Staten Island, NY

11.27.82: L'Amour, Brooklyn, NY

12.3.82: Agora Ballroom, New Haven, CT

12.4.82: Agora Ballroom Hartford, CT

12.10.82: Final Exam, Randolf, NJ

12.17.82: The Tube TV, Newcastle, UK

12.18.82, 12.19.82, 12.20.82: Marquee Club, London, UK

12.26.82: Hammerheads, West Islip, NY

12.27.82: Mid Hudson Civic Poughkeepsie, NY—Sick Fucks opened

12.28.82: Gemini II, Yorktown Heights, NY

12.29.82: The River, Trenton, NJ

12.30.82: Agora Ballroom, New Haven, CT

12.31.82: Paramount Theatre, Staten Island, NY

1.6.83: Fountain Casino, Aberdeen, NJ

1.21.83: Agora Ballroom, New Haven, CT

1.27.83: Mad Hatter (SB), Stony Brook, NY

1.28.83: Fountain Casino, Aberdeen, NJ

1.29.83: Gemini II, Yorktown Heights, NY

2.2.83: Day 1 of recording

3.5.83, 3.6.83: Marquee Club, London, UK

4.6.83: Record for Top, Olympic Studios, Guildhall, Portsmouth, UK

4.7.83: Rock City, Nottingham, UK

4.8.83: Queensway Hall, Dunstable, UK

4.10.83: Royal Court Theatre, Liverpool, UK

4.11.83: Victoria Hall, Hanley, UK

4.12.83: Manchester Apollo, Manchester, UK

4.14.83: Nite Club, Edinburgh, UK

4.15.83: The Mayfair, Newcastle, UK

4.16.83: St Georges Hall, Bradford, UK

4.17.83: University, Sheffield, UK

4.18.83: The Odeon, Birmingham, UK

4.19.83: Lyceum Ballroom, London, UK

4.20.83: Top of the Pops, London, UK
5.28.83: Queensway Hall, Leeds, UK—w/Anvil, Saxon, Girlschool, Battle Axe
6.3.83: Top of the Pops, London, UK
6.7.83: Recorded "Top of the Pops"
6.8.83: Top of the Pops, London, UK
6.30.83: L'Amour, Queens, NY
7.1.83: Agora Ballroom, New Haven, CT
7.2.83: Mid Hudson Civic, Poughkeepsie, NY
7.3.83: Fountain Casino, Aberdeen, NJ
7.7.83: The River, Trenton, NY
7.8.83: Dynasty, Staten Island, NY
7.9.73: Gemini II, Yorktown Heights, NY
7.10.83: Final Exam, Randolf, NJ
7.15.83: Circus Circus, Bergenfield, NJ
7.16.83, 7.17.83: L'Amour, Brooklyn, NY
7.22.83: Unknown, Salt Lake City, UT—Tour with Blackfoot, Krokus
7.23.83: Red Rocks, Denver, CO
7.24.83: Unknown, Albuquerque, NM
7.26.83: Unknown, Tuscon, AZ
7.27.83: Unknown, Temple, AZ
7.28.83: Unknown, San Diego, CA
7.29.83: Hollywood Pallac, Los Angeles, CA
7.31.83: Unknown, Sacremento, CA—End of tour with Blackfoor, Krokus
8.6.83: The Rainbow, Denver, CO
8.8.83, 8.9.83: Cardi's, Austin, TX
8.10.83: Cardi's, Beaumont, TX
8.15.83: The Chance, Poughkeepsie, NY
8.17.83: The Beacon Theatre, New York, NY
8.20.83: Monster of Rock Donnington, UK—w/Dia, Whitesnake, ZZ Top
8.28.83: Dallymount Park Dublin, Ireland—w/Mamas Boys, Motorhead, Black Sabbath
9.1.83: Paradiso, Amsterdam, Holland—w/Anvil
9.2.83: Westfalenhalle, Dortmund, Germany
9.3.83: Stadion, Kaiserslautern, Germany
9.4.83: Zeppelinfeld, Nurnberg, Germany—w/Ozzy, Meatloaf, Whitesnake, Think Lizzy, Motorhead, Saxon, Blue Oyster Cult
9.6.83: Vorst National, Brussels, Belgium
9.8.83: Palais D'Hivre, Lyon, France
9.10.83: Festival, Mulhouse, France CANCELED due to weather
10.11.83: Uptown Theatre, Kansas City, KS—w/Queensryche
10.13.83: Unknown, Debuke, IA—w/Queensryche
10.15.83: Haymaker's, Chicago, IL—w/Queensryche
10.16.83: Eagle's Nest, Milwaukee, WI—w/Queensryche
10.17.83: Top of the Rock Grand Rapids, MI—w/Queensryche
10.19.83: Harpo's, Detroit, MI—w/Queensryche
10.20.83: Unknown, Columbus, OH—w/Queensryche
10.21.83: Engineer's Auditc Cleveland, OH—w/Queensryche
10.22.83: Rooftop Sky Roa, Buffalo, NY—w/Queensryche
10.24.83: Paradise Theatre, Boston, MA—w/Queensryche
10.26.83: Wax Museum, Washington, DC—w/Queensryche
10.27.83: Stanley Theatre, Pittsburgh, PA—w/Queensryche
10.29.83: The Chance, Poughkeepsie, NY—w/Queensryche
10.31.83: Agora Ballroom, Hartford, CT—w/Queensryche

11.1.83: The Ritz, New York, NY—w/Queensryche 2 Shows— one dry, one not
11.4.83: Concert Hall, Toronto, Canada—w/Queensryche
11.5.83: Unknown, Ottawa, Canada—w/Queensryche
11.6.83: The Spectrum Montreal, Canada—w/Queensryche
11.7.83: Unknown, Quebec City, Canada—w/Queensryche
11.23.83: Fountain Casino, Aberdeen, NJ
11.24.83: Agora Ballroom, New Haven, CT
11.25.83: L'Amour, Queens, NY
11.26.83: L'Amour, Brooklyn, NY
11.27.83: JB Rock III, Middletown, NY
12.10.83: Tower Theatre, Philadelphia, PA
12.27.83: Unknown, Baltimore, MD
12.28.83: L'Amour, Brooklyn, NY
12.29.83: Roller Rink, Sayville, NY
12.30.83: Fountain Casino, Aberdeen, NJ—w/Metallica (their first East Coast show ever)
12.31.83: Agora Ballroom, Hartford, CT
4.20.84: L'Amour, Brooklyn, NY
4.21.84: L'Amour, Queens, NY
5.19.84: Orange County Festival, San Bernadine, CA—Taping for live MTV concert special
5.22.84: Filmed Video,Hollywood, CA
5.29.84: Filmed Razzama, Newcastle, UK
6.6.84: Stadsgehpprzaal, Leiden, Holland—w/Metallica
6.7.84: Volksbildungsheim, Frankfurk, Germany—w/Metallica
6.8.84: Jumbo, Oldenzall, Holland—w/Metallica
6.9.84: Evenementenhal, Zwaagwesteinde, Netherlands—w/Metallica
6.10.84: Sportsfields,Poperinge, Belgium—w/Metallica
6.11.84: Markthalle, Hamburg, Germany
6.13.84: University of E. Anglia, Norwich, UK
6.15.84: Hammersmith Odeon ,London, UK
6.19.84, 6.20.84: Hammersmith Odeon ,London, UK—Live release
7.11.84: Unknown, Bangor, ME—w/RATT and Lita Ford
7.13.84: Agora, Hartford, CT—w/RATT and Lita Ford
7.14.84: Kingston Fairgrounds, Kingston, NH—w/RATT and Lita Ford and Cheap Trick
7.15.84: The Pier, New York, NY—w/RATT and Lita Ford
7.16.84: Allentown Fairgrounds, Allentown, PA—w/RATT and Lita Ford
7.18.84: Auditorium Theatre, Rochester, NY—w/RATT and Lita Ford
8.12.84: Civic Center, Pittsburgh, PA—w/Dio
8.14.84: Civic Center, Baltimore, MD—w/Dio
8.15.84: Nassau Collesiur, Nassau, NY—w/Dio
8.17.84: Verdun Auditorium, Montreal, Canada—w/Dio
8.18.84: Coliseum, Quebec, Canada—w/Dio
8.20.84: Civic Center, Providence, RI—w/Dio
8.21.84: New Haven College, New Haven, CT—w/Dio
8.23.84: Mid Hudson Civic Center, Poughkeepsie, N—w/Dio CANCELED
8.24.84: Centrum, Worcester, MA—w/Dio
8.25.84: Spectrum, Philidelphia, PA—w/Dio 8.27.84:
8.27.84: Filmed Video for, Los Angeles, CA
8.28.84: Hara Arena, Dayton, OH—w/Mamas Boys, RATT, Y&T
9.3.84: Collesium, Evansville, IN—w/Mamas Boys, RATT, Y&T
9.4.84: Col Ballroom, Davenport, IA

9.5.84: Unknown, Omaha, NE
9.6.84: Filmed for TV show, Los Angeles, CA
9.10.84: Palladium, Hollywood, CA
9.18.84: Civic Auditorium, San Jose, CA—w/Y&T
9.19.84: Civic Auditorium, San Jose, CA—w/Y&T
9.21.84: Unknown, Bakersfield, CA—w/Y&T, Lita Ford
9.22.84: Unknown, Las Vegas, NV—w/Y&T, Rex Havoc
9.27.84, 9.28.84: Starry Night's, Portland, OR
10.4.84: Albuquerque Civic Ceneter, Albuquerque, NM
10.6.84: Unknown, Lubbuck, TX—w/Dokken, Y&T
10.7.84: Unknown, Amarillo, TX—Dee arrested for obscenity
10.8.84 Unknown, El Paso, TX
10. 9.84: Unknown, Midland, TX
10.11.84: Kiefer UNO Lakefront Arena, New Orleans, LA
10.12.84: North Hall, Memphis, TN
10.14.84: Unknown, Nashville, TN
10.24.84: Orpheum Theatre, Boston, MA
10.25.84: Starry Night's, Portland, OR
11.24.84: Metro Centre, Halifax, Canada—w/Iron Maiden
11.26.84: Coliseum, Quebec City, Canada—w/Iron Maiden
11.27.84: Forum, Montreal, Canad—w/Iron Maiden
11.28.84: Civic Center, Ottawa, Canada—w/Iron Maiden
11.30.84: Maple Leaf Gardens, Toronto, Canada—w/Iron Maiden
12.1.84: Arena, Sudbury, Canad—w/Iron Maiden
12.3.84: Arena, Winnipeg, Canada—w/Iron Maiden
12.4.84: Agri Dome, Regina, Canada—w/Iron Maiden
12.6.84: Northlands Coliseum, Edmonton, Canada—w/Iron Maiden
12.7.84: Corral, Calgary, Canada—w/Iron Maiden
12.9.84: PNE Coliseum Vancouver, Canada—w/Iron Maiden
12.10.84: Coliseum, Seattle, WA—w/Iron Maiden
12.11.84: Coliseum, Portland, OR—w/Iron Maiden
12.13.84: Salt Palace, Salt Lake City, UT—w/Iron Maiden
12.15.84: McNichols Arena Denver, CO—w/Iron Maiden CANCELED
12.17.84: Kemper Arena, Kansas City, MO—w/Iron Maiden
12.18.84: Kiel Auditorium St. Louis, MO—w/Iron Maiden
12.19.84: Mecca Arena Milwaukee, WI—w/Iron Maiden
12.20.84: Metro Centre Minneapolis, MN—w/Iron Maiden
12.21.84: Rosemont Horizon, Chicago, IL—w/Iron Maiden
1.3.85: Gardens, Cincinnati, OH—w/Iron Maiden
1.4.85: Joe Louis Arena, Detroit, MI—w/Iron Maiden
1.5.85: Ohio Centre, Columbus, OH—w/Iron Maiden
1.6.85: Richfield Coliseum, Cleveland, OH—w/Iron Maiden
1.7.85: Memorial Auditorium, Buffalo, NY—w/Iron Maiden
1.14.85: Civic Center, Hartford, CT—w/Iron Maiden
1.15.85: Centrum, Worcester, MA—w/Iron Maiden
1.28.85: Capitol Center, Landover, MA—w/Iron Maiden
1.29.85: Spectrum, Philidelphia, PA—w/Iron Maiden
1.31.85: Coliseum, Columbia, SC—w/Iron Maiden
2.1.85: Freedom Hall, Johnson City, TN—w/Iron Maiden
2.2.85: Omni, Atlanta, GA—w/Iron Maiden
2.3.85: Mid South Colise, Memphis, TN—w/Iron Maiden
2.5.85: Municipal Auditorium, Nashville, TN—w/Iron Maiden
2.6.85: Coliseum, Knoxville, TN—w/Iron Maiden
2.8.85: Coliseum, Charlotte, NC—w/Iron Maiden
2.9.85: Coliseum, Greensboro, NC—w/Iron Maiden
2.10.85: Auditotium, Greensville, SC—w/Iron Maiden
2.12.85: Memorial Coliseum, Jacksonville, FL—w/Iron Maiden
2.14.85: Lee County Arena, Ft. Myers, FL—w/Iron Maiden
2.15.85: Hollywood Sportatorium, Miami, FL—w/Iron Maiden
2.16.85: Civic Center, Lakeland, FL—w/Iron Maiden
2.17.85: Bayfront Center, St. Petersburg, FL—w/Iron Maiden
2.19.85: UTC Arena Tour, Chattanooga, TN—w/Iron Maiden
2.20.85: Boutwell Auditorium, Birmingham, AL—w/Iron Maiden
2.21.85: Von Braun Coliseum, Huntsville, AL—w/Iron Maiden
3.1.85: Unknown, Tokyo, Japan
3.2.85: Unknown, Osaka, Japan
3.3.85: Unknown, Nagoya, Japan
3.6.85: Unknown, Auckland, New Zealand
3.8.85: Unknown, Sydney, Australia
3.10.85: Unknown, Melbourne, Australia
3.11.85: Unknown, Brisbane, Australia
3.13.85: Filming for Pee Wee Herman's "Big Adventure"
3.14.85, 3.15.85, 3.16.85, 3.17.85: Long Beach Arena Long Beach, CA—w/Iron Maiden
3.19.85: Lawlor Events Center, Reno, NV—w/Iron Maiden
3.20.85: Selland Arena, Fresno, CA—w/Iron Maiden
3.21.85: Cow Palace, San Franscisco—w/Iron Maiden
2.23.85: Sports Arena, San Diego, CA—w/Iron Maiden
3.24.85: Compton Terrace,Tempe, AZ—w/Iron Maiden
6.15.85: Begin pre-production for "Come Out and Play"
1.10.86: Cumberland Auditorium, Portland, ME
1.12.86: The Coliseum, New Haven, CT
1.14.86: Civic Arena, Pittsburgh, PA
1.15.86: War Memorial, Rochester, NY
1.16.86: Maple Leaf Arern Toronto, Canada CANCELED
1.18.86: The Spectrum, Philidelphia, PA
1.19.86: Civic Center, Glens Falls, NY
1.21 .86: The Centrum, Worcester, MA
1.22.86: Capitol Center, Largo, MD
1.24.86, 1.25.86: Radio City Music New York, NY
1.28.86: Richmond Colise Cleveland, OH
1.29.86: Pavilion, Chicago, IL
1.30.86: Cobo Arena, Detroit, MI
1.31.86: Mecca Auditorium, Milwaukee, WI
2.3.86: Unknown, Minneapolis, MN
2.4.86: Unknown, Cedar Rapids, IA
2.5.86: Unknown, Kansas City, MO
2.8.86: Unknown, Houston, TX
2.9.86: Unknown, San Antonio, TX
2.10.86: Unknown, Dallas, TX
2.12.86: Unknown, El Paso, TX CANCELED
2.14.86: Unknown, Denver, CO CANCELED
2.16.86: Sports Arena, San Diego, CA CANCELED
2.17.86: Unknown, San Bernadine, CA CANCELED
2.19.86: Unknown, Los Angeled, CA CANCELED
2.21.86: Unknown, San Francisco, CA CANCELED
2.22.86: Unknown, Sacramento, CA CANCELED
2.25.86: Unknown, Portland, OR CANCELED
2.26.86: Unknown, Spokane, WA CANCELED
2.28.86: Unknown, Seattle, WA CANCELED

3.2.86: Unknown, Salt Lake City, UT *CANCELED*
3.4.86: Unknown, Omaha, NE *CANCELED*
3.5.86: Unknown, Des Moines, IA *CANCELED*
3.7.86: Unknown, St. Louis, MO *CANCELED*
3.8.86: Unknown, Cincinnati, OH *CANCELED*
3.9.86: Unknown, Indianapolis, IN *CANCELED*
3.11.86: Unknown, Buffalo, NY *CANCELED*
3.12.86: Unknown, Providence, RI *CANCELED*
3.22.86: TV Show on Channel 3
3.23.86: Gaumont Theatre, Ipswich, UK
3.24.86, 3.25.86: Hammersmith Odeon, London, UK
3.28.86: Isstadion, Stockholm, Sweden
3.29.86: Scandinavium, Gothernburg, Sweden
3.31.86: Drammenshalle Oslo, Norway
4.1.86: Saga, Copenhagen, Denmark
4.2.86: Olympen, Lund, Sweden
4.4.86: Vejlby Risskov H Aarhus, Denmark
4.6.86: Stadthalle 2, Bremen, Germany *CANCELED*
4.7.86: Halle Gartlage, Osnabruck, Germany *CANCELED*
4.9.86: Grugahalle, Essen, Germany
4.10.86: Eberthalle, Ludwigshafen, Germany
4.12.86: Circus Krone, Munich, Germany
4.13.86: Hemmerleinhalle, Nurnberg, Germany
4.14.86: Stadthalle, Offenbach, Germany
4.16.86: Sporthalle, Stuttgart, Germany
4.19.86: Victoria Hall, Hanley, UK
4.20.86: Royal Centre, Nottingham, UK
4.21.86: Apollo, Manchester, UK
4.22.86: Playhouse, Edinburgh, UK
4.23.86: Odeon, Birmingham, UK
4.25.86: Jaap Edenhall, Amsterdam, Holland
4.27.86: Forest National, Brussels, Belgium
4.28.86: Casino, Paris, France
6.20.86: Festival, Vaala, Finland
6.23.86: Palazzetto dello Sport, Bologna, Italy
6.24.86: Teatro Tenda, Milan, Italy
9.18.87: Unknown, Burlington, VT
9.20.87: Unknown, Albany, NY
9.22.87: Mid Hudson Civic, Poughkeepsie, NY
9.23.87: Unknown, Utica, NY
9.25.87: Leroy Theatre, Providence, RI *CANCELED due to power outage*
9.26.87: Orpheum Theatre, Boston, MA
9.29.87: Tower Theatre, Phililedlphia, PA
9.30.87: Warner Theatre, Washington, DC
10.3.87: Felt Forum, New York, NY
10.4.87: Music Hall, Cleveland, OH
10.7.87: Royal Oak Theatre, Detroit, MI
10.8.87: Holiday Star Theatre, Merrillville, IN
10.9.87: Unknown, Milwaukee, WI
10.10.87: Orpheum Theatre Minneapolis, MN—*Final Show Before Breakup*
6.7.00: Tavern on the Green, New York, NY—*Party for Jason Flom*
11.28.01: Hammerstein Ballroom, New York, NY
12.13.02: Don Hil's Club, New York, NY
4.4.03: L'Amour, Brooklyn, NY—*w/Bent Brother*

4.11.03: The Downtown, Farmingdale, NY—*w/Bent Brother*
4.12.03: The Chance Poughkeepsie, NY—*w/Bent Brother*
4.27.03: Tuxedo Junction, Danbury, CT
4.30.03, 5.6.03: USO Tour, Korea
6.8.03: Sweden Rock, Solvesborg, Sweden
6.27.03: Z7 Pratteln, Pratteln, Switzerland
6.28.03: Bang Your Head!, Balingen, Germany
8.2.03: Wacken, Wacken, Germany
10.24.03: Hampton Beach, Hampton Beach, NH
10.26.03: Webster Theater, Hartford, CT
10.27.03: Beacon Theater, New York, NY
10.30.03: House of Blues, Chicago, IL
11.1.03: Royal Oak Music, Royal Oak, MI
1.31.04: Double D's, Morristown, NJ
5.27.04: Jaxx, Springfield, VA
5.29.04: River Fest, Somerset, WI
6.18.04: Summer Rock, Budapest, Hungary
6.19.04: Waldrock, Holland
7.9.04: Meadowbrook Farm, Gilford, NH
7.10.04: Capitol Federal Park, Bonner Springs, KS
7.16.04: Yellowstone Bike, Yellowstone, MT
8.13.04: Mid-Hudson Civic Center, Poughkeepsie, NY
8.14.04: Penn's Peak, Jim Thorpe, PA'
9.23.04: Oneida Casino, Green Bay, WI
11.13.04: Monterrey Metal, Monterrey, Mexico
11.29.04: The Downtown, Farmingdale, NY—*w/Bent Brother*
12.4.04: The Chance, Poughkeepsie, NY—*w/Bent Brother*
4.25.12—5.4.12: *Time Period of Possible Promotion Activities for Jim Bean/Hornitos*
6.2.12: Trondheim Rock Trondheim, Norway
6.8.12: Sweden Rock, Solvesborg, Sweden
6.14.12: Azkena Rock Festival, Vitoria, Spain
6.16.12: Steamboat Days, Burligton, Iowa
6.23.12: Graspop, Dessel, Belgium
7.5.12: Arena, Moscow, Russia
7.7.12: Skanevik Blues Festival, Skanevik, Norway
8.4.12: Clearfield County, Clearfield, PA
12.9.12: The Emporium, Patchogue, NY—*Benefit for Hurricane Sandy*
4.13.13: Metal Fest, Santiago, Chile
4.14.13: Live N Louder, Sao Paulo, Brazil
5.4.13: M3, Columbia, MD
5.11.13: Old Bridge Metal, Freehold, NJ
6.15.13: Republic of Texas, Austin, TX
6.21.13: Hellfest, Glisson, France
6.28.13: Graspop Metal Meeting, Dessel, Belgium
7.18.13: Rock USA, Oshkosh, WI
7.27.13: Skogsrojet, Rejmyre, Sweden
12.14.13: Rockklassiker Live, Sandviken, Sweden
3.15.14: Unknown, Mexico City, Mexico *CANCELED*
5.15.16: Las Vegas Rock Awards, Las Vegas, NV
5.17.14: Starland, Sayreville, NJ
6.12.14: Copehell, Copenhagen, Denmark
6.14.14: Download, Leicestershire, UK
7.5.14: Rock Fest, Barcelona, Spain
7.11.14: Sommav Rock, Svedala, Sweden
7.12.14: Bang Your Head, Ballingen, Germany

7.25.14: Fox & Friends, New York, NY
8.2.14: Rock Fest, Graz, Austria
8.7.14: Summar Festival Klaksvic, Faroe Islands
8.9.14: Alcatraz Fest, Kortruck, Belgium
8.10.14: Heavy Montreal, Montreal, Canada
9.5.14: Best Buy Theatre, New York, NY
5.30.15: Hard Rock Hotel, Las Vegas, NV
6.13.15: Starland Ballroom, Sayreville, NJ
6.19.15: Tons of Rock Festival, Halden, Norway
6.20.15: State Prison Motorcycle Festival, Horsens, Denmark
6.27.15: Topfest, Piestany, Slovakia
6.28.15: Kavarna, Kavarna, Bulgaria
7.2.15: Toreboda Festival, Toreboda, Sweden
7.24.15: Rock Fest, Barcelona, Spain
8.29.15: Woot Stock, Prince George, BC Canada
9.12.15: RockTember, Grand Casino Hinckley, MN
5.15.16: Hair Metal Awards, Las Vegas, NV
6.10.16: Sweden Rock, Solvesborg, Sweden
6.12.16: Nova Rock, Pannonia Fields, Austria
6.18.16: Hellfest, Cusson, France
6.19.16: Graspop Metal Meeting, Dessel, Belgium
6.24.16: Rock Fest, Montebello, Quebec, Canada
7.14.16: Guitare en Scene, Saint-Julien-Et-Genevois, France
7.15.16: Bang Your Head!, Balingen, Germany
7.17.16: Rock Fest, Barcelona, Spain
7.23.16: Corona Hell & Heaven, Mexico City, Mexico
7.31.16: Rock the City, Bucharest, Romania
8.5.16: Porisphere, Pori, Finland
8.6.16: Wacken open Air, Wacken, Germany
8.12.16: Bloodstock Open, Derbyshire, UK
8.14.16: Alcatraz Hard Rock & Metal Festival, Kortrijk, Belgium
10.1.16: Rock Carnival, Lakewood, NJ
10.5.16: Cathouse Reunion, Los Angeles, CA
11.16.16: Monterey, Mexico—w/*KISS*

45 Canceled Dates
14 Recording & Rehersal Days
2295 Performance Days

Club	Number of Times
Satalite Lounge	11
Wreck Room	2
Spruce Goose	4
Colony III	16
Mad Hatter EQ	118
Sunshine In	2
TG	4
Capricorn	13
Searchlite·	19
Sahara	21
Hunter Village	13
Joker II	23
George Inn	4
Dodds	35
Dodds Crest	4
Caspers	6
Joker	6
Mr. T	37
Liberty Bell	8
Pourhouse	4
Electric Elephant	24
OBI East	8
Rumbottoms	19
Ubie	30
Inner Circle	3
Beggars B	19
Maxi's	109
Chaucer Ale House	19
1890	14